Sanity Secrets *for* Stressed-Out Women

Sue Augustine

HARVEST HOUSE PUBLISHERS

EUGENE, OREGON

Cover by Left Coast Design, Portland, Oregon

Cover photo © iStockphoto

SANITY SECRETS FOR STRESSED-OUT WOMEN

Published by Harvest House Publishers
Eugene, Oregon 97402
www.harvesthousepublishers.com

Library of Congress Cataloging-in-Publication Data

Augustine, Sue.
Sanity secrets for stressed-out women / Sue Augustine.
p. cm.
ISBN 978-0-7369-2417-7 (pbk.)
1. Christian women—Religious life. 2. Stress (Psychology)—Religious aspects—Christianity. I. Title.
BV4527.A93 2009
248.8'43—dc22

2008028532

Printed in the United States of America

09 10 11 12 13 14 15 / BP-NI / 10 9 8 7 6 5 4 3 2

Contents

PART 1

Is Your Life Out of Control?

1

Escape the Lunacy

Somewhere along this frenzied journey called modern-day life, we've lost our sanity. In fact, a friend of mine has a magnet on her refrigerator that says, "Out of my mind. Be back in one hour." But she wants to know why she has to return so soon. And she's not alone. More and more women tell me they long to escape, even temporarily, to a slower-paced, simpler time. If there is one expression that describes the condition of women's lives today, it is "stressed out." In fact, many of us are getting stressed out over being so stressed out.

❊ ❊ ❊

Some mornings it seems hardly worth the effort to take the cat off your face. (You have to be a cat owner to know this is how they get your attention in the morning.)

This book is as much for me as it is for you. I am not immune to the types of pressures life throws at us. Although I write and speak about stress solutions, I face the same daily stressors as everyone else. But I've discovered some innovative sanity secrets through research, reading, and life experience that help me stay sane...and they will help you too.

Although most of the time I'm so excited about my life I can hardly stand it, there are times when I have to guard against bouts of frustration, discontent, and world weariness. I get irritated, annoyed, agitated, worried, and disappointed over the same things that probably upset you: there's never enough time, I need to lose weight, I can't find things when I need them, where is the romance, what was I thinking when I married him (and why won't he read *his* relationship manual), the car needs to go in for repairs again, the kids are driving me nuts, why did I think I'd be any good at this job, will I ever get totally organized, the phone never stops ringing, will there be enough money for retirement, I need a vacation!

Some mornings it seems hardly worth the effort to take the cat off your face. (You have to be a cat owner to know this is how they get your attention in the morning.) If you've ever had "one of those days," or weeks, or lifetimes, you know that sometimes the only answer seems to be to run away from home, leave town, and start over again. Some days I'm convinced that if I could just dye my hair, get new ID, and escape to a Caribbean island, maybe I could regain some of my sanity and begin anew. But the old axiom "Wherever you go, there you are!" reminds me that although it's not easy to find happiness within myself, it's impossible to find it elsewhere.

For many of us, life has become a pressure cooker of excessive demands, unrealistic expectations, and nearly impossible standards. Being a woman means there is always more than plenty to do—more than enough people to help or deal with, appointments, activities, and unfinished tasks competing for our attention. While traveling as an international motivational speaker, I began sharing with women audiences that I was writing a book on "sanity secrets for surviving daily pressures, overcoming physical burnout, and conquering inner turmoil." Almost every woman responded by asking, "How soon can I have a copy? I need that book yesterday!" Each week I hear from women who tell me they feel overworked, overextended, overwhelmed, overloaded, undervalued, and unappreciated. From nearly every angle, women are burned out, worn out, and weary. In fact, being frustrated, frayed, frazzled, and fatigued most of the time has become the new normal.

What I want us to do in this book is take a step back and see this insanity for what it really is, take lessons from the way life used to be, learn some wisdom of the ages, and move forward to becoming the level-headed, even-tempered, calmer, saner, more balanced women God created us to be.

How to Use This Book

You've got enough stress in your life right now (or you wouldn't be reading this book), so learning how to implement these sanity secrets isn't meant to be an additional source of tension. I suggest reading this book in short sessions and only reading as much as you can take in and act on within the next week or two. I have divided the information into bite-size segments to make it easy-to-read and conducive to putting the principles into action. At the end of most Sanity Secret chapters are "Sanity Savers & Survival Hints" sections. These are extra tips and ideas I've tested and put into practice in my life…and they'll help you in your quest for a stress-free life.

This book has four parts, and following each one there is a section called "The First Resort"—an encouragement to turn to God through prayer in times of distress…rather than asking for divine guidance as a last-minute last resort. These inspiring thoughts, uplifting ideas, and biblical insights will help you transform your life by bringing it into balance—mentally, emotionally, and spiritually.

My desire is that this book will be a refuge from the world for you, a retreat from the pressures of life and a haven for a few minutes out of your day. I hope you'll relax just a bit while discovering the principles and tools that will help you reclaim your life and put it on solid footing once again.

Here are some ways to get maximum results from this book:

- As you read each segment, keep in mind your current situations, circumstances, and challenges at home and at work. Relate all the information to your life. Ask, "How can I use these ideas to overcome the stressors I'm facing now?" and "How will these concepts improve my life?"

- Use a highlighter to emphasize ideas and points that stand out and are especially meaningful to you. When you go back later to review, you'll be able to spot those special concepts right away.
- Keep a pen and spiral-bound notebook handy. As you read, make summary notes of the points that are particularly pertinent to your life. You'll end up with a shorter version of the book with the specific ideas you plan to incorporate into your life. This will be easier to review any time you need a quick refresher.
- As you read, note the specific goals you want to achieve.
- As tempting as it may be, resist thinking, *I know lots of people who really need these ideas!* While it's true that others would benefit from these sanity secrets, you're the one reading this book. For now, take the information personally. Once you experience results in your life share the ideas with others and include your personal insights.
- Implement the Sanity Savers & Survival Hints. Use the information as a personal goal planner.
- Put new strategies into practice as soon as you can. Knowledge is great, but it's only potential success until it's combined with action. Doing what you know brings success.
- Expect great results! There's an adage that says, "When the student is ready, the teacher will appear." We have many teachers over the course of our lifetimes. Let this book be one of them for you.
- When it comes to making changes, give yourself time. It's natural to feel uncomfortable when attempting anything new or different, so don't get discouraged if it's a bit difficult at first. It takes about three weeks to develop a new habit pattern. Be patient. You will experience a calmer, more relaxed life in about 21 days.

Are you at your wit's end? Then I hope you take a step away from the lunacy and embrace a simpler, saner pace where what matters and what doesn't will be easier to see. If you're sick and tired of being sick and tired, get ready to be renewed, refreshed, and recharged! If you're fed up with being inundated, snowed under, and weighed down by information, deadlines, never-ending to-do lists, obsessions, fads, crazes, clutter, and too many decisions, separate yourself from the noise that surrounds you and listen for the sound of wisdom coming from inside you...from the still, small voice of God, who will give direction and new meaning to your life. Putting the sanity secrets to work in your life will decrease the craziness you experience and increase your joy.

❁ ❁ ❁

I don't suffer from insanity; I enjoy every minute of it

BUMPER STICKER

Why and How I Can Help You

A large international seminar company organized the very first stress-management workshop I ever presented. I prayed that at least 20 people would be interested in attending. More than 700 participants showed up! I was so stressed from the size of the audience that I don't remember one word I said. Since then I've had many opportunities to present my program to thousands of people. Based on positive feedback from participants about the results they experience and my own observations, I'm confident you'll find the material timely, relevant, and helpful. Over the past 20 years I've developed and updated the content many times to keep it current and applicable to today's lifestyles.

For quite a while now audience members have continued to ask for a book on managing stress. While I'm not an expert when it comes to the psychology of stress management, this book is written from personal experiences—mine and others—plus the wisdom and principles found in God's Word and extensive research I've done while preparing for and presenting stress-management workshops in professional and corporate settings, on cruise ships, in churches, and at women's retreats.

Defining the Sanity Secret Philosophy

"Sanity secrets" are the self-nurturing steps you can take to fortify yourself for the upcoming struggles and ongoing challenges you face that rob you of peace of mind and throw you off balance. The sanity secrets philosophy is simple: "Pinpoint your stress triggers and make changes in your thoughts, beliefs, actions, and lifestyle to nurture your life back into balance and wellness so you'll cope well during times of distress." For those times when things go wrong, be prepared by treating yourself right.

❁ ❁ ❁

Quit taking this life on earth so seriously.
Nobody gets out of it alive anyway.

Stress is taking its toll on us, and part of it is because we've bought into the message that we're capable of doing everything for ourselves. These days, due to the feminist movement, we can pay for our own meals, open our own doors, carry our own luggage, and give up our own seats on the last lifeboat. We've also been fed warped messages about what we *can do* and what we *should do*. The problem started when we distorted the truth that "women can be anything" into the mandate that "women should do everything." And when we fall short of that ideal, we feel disappointed in ourselves. There is a big difference between "can be" and "should do"!

In our high-tech and fast-paced culture, it's easy to get stressed out, off balance, and caught in the trap of believing the messages all around us that encourage us to do more and be more. For starters, not only are we rushing about at breakneck speed attempting to get everything crossed off our never-ending to-do lists, we're also doing it wearing three-inch heels. Talk about getting off balance! Our minds are always busy and filled with concerns about the future, our children and grandchildren, our relationships, health issues, time pressures, finances, and social responsibilities. And then there's all that is going on in other parts of the world that we hear about on the news.

Some of us work in careers or professional positions where we must constantly adapt to new procedures, handle personality conflicts, and cope with looming deadlines. Others must deal with busy toddlers, teenagers exhibiting "hormonal crazies," or aging parents with serious health and financial concerns. In some cases it's all of these. Perhaps you have a husband who constantly works overtime, or is often away from home on business trips, or is preoccupied with a hobby or sport that takes precedence over all other matters. Maybe you have no spouse at all to alleviate some of the social and financial pressures. Are you a single mother bearing the full responsibility of being the mom, dad, breadwinner, and homemaker all wrapped into one?

Add to these the increasing external pressure of having to accomplish more in less time, and it seems any opportunities to slow down, take your time, enjoy some pampering and nurturing retreats, make time for family and friends, and complete activities at your own pace are rare. For some they never occur at all.

Learning and implementing sanity secrets when you're feeling tense and stressed means finding ways to live stress free within the chaos rather than wishing it would all go away. It involves finding time for the important things in your life and discovering coping mechanisms to help you deal with those circumstances and situations that are clearly (or not so clearly) beyond your control. Sanity secrets equip you to:

- nurture your inner self
- acquire a positive mental perspective toward your life and future
- discover the inner peace and freedom you long for

What It Is and Isn't About

Sanity Secrets for Stressed-Out Women will help you develop a system of proven approaches, time-honored wisdom, and practical principles you can implement when stress threatens to overwhelm you. By putting them into practice regularly, the sanity secrets can soften future stressful circumstances too. Sanity secrets go well beyond the conventional stress-management strategies that encourage deep breathing, progressive relaxation, exercising, drinking pure water, and eating a healthy diet, although all of these traditional methods are important and will be touched on in various chapters.

You'll be discovering ways to *control* your stress responses and *minimize* the negative effects of stressful situations and circumstances before stress takes over. What you won't find are suggestions for eliminating all the causes of your stress. I know, it would be wonderful and convenient to wave a magic wand and see all the situations, circumstances, and people that make us crazy disappear. But here's the thing: The stress in our lives—and on this planet, for that matter—is not going away. So we need tools and inner strength to deal with it rather than wasting valuable energy and time wishing it would magically vanish.

> Sanity secrets: principles and ideas that minimize the negative effects of living in our chaotic world and help us balance priorities, renew our enthusiasm, and enjoy life.

You also won't find ideas for coping with loss, dealing with grief, managing anger, or overcoming a harmful past. There are many great books available to help in those specialized areas, although most of the principles presented here will be helpful if you find yourself in such circumstances.

What can this book about stress survival do to help you? In these sanity secrets you'll discover practical, straightforward approaches to minimize the negative effects of living in our chaotic world. You'll find an abundance of concepts to help you balance your priorities, renew your enthusiasm, and find time to enjoy the truly important relationships and activities you value most.

In addition, sanity secrets provide ways to stay calm in a crisis, recognize and release earlier experiences that are still causing stress today, and move freely into a future filled with peaceful possibilities. By caring for your physical body, resting your mind, and drawing on the spiritual strength you gain from trusting in God, you can feel rejuvenated and see your struggles, disappointments, and challenges with a fresh perspective. Along the way, you'll discover specific suggestions and tools that deal with issues such as physical relaxation, nutrition, fitness, and definite thought processes for maximizing energy, minimizing stress, and promoting vibrant health, energy, and vitality.

You will never be problem-free as long as you are alive on this planet.

That's an unfortunate truth. In fact, each and every one of us is currently in one of three places: right in the middle of dealing with a serious problem, just finishing up handling a major problem, or heading toward the next big problem. So if you aren't facing a crucial issue or concern right now, don't assume this book isn't for you. Trouble is on its way, I promise. And when your current problems finally go away, new ones will soon arrive. Sometimes it seems we're allowed a brief reprieve in-between, a chance to coast for a bit before the next one appears. Often the new problems that come along are much worse than the ones we could hardly wait to get rid of. Many of us tend to put our lives on hold until the problems go away. But we'll never be completely stress free until the day our friends file past us whispering, "My, doesn't she look natural?" So instead of waiting for that momentous day, let's find out how to have peace in the midst of the storms of life.

Defining Peace

Many women tell me what they are truly seeking in a stress-free existence is genuine inner peace. If that sounds like you, how would you describe the peace you crave? What does it look like? A pastor friend of mine gave an illustration in one of his sermons that created such a visual image I'll never forget it. According to the story, many years ago two renowned artists were each asked to paint a picture depicting their personal interpretation of true peace. The first artist's painting portrayed an idyllic woodland scene complete with tranquil streams; a small babbling brook; clear, sunny skies; and birds nesting serenely in the treetops. The second artist's picture of peace took a completely different slant. In his work he painted a violent storm scene with intense, raging winds; dismal, ominous clouds; and fierce ocean waves lashing their fury against a rocky cliff. Tucked in the midst of it all, in a small cleft in the rock, was a tiny bird—safe, unruffled, and protected from the turbulence surrounding it. This seems to be a much truer rendition of inner peace in our chaotic world. Even in the fiercest storm there can be a calm, silent center in a cleft in the rock.

We can take inspiration from this by appreciating the serenity and tranquility we experience when we're trusting in our heavenly Father, who cares for our every need. As our responsibilities, problems, and concerns whirl around us out of control, threatening to knock us off balance, we are warmed and comforted by the inner serenity and profound sense of peace we have knowing we're tucked away with God. He's in control, and our true tranquility comes from his promise to never leave or forsake us (Deuteronomy 31:6). He gives us peace that passes all understanding. All we need to do is trust him implicitly. With this newfound tranquility, we can face our fears with confidence; build strong, healthy ties with family and friends; and valiantly confront the difficult times brought about by hardship and adversity. Aside from all this, we can share our peace with others caught in the storm and help quiet the tempest they find themselves in…even if it's only for a season.

Although we yearn for those times when we can physically escape to a more restful, peaceful environment, stress-free living is far more than simply spending the weekend at a spa or resort or taking two weeks out of the year to lie on a beach and bury ourselves in a good book. As valuable as taking a break from routine can be for short-term stress relief, true inner peace comes only after we've learned to deal with life's natural ebb and flow and restored the balance between body, mind, and spirit. We can accomplish this by applying a few basic-yet-essential sanity secrets to our everyday living. This way we can separate ourselves from the hectic, worrisome pace of modern living and make these stress-free principles an integral part of our lives.

2

Yearning for Sanity

What I find myself longing for these days, and what I think most women long for, is a return to sanity. My thesaurus says other words for *sanity* are *mentally healthy, whole, sound, fit,* and *normal.* When we are healthy and whole, we act reasonably and have rational responses to tensions and pressure situations. It's not hard to understand our deep, inner pining for a saner, calmer, relaxed, and more serene way of living when we look closely at the insanity going on in our lives today.

Does this scenario sound familiar? Women are expected to climb the corporate ladder during the week; work out at the fitness club every morning; go for a walk during lunch hour; stop by the dry cleaners, shoe repair, post office, and library after work; drop off and pick up the kids at music lessons and sports practices; cook nutritious suppers that don't make anyone gag; keep the corn from touching the potatoes; kiss boo boos; and help Junior construct an Indian hut model using six toothpicks, one tortilla, and a Magic Marker for the science fair project tomorrow. (We get pretty good grades too!) We know every detail of our kids' lives, while our husbands seem to be vaguely aware that some short people are living in the house.

Women also feel pressured to keep an orderly home; entertain guests in the evenings; and spend our weekends making kettles of meatless soups and vegetarian casseroles, baking multigrain muffins, separating mountains of clean laundry from the dirty stuff, and organizing the paper clutter from the previous week before the new piles begin. And to top it all off, with the ounce of strength we have left in our tired, aching bodies, we attempt to turn into love goddesses for our hubbies after dark. *Whew!* It's no wonder women fall into the trap of thinking we aren't measuring up when we find we can't fulfill all these expectations, ideals, and standards—even though we know innately they are unrealistic and virtually impossible to do.

A Typical Day

Let's take a deeper look at what happens during an average day in the lives of twenty-first-century women.

We wake up to a noisy alarm clock (or a crying baby or squabbling kids) in a room with closed windows and some sort of electronic air cleaner because we wouldn't dare take the risk of breathing some form of pollution while we sleep. We drag ourselves out of bed, stumble into the bathroom, and find that brushing our teeth is not going to be a simple matter. There's the organic, 100-percent natural toothpaste, plus one with whitening power, and another that fights cold sensitivity. Don't forget the mouthwash with added fluoride protection, whitening strips, a waterpick, and the dental floss we keep promising the hygienist we will use twice daily.

After that, we prepare for our morning shower and are faced with a multitude of choices. We have the raspberry refreshing shower gel, grapefruit-mango foaming bath essence, wild strawberry body scrub, peach-coconut facial mask, green apple clarifying shampoo, avocado volumizing shampoo, vanilla moisturizing conditioner, oatmeal-kiwi glycerin soap, almond facial moisturizer, tangerine hand lotion, lavender foot cream, herbal bouquet relaxing aromatherapy oil... Wait a minute, are we having a shower or making a fruit cobbler? Anyway, you get the drift. With all these options, a trip to the supermarket would be a lot easier on our brains first thing in the day.

Later, after reaching for the antiperspirant, we remember the media warnings about possible dangers from all the chemicals and aluminum in there, so we make a mental note to add plain, old-fashioned "deodorant" to the shopping list and simply take our chances for today. Keeping in mind that multitasking is very important in today's world, consider this helpful suggestion made in an article I read not long ago. It recommended we keep an old toothbrush handy in the shower so we can clean the grout between the tiles while our hair conditioner is working. The writer also suggested we get a waterproof iPod so we can listen to motivational messages to stimulate our minds while we're stimulating our bodies with an all-natural loofah sponge. The article went on to encourage us to get an early start on our fitness regime by doing a few deep knee bends and squats while using the blow dryer, curling iron, or hair straightener. Call me peculiar, but I think this type of multitasking is more outrageous and laughable than any episode of a TV sitcom!

At this stage, we haven't even really started our day, and yet we've already been required to put out more effort and make more decisions than the president of a large country. What's more, we feel terrible about ourselves because someone who needs this much help can't possibly be in any condition to venture out into the world. We'd love to crawl back into bed and pull the covers over our heads, but we can't because we've been programmed that "the early bird gets the worm" and "if you snooze you lose." So we dress quickly and get ready for breakfast.

Now, there's no such thing as a simple breakfast. It must be sugar-free, fat-free, low in calories, and high in fiber. So we forgo the eggs because of our cholesterol levels and pass up the bacon because of the saturated fat. Instead, we toast some multigrain bread and eat it dry—no butter, no jam. Maybe our vitamin pills can make up any slack. Aside from our one-a-day multivitamin, there's an additional one to activate our brains, one to improve our memories, one to pick us up, and another to calm us down. Naturally, we wash them down with bottled Evian rather than the polluted sludge we've been told is coming out of our tap.

Wow! What a tremendous number of choices, obscure details, trivia, doubts, fears, and insecurities we face just to get started on an average day. No wonder we feel burned out, worn out, and weary. In the workshops I conduct, my motivational speaking, and the books I write, my goal is to help people relieve stress by discovering how abnormal and unnecessarily complex and nerve-racking the daily ins and outs of our lives have become.

We need to get back to sanity—to the ability to make sound, rational decisions for ourselves, to be level-headed, sensible, and practical when it comes to running our affairs. The opposite of being sane is to be unreasonable, ridiculous, or absurd. Insanity means lacking the ability to think logically and with reason. Let's face it—somewhere along the way we've lost our sanity—the proof is in our unbalanced lives, out-of-control emotions, and continual striving toward having it all.

Over the past several years we've seen a craving for sane living revealed in a shift toward simplicity and minimalism and a move toward spiritual awareness. It's not hard to understand this trend when we look closely at what's going on today. Each year we spend billions of dollars on stress management. Billions! Therapists, counselors, speakers, seminar leaders, workshops presenters, and authors help people cope with every type of stressor, including feelings of being overwhelmed, overloaded, overstretched, overworked, and under pressure. We've become a society obsessed with how dreadful and appalling life is rather than giving our attention to the joys around us or discovering ways to celebrate life and reflect on how wonderful it is. In libraries, bookstores, on the internet, on television, and on radio there is information available on every stress survival topic. Maybe you'd like to read one of these imaginary self-help books?

Show Me a Functional Family

Hurry Up and Slow Down

12 Steps to Going 24 Hours with No TV

He Said, She Said—So Who's Listening?

I'm Okay, You're Irrational

Men Are from Mars and They're Not Going Back

Would You Like Cheese with Your Whine?

If They Can Send a Man to the Moon,
Why Can't They Send 'Em All?

Amazing New "Exercise–Weight Loss" Connection

How to Stop Your Family from Driving You Nuts

Quit Trying to Ruin My Life, but First, Could You
Drive My Friends and Me to the Movies?

Although these books were never written (that I know of), millions of dollars are invested annually to show people the way to achieve stress-free lives. I have to smile when I think of my parents and grandparents and how they knew so many valuable ways to stay calm, feel relaxed, and create comfort. They didn't have Dr. Phil or Oprah to show them how to achieve a peaceful, satisfying, hassle-free, rewarding life. They didn't need to be told to focus on intangibles such as moderation, self-control, charity, compassion, generosity, family ties, connection in relationships, laughter, creativity, imagination, courtesy, consideration, good manners, and respect. In their generation, these were givens. These values came intuitively, were presented by society, and enforced by parents. Why were these qualities considered much more important to former generations than to ours? And what can we do to clarify the values in our own lives to bring back what's really important?

We tend to blame our stress on the fact that we live in a time that is much more difficult and challenging than it was for past generations. Have we forgotten that those generations faced world wars, the Great Depression, racial intolerance, sexual inequality, intense and prolonged physical labor, and in some cases extreme levels of poverty? Most of us are not stressed because we face life-threatening circumstances every day. Our insanity comes from losing touch with reality and failing to acknowledge the things that are of true value. We aren't sure anymore what is really important. It's difficult to tell the difference between our wants and our needs.

Our hectic pace—along with nonstop mass marketing, technology that demands an immediate response, and constant information about all that's happening in the world—has obscured rational thinking and common sense. Is some or much of our insanity and suffering coming from being a generation steeped in excess and overindulgence?

Even so, in many ways we're longing to live the life that people had in the 1950s, or at least what is idealized as 1950s culture. Some women familiar with that era tell me they yearn for the sanity that went along with the life embodied by the fictional June Cleaver and Betty Crocker. Apron-wearing women stayed home; kept organized houses; cooked delicious meals for their families; visited with friends; cared for their husbands; and spent valuable time teaching their children manners, ethics, and morals.

Speaking as someone who grew up in that era, it truly seemed to be a generation a lot saner than ours.

Kids in that time period would walk home after school to find the house filled with the delicious aromas of supper simmering on the back burner and a homemade dessert baking in the oven. There'd be an after-school snack of chocolate milk and oatmeal cookies warm from the oven, and other family members...along with the dog...were waiting there to greet them. After enjoying a home-cooked dinner served from platters and bowls around the kitchen table, the kids would play tag and hide-and-seek outside, running all over the place until dark, and then beg their parents for "just five more minutes" before coming in for bed. Bedtime meant a warm bath, a snack, a story read by a parent, and nighttime prayers. On Saturday mornings they'd grab a sack lunch of peanut butter and banana sandwiches, chocolate brownies, a thermos of ice-cold milk, and apples; get on their bikes; and take off for the day to the local swimming pool or to explore the neighborhood with friends. The next day they were off to Sunday school and then to Grandma's for a traditional Sunday dinner.

The closest we get to that nowadays is watching a TV commercial showing a couple getting excited about the pizza being delivered to the door or families jumping for joy over their trip to a fast-food restaurant.

> People were satisfied with simplicity. They were connected with their personal values. They were in close touch with family, friends, and community.

One professional woman wrote to me about wanting to minimize the stress in her life since taking on an executive position in her career. She talked of the fond memories she had of a simpler time when, as a stay-at-home mom, the children were asleep for their afternoon nap, a roast was in the oven, the folded laundry smelled of fresh air from being hung on the clothesline that morning, and a home-baked apple pie was cooling in the breeze of an open window. Aromas of floor wax and furniture polish wafted through the house, and she had time to put her feet up and browse through a magazine or get into a good novel while sipping a steamy cup of tea before the little ones got up from their nap. As much as she didn't want to give up her modern conveniences or her corporate position, she longed for some of the sanity, inner peace, and sense of completion of days gone by.

The world wasn't so much kinder to those other generations. For many, there were terrible hardships. Maintaining a household required long hours and lots of hard, physical work. Poverty was common, opportunities and possibilities were narrower, and many choices limited. The world was smaller in scope. Then what's the main difference between what's happening now and what took place in our grandparents' generations? It was saner in those days because people were satisfied with simplicity. They were connected with their personal values. They were in close touch with family, friends, and community.

Even if it were possible to go back, no woman I know would choose to live in the days before blow dryers, curling irons, automatic washing machines, disposable diapers, dishwashers, microwave ovens, cordless phones, palm pilots, voice mail, fitness clubs, TVs, CDs, DVDs, HDTVs, MP3s, iPods, the internet, Blackberries, and email. Or would we? In any case, there are lessons to be learned from yesterday's lifestyle. Let's strike a balance between the opportunities and possibilities of today's world and the sanity of yesterday. By using the sanity secrets, we'll have less stress and more joy.

3

What Is This Thing Called Stress?

I can honestly say I don't remember hearing my parents use the "S" word to describe themselves or their circumstances when I was growing up. It's only lately that people have begun to describe their condition as stressed out. In the "olden days," people may have said they were at their wit's end, worried, nervous, or concerned over some matter. They might have referred to feeling tense in their marriages, apprehensive about an upcoming event, fearful of the future, or anxious about being parents. My mother used to say we kids were the cause of her "screaming meemies"! (It wasn't until I had children of my own and experienced tsunami-like stress that I fully understood that expression.) But rarely, if ever, did my parents or other adults I knew use the word *stress* to describe what they were experiencing.

Originally *stress* was an engineering term that referred to the amount of pressure steel could withstand. Stress is a state of dynamic tension created when we respond to perceived demands and pressures from outside and within ourselves. It's normally *how we feel about a situation* that determines whether it will cause stress—not the situation itself.

How much pressure can we withstand? Physically, mentally, and emotionally we've been miraculously created and designed to survive an incredible amount. But if the tension we tolerate daily continues to build without a respite, sooner or later we will break under the load. A chair is built to withstand a certain amount of pressure, and a person can sit on one for days at a time without any problem. We could probably even put another person on the same chair…or perhaps several people. But eventually, if we keep adding more and more bodies, the chair is going to collapse. That's what happens to us. In our modern world we are under increased and often prolonged pressure. We continue to pile on ourselves more demands, responsibilities, obligations, and activities. Add to that the resulting problems that go along with living, plus the hassles and tension of relationship conflicts, the occasional emergency or crisis, and the normal daily upsets, and it's easy to see why we finally crash.

But it's not the stress that ruins us; it's the prolonged pressure…and the fact that we keep loading it on without taking care to renew ourselves or setting aside time for us to recharge. When we live in a perpetual state of overload, push beyond our limitations, and feel as though we are on the verge of collapse, we run into significant problems.

There are some truths about stress that will enable us to understand the challenges and difficulties that cause pressure and take action against them.

Seven Truths About Stress

1. *Stress is not always harmful to your health.* Stress is a natural part of being human. And stress in and of itself is not a bad thing. We need a little tension, or spice, in our lives to keep us stimulated and interested in the world around us. It's what keeps us alert and bright. In the long-ago past, this tension helped keep us one step ahead of predators and other dangers to our survival. Even today stress can function as a source of motivation and a catalyst in the problem-solving process. Athletes and Olympic champions say they count on having some stress to help them perform at peak levels. My husband is a drag racing driver, and he needs a measure of stress to keep him alert and focused (especially when he's packing his parachute!). Entertainers, musicians, and actors would be concerned if they didn't have a little stress before a performance because it gives them an edge that helps them perform at their best. Most of us function better with the stress of a looming deadline, and students are known to study more effectively when they have the pressure of an upcoming

exam. (I wonder if it's stress that keeps some high school and college seniors alive!)

Very simply, our daily responses to change, challenges, and surprises are stress related. When we become excited, the hormone *adrenalin* (aka epinephrine) turns on our alertness, helping us to focus on the event at hand. If you were a brain surgeon about to operate or a pilot landing a jumbo jet—trust me, a little added tension would be good for you and everyone involved. Stress is to life what tension is to the violin string—too little and the music is dull; too much and the string snaps. The problems come when we're in a heightened "alert state" with muscles tense day-in, day-out, month after month. So the issue is not whether we *have* stress but rather how we *deal* with *excess* stress.

2. *Not all stress comes from negative events.* We tend to think tension and pressure come from unpleasant situations. Yet even events and circumstances we look forward to can cause stress. Ask any new bride and groom. Planning a vacation, buying a new home or car, having a baby, going back to school, getting a promotion, changing job positions, and retiring are all exciting and meaningful experiences, but they each bring stress.

We look forward with great anticipation to spending the holidays with family and friends, yet often, after it's over, we wonder how we ever got through it or if it's worth doing again next year. Have you ever returned from time off work feeling that you now need a vacation to recover from your vacation? Positive events can be stressful. Even a good exercise program or a great game of golf or tennis puts stress on our bodies.

> Having dreams come true can be stressful even though we probably wouldn't change a thing.

Although it wasn't always true, today I can tell you I'm living my dream—traveling the world as a motivational speaker and author and being a loved and loving wife and mom. At work I present programs internationally at conferences, corporate staff-training events, and women's retreats, as well as on cruise ships sailing to Hawaii, Alaska, Bermuda, and the Caribbean. My books have helped thousands of individuals make positive, life-changing choices. Some of my books have even become bestsellers. I work with a wonderful publisher who offers me the opportunity to continue writing. Yet because my dream has come true, I now deal with the stress of deadlines, due dates, jet lag, and other pressures I never imagined. Traveling through different time zones and dealing with flight cancellations, delays, and missed connections are stressful. And spending nights away from home and missing family and family-related events adds to the tension.

Doing what I love to do also involves many long hours spent in my office. I'm on the phone, answering emails and other correspondence, researching and designing new materials, and preparing contracts and invoices.

Having dreams come true can be stressful even though we probably wouldn't change a thing.

3. *Stress can come from unlikely sources.* We don't normally think of thermal stress, which is when our body temperature experiences sudden and extreme change by moving from hot temperatures to cold or vice versa. When you go from an air-conditioned home, car, office, or shopping center into the sweltering outdoor heat or come into a warm environment after being outside on a blustery day, your body undergoes stress.

There are also electromagnetic radiations emitted from common household items, including televisions, radios, computers, microwave ovens, cordless and cell phones, cars, electric blankets, and many other modern conveniences, that put stress on the delicate balance of our biological functions and our immune systems. Aside from these, there are TV and telephone satellites, international telecommunication centers, and the latest radar technology, as well as water pollution and food additives that add to our problem. Even the air, sun, and rain aren't what they used to be.

Although these issues are invisible and it's difficult to measure the effects of pollution, toxic waste, chemicals, the greenhouse effect, extreme weather, and electromagnetic forces on our bodies, the stresses are real and can have a noticeable effect on our health.

4. *Stressful living seems worse nowadays.* Since the world is much more complex today, we certainly tend to believe that life is more stressful. However, the amount of stress each of us attracts into our daily lives has a lot more to do with our thoughts, beliefs, habits, lifestyles, and daily

choices. Good stress management is really life management and taking control of our lives. It's all about balance, time effectiveness, and healthy self-care, as you'll discover in the following chapters.

5. *Stress is different for everyone.* Situations that cause you to feel stressed out might have no impact on someone else. While cooking, baking, or having people over for dinner may be a relaxing hobby for one person, another would find it extremely stressful. When you see how a friend or family member handles pressure and tension, you may be tempted to compare yourself and wonder where you went wrong. But when it comes to stress, we are all different even when we're related. Our lives are unique and our situations are different. Our family dynamics, past programming, and reactions are all distinctive. Even if two people were experiencing similar distressing circumstances, their responses would not be identical. Each of us responds to pressure in a way unique to us. That's why there are no universally effective stress reduction techniques.

We need to develop a personalized system made up of various proven practices, valuable approaches, and time-honored methods adapted to our style.

6. *All stress symptoms deserve and require attention.* Falling into the trap of believing minor symptoms can be ignored is easy. Headaches, backaches, stiff muscles, teeth grinding, jaw clenching, angry outbursts, heartburn, and insomnia can be early warning signs that your life is getting out of control and you need to make some changes to manage the stress. Even when there are no obvious symptoms, stress can be taking its toll. Don't be fooled. If you've developed the habit of camouflaging or numbing your symptoms with medication, alcohol, sugar, caffeine, food, shopping, gossiping, or television watching, you are sedating the very symptoms that could act as alarms, warning you of potential danger so you can save your life. You can go through your days without giving stress much thought until it overwhelms you...or you can choose to do something and head it off now.

7. *Harmful stress can drive us to despair.* Most of the time, when we talk of stress, we are referring to *distress*—the feeling we have when the tension

we experience is consistently high. When our bodies are placed under physical or psychological stress over a sustained period of time, it increases the production of hormones, including adrenaline and cortisol. These hormones produce marked changes in your heart rate, blood-pressure levels, metabolism, and physical activity. Although this physical reaction can help you function more effectively when you're under pressure for short periods of time, it can be extremely damaging to your body in the long run.

While some stress is advantageous in keeping us on our toes and even desirable in certain situations, negative stress can be devastating. According to studies and surveys, over 80 percent of all visits to the doctor have to do with stress-related complaints. Many common ailments, including allergies, arthritis, headaches, and back problems, can often be traced back to stress. Stress has been linked to the leading causes of death, including heart attacks and strokes. Research shows that job stress costs companies billions of dollars each year through absenteeism, lost productivity, insurance claims, and reduced levels of performance. People may be physically present but mentally absent due to stress-related complaints, and that's when accidents happen and mistakes are made. Anything that can be done to reduce the damaging effects of stress makes workers happier and organizations wealthier.

No one can completely escape the effects of stress. It influences all of us at some time in our lives. Yet it's possible to maximize our efforts while minimizing our stress levels. We want to manage stress so that it continues to stretch us toward our personal goals without damaging our physical and mental health, personal relationships, and future success opportunities.

Different Types of Stress

Do you have any idea how many books are out there covering the different types of stress? Neither do I. But I imagine it's a huge number. That's what makes stress management seem so complicated and confusing. One way to lessen the confusion is to identify and recognize the various types of stress that affect our lives. As you read, remember that self-testing can become yet another source of stress, so what follows is meant as a *general* guide to understanding where stress comes from.

Ongoing stress: This is the most common form of stress and comes from the tension of current day-to-day demands, along with the anticipation of upcoming pressures. This stress is caused by the fender bender that put your car in the body shop, the washing machine that quit midcycle, the important papers that have gone missing, a crucial deadline coming up quickly, a phone call from the principal about a problem your child is having at school, and so on. There is usually some combination of several stress emotions—anger or irritability, anxiety or apprehension, and depression or hopelessness. Interestingly, this type of stress can actually be helpful in small doses, motivating you to change directions, take action, and make healthy changes. But too much is exhausting. Even positive events, such as being the chairperson for a professional association, volunteering to coach your kid's baseball team, or playing a role in a community or church stage production, can be exhilarating and energizing in the beginning. But when you're constantly in a position where you feel pushed close to or beyond your limits to keep up, you'll eventually feel overwhelmed and burned out.

Immediate urgency stress: This stress comes from trying to squeeze a size 12 body into a size 8 sequined evening dress (it fit perfectly last year) just minutes before you need to leave for a dinner party. It's a direct crisis, and an independent incident probably not connected with any others. This type of stress often comes from wanting to do or be more than is possible. It is a result of constantly being in a rush and living in a continual state of urgency, chaos, and crisis. When you don't have time to plan, take on too much, or always have too many irons in the fire, you won't be able to organize or manage the many self-inflicted demands and pressures clamoring for your attention. You then become short-tempered, irritable, anxious, and tense. Your world becomes a very stressful place to live.

Chronic stress: This stress is your greatest enemy. It is the grinding type that irritates and aggravates day after day, year after year, until it eventually wears you away. Long-term, chronic stress wreaks the most havoc by destroying your body, your mind, your spirit, and ultimately your life. It happens when you feel trapped in a job you despise, an unhappy marriage, a dysfunctional family, or a condition of debt or poverty. If you live in a state of hopelessness and despair, never seeing a way out of a miserable situation, it's tempting to give up looking for solutions. One of the goals in this book is to restore your hope. God says in Jeremiah 29:11, "I know what I'm doing. I have it all planned out—plans to take care of you, not abandon you, plans to give you the future you hope for."

It's been said that hope is the oxygen of the soul. Long-term stress can rob us of hope and literally take away our breath. Hopelessness is the root of many of today's psychological disorders. But there is a light at the end of the tunnel—and it is not a train!

Are you overstressed? Has it been a long-term condition? Let's find out where your personal stress level stands.

This Is Only a Test

Try this little test. It will give you a *rough* estimate of how much stress you are currently experiencing. On a scale of 1 to 5, rate how often you feel this way, with number 1 being never and number 5 being very often.

____ I have so many challenges and difficulties that I will never overcome them.

____ Life is so complex that I can't figure it all out.

____ Clutter is piling up so high I fear I'll never conquer it.

____ I'm frustrated and angry over things that are beyond my control.

____ I can't cope with all the things on my never-ending to-do list.

____ I feel incapable of getting control over the truly important things in my life.

____ I'm upset and/or hurt over something that happened without warning.

____ Things never seem to go my way.

____ I'm ill-equipped to handle the daily annoyances and irritations in life.

____ I can't stay on top of my schedule and priorities.

____ I doubt whether I can get a grip on my personal problems.

____ I'm hesitant about taking a stress quiz that has no reliable scoring system.

Just kidding about that last one! Hey, I'm a writer, not a mathematician. However, if you have a lot of fours and fives in this list, you have a high stress level.

Most of our stress is control based. When things happen that we perceive to be beyond our control, we feel pressure. Regardless of what your stress score is, you are no doubt experiencing some pressure and tension in your life, so keep reading. There are sanity secrets that can improve your reactions to even the everyday stresses in your life.

4

Measuring Your Stress Susceptibility

We are in charge of the stress in our lives. It may not always seem like it, but the level of stress we experience has more to do with the choices we make than the pressures we face. By our lifestyle choices, we *choose* whether we will be vulnerable or resistant to stress and burnout. If you're under a lot of stress right now, this may not seem like a very comforting thought—but it can be a liberating one. There are steps and precautions you can take to safeguard against becoming susceptible to the negative effects of stress. Why not take this simple stress test? The more you can check, the less vulnerable and more stress-resistant you are. After the test we'll examine each statement more closely.

Testing...Testing...

Place a check mark by the statements that are generally true in your life.

____ When I'm down, I have at least one close, confiding friend who will really listen.

____ I can ask for help when I need it.

____ I have at least one relative nearby on whom I can depend in times of need.

____ I take time for friendships and make an effort to nurture them.

____ I get six to eight hours of sleep at least four nights per week.

____ I eat at least one balanced, hot meal per day, including something fresh and unprocessed and preferably prepared at home.

____ I have plenty of fun times alone or with friends when I laugh till I cry.

____ I'm able to release negative emotions and speak openly about my feelings when upset, angry, worried, or fearful.

____ I'm able to talk candidly with the people I live with about daily living concerns.

____ I have something fun to look forward to each day, each week, each month.

____ I'm organized and manage my time effectively.

____ I plan quiet time for myself every day to relax.

____ I take steps to ensure I'm in good health.

____ I get enough "fun" exercise to achieve and maintain my desired level of fitness.

____ I generally have an optimistic outlook on life.

____ I gain strength from my faith and relationship with God.

____ I regularly attend church.

____ I have a daily time of meditation and prayer.

How did you do? The fewer check marks you have, the higher your stress susceptibility. This test isn't meant to make you feel bad or guilty. It's just a gentle prompting and encouragement to get into the habit of caring for yourself.

Let's look closely at the 18 statements in the quiz and check the corresponding sanity secrets to see if you're protected from the consequences or at risk for harmful results. Each of the behaviors and practices we'll look at can improve your resistance and lower your vulnerability so you can better withstand stress. They are our first line of defense. If you didn't score as well as you'd like, you can turn things around by using the list as a goal-planner to set some future targets for yourself. Take one at a time, and make your goal realistic and achievable so you feel comfortable aiming toward it.

1. *When I am down, I have at least one close confiding friend who will really listen.* Numerous studies have shown that women who experience severe stress without having a close, confiding friend are ten times more likely to become depressed than equally stressed women who have close friends. There are times when you need to talk, to rant a bit, to share. A confiding friend is someone you can trust with your deepest, innermost thoughts, your worst fears, your greatest doubts, and your highest dreams. She'll always provide support, boost your morale, and give your mental health a lift just by being here. I like this saying: Friendship is a single soul dwelling in two bodies.

2. *I can ask for help when I need it.* It takes courage to ask for help. For some of us it's like admitting we aren't capable of doing what needs to be done. One big step toward regaining your sanity is realizing you can't go it alone. There are times when you will need to delegate tasks, hire outside help, or simply ask for a helping hand. When you ask for emotional support, choose carefully the people with whom you share your concerns, fears, doubts, and insecurities. They should be women you can be emotionally confidential with, who will respectfully listen, remain trustworthy, and openly share in return.

3. *I have at least one relative nearby on whom I can depend in times of need.* Your family can be a support group who knows everything about you and loves you anyway! There's a built-in history that requires no explanation or apologies when it comes to who you are and how you are handling the stress you're experiencing. A loving family accepts you and offers unconditional love, emotional support, and practical help when

you're under pressure or in a crisis. Your family members can be your oldest, closest, and most trusted friends. Mom, dad, sisters, brothers, aunts, uncles, and cousins are the ones with whom you share treasured memories—vacations, pets, teachers, schools, special holiday gatherings, Friday night spaghetti and meatball suppers, and evenings of popcorn and games around the kitchen table. Not all families support each other, but having even one relative who is an encouragement to you and will be there to provide emotional support when you need it can help ease the pressure when you feel you can't cope.

4. *I take time for friendships and make an effort to nurture them.* When the Beatles sang "I get by with a little help from my friends," they knew what they were singing about. Women are especially relational. We really do need each other. Friends understand what we're going through, the stresses we face, how we feel about them, and the way we react.

If there is a man in your life, chances are he just doesn't get you. Why? He's not wired to get it! There are some things only another woman can identify with and appreciate. Let your friends know how important they are to you. As you keep in touch with old friends, new ones will enter in. Your life changes over the course of time, and friends will change too. Taking care of yourself doesn't mean doing it all alone. We long to be heard, valued, and understood. We must share aspects of our lives with others. Realizing we aren't alone is comforting and helps us put our problems and challenges into perspective.

Realizing we're not alone is comforting and helps us put our problems into perspective.

5. *I get six to eight hours of sleep at least four nights per week.* Not everyone has the same sleep requirements. Some women can get by with amazingly little sleep. Most of us, though, need a full night's sleep at least several times a week to successfully handle daily stressors. You can get by with less sleep for a while, but eventually you will pay the price. Without enough sleep, you become tense, irritable, and edgy until you finally get enough sleep to feel rested, which can take several weeks.

6. *I eat at least one balanced, hot meal per day, including something*

fresh and unprocessed and preferably prepared at home. A hot, well-balanced, home-cooked meal enjoyed while sitting at the dinner table can do wonders for your ability to resist stress. Pleasurable conversation and satisfying interaction with loved ones over a tasty meal do a great job of fending off negative stress. Eating on the run can diminish your ability to cope with pressure situations. Fast food doesn't provide the nutrients you need. When you're under a lot of stress, you need to add more foods containing B and C vitamins while cutting back on sugar, salt, and fat. Rather than grabbing something from the fast-food drive-through or eating prepared and packaged foods that offer little nutritional value, aim to have at least one sit-down, home-cooked meal each day.

7. *I have plenty of fun times alone or with friends when I laugh till I cry.* It's estimated that children laugh on average 500 times a day. In contrast, adults only laugh about half a dozen times in 24 hours. I'm talking genuine laughter, not the hysterical, out-of-control variety that ends in giant, inconsolable sobs as you lie in a heap on the just-mopped kitchen floor now covered in some unrecognizable sticky substance. We adults have a long way to go to meet our daily laughter quotient. It's been said that having a good laugh is like jogging on the inside. The Bible says, "A cheerful heart is good medicine, but a broken spirit saps a person's strength" (Proverbs 17:22 NLT). Laughter promotes good health, whether it's planned or spontaneous.

8. *I'm able to release negative emotions and speak openly about my feelings when upset, angry, worried, or fearful.* Turning your emotions inward and bottling them up is mentally and physically damaging. If you don't like to talk when you're stressed, you may be *decreasing* your resistance. Communicating your emotions in appropriate ways is vital to your health. If you find it difficult to express yourself when you're upset, worried, or angry, put your feelings in writing first. Then when you're ready to express yourself verbally, practice being assertive rather than aggressive. Being assertive means you stand up for your rights while being sensitive to the rights and feelings of others. It's a nonoffensive approach that allows others to speak up about their feelings as well, allowing all parties to better understand each other.

9. *I'm able to talk candidly with the people I live with about daily living concerns.* Running a household is a team effort. You may want to hold regular monthly family or household meetings to address issues such as chores, schedules, money matters, and home organization so the household can be run without conflict and confrontation. If you avoid talking about problems and daily hassles, they become a chronic source of resentment and hostility. Teamwork makes life go smoothly and easily. You might not solve problems on the spot, but you will prevent a build-up of complaints that could explode later on.

10. *I have something fun to look forward to each day, each week, each month.* Doing something just for fun is not only enjoyable at the time, it's an effective way to recover from the effects of stress and improve your resistance to future pressures. Find something pleasurable you can look forward to at the end of each day. It doesn't have to cost a lot of money or take much time. It might be watching a funny movie or a classic that's an old favorite, soaking in a warm bubble bath in a candlelit bathroom, reading a good novel, doing a crossword or jigsaw puzzle, or taking your dog for a walk. Once a week plan to work on a hobby, take an education course, visit a museum or art gallery, meet with friends to play board games, or get out into the country for a nature hike. Once a year plan a trip, organize a reunion with family or friends, or go to the ballet, opera, theater, or a concert.

Too often we feel guilty taking the time or money to do things just for fun. When you make time for fun, your whole body relaxes and you end up experiencing less stress from the demands and pressures of daily living.

11. *I'm organized and manage my time effectively.* There will never be more hours in a day, but you can make better use of the time you have. When you have too much to do in too little time, it's a guaranteed recipe for stress. Being disorganized saps your strength and energy. Organizing your time means setting priorities, planning ahead, being willing to delegate certain tasks, enlisting support, and hiring help when necessary. By scheduling and prioritizing, you'll be able to spend your time on the things that matter most to you. By knowing which time of day you function best,

setting realistic deadlines, and taking time each day to think and relax, you'll protect your time and avoid time-wasting activities.

12. *I plan quiet time for myself every day to relax.* If you think you haven't got time to relax, either you're too busy for your own good or you have a distorted view of efficiency. *Relaxing is not goofing off.* It's essential if you want to handle daily pressures effectively. Women who take care of themselves with a time of quiet relaxation during the day report they sleep better at night, have more energy, are more likely to stay calm in chaos, and are more creative problem-solvers. Your quiet time might be spent praying, meditating, reading, gardening, taking a stroll, studying the Bible, or simply doing nothing. Silence and solitude are great stress relievers. Even 15 minutes of quiet time each day can rest your mind and body.

13. *I take steps to ensure I'm in good health.* When life gets too hectic, it's tempting to take shortcuts where your health is concerned. A healthy body is the first line of defense against the harmful effects of stress. Without your health, your resistance is weakened and may even work against you. When you always feel under the weather, it interrupts your sleep, drains your energy, and is an additional source of uncertainty or anxiety. Don't let worsening health symptoms and neglect due to lack of time add to your pressure.

14. *I get enough "fun" exercise to achieve and maintain my desired level of fitness.* Exercise benefits you in many ways. Aside from the obvious—strengthening your heart, improving circulation, controlling weight, building muscle, improving posture and balance, and promoting flexibility—it has mental and emotional benefits by releasing endorphins and creating a sense of peace and well-being. Whether it's walking, cycling, swimming, tennis, or aerobics classes, pick any exercise activity you enjoy so you'll be more likely to stick with it.

15. *I generally have an optimistic outlook on life.* "An optimist sees an opportunity in every obstacle while a pessimist sees an obstacle in every opportunity." Optimists view even upsetting situations as opportunities for personal growth rather than sources of stress. They come through a

stressful situation focusing on the positive lessons they've learned and what they will do differently next time. Optimists focus on problem-solving situations that are within their control and devising coping mechanisms for those beyond their control.

16. *I gain strength from my faith and relationship with God.* In order to be effective, stress survival involves the balance of body, mind, and spirit. Picture a three-legged stool. When any one of the three elements is missing, the stool topples over. Many people work on getting physically and mentally fit while leaving out that most important aspect. Someone once said we are all born with a God-shaped hole in our hearts that we try to fill with everything else—relationships, money, possessions, fame, and success. Until we invite God to fill that hole, we will always feel a longing and emptiness. A personal relationship with God means you can turn your worries and cares over to him. You don't need to walk alone. With God handling your affairs, you can have his peace that passes all understanding.

17. *I regularly attend church.* By getting together to worship with others who have the same beliefs, your faith will be strengthened. The friends you make at church form a strong support group you can call on and trust during times of high stress. Social events at church provide opportunities to mix with like-minded people. You'll find opportunities to give back by offering your gifts and talents. We all have a deep, inner longing to be acknowledged. In the Father's house you will be accepted and loved.

18. *I have a daily time of meditation and prayer.* One of the most powerful forms of meditation is prayer. Prayer simply means talking with God. Imagine having coffee with your heavenly Father! It's not only calming and relaxing when you're in a state of distress, but it allows you to release your worries knowing he hears your requests and the cries of your heart. He has promised that he will never leave you or forsake you. You are not alone. Communing with God is a great privilege and the cornerstone of stress survival.

How many of those activities are in your life today? Are there any you want to add? What are they? What steps can you take this week to implement them? Write them down.

Now that you have a good view of your lifestyle as it is now, let's look at where your main stressors are coming from. Read the following and put a check mark beside the ones that bring about the most stress for you.

Stress Sources

____ attempting to balance family, work, and personal activities

____ trying to find time for myself

____ being overcommitted at work and home

____ having too many social obligations

____ relationship conflicts

____ marital differences or difficulties

____ childcare responsibilities

____ child disciplinary problems

____ being single

____ being a single mother

____ having a blended family

____ stepparenting

____ financial pressures and concerns

____ family or domestic violence

____ family get-togethers

____ trouble with in-laws

____ having a retired spouse

____ poor self-image and low self-esteem

____ weight problems

____ changes or challenges at work or school

____ operating my own business

____ working from an office at home

____ pressures of being a boss/manager/supervisor/business owner

____ conflict with bosses or employees

____ ____

____ ____

____ ____

Major life changes, challenges, and emergencies are additional sources of stress.

____ getting married

____ relationship breakup

____ divorce

____ getting remarried

____ having a baby

____ raising a child with a disability

____ loss of job/income

____ retirement

____ declaring bankruptcy

____ child leaving home

____ moving from your house

____ moving geographically

____ major accident

____ major illness or injury

____ breakdown of car or major appliance

____ ____

____ ____

____ ____

The bottom line is that all change is stressful, whether it's desirable and beneficial or disturbing and uninvited. Some situations can be planned for, such as weddings and moves, while others can't, such as accidents and sudden illness. Experts tell us that experiencing three or more major life change events in a 12-month period, over and above the typical ongoing stressors, constitutes an overload of stress in a person's life. However, the everyday variety of stress problems may be more of a concern because they can remain hidden.

The First Resort

Too often we wait until we are stressed out, worn out, and burned out before we call out to God in prayer for the help we need. Although he should be the first place we turn, going to God is frequently our last resort and final course of action. Often we wait until we're at our wit's end and have exhausted all our human resources, as frail as they are, before finally looking to our heavenly Father for answers. Even when we're overwhelmed, overloaded, and overextended, why do we still believe we can or must handle everything on our own? When we finally come humbly before God and embrace him as sovereign Lord, we learn from him. We gain strength from him. If this were our first resort, and not the last, think of the stress and insanity we would avoid! Jesus calls us to a place of rest:

> Are you tired? Worn out? Burned out on religion? Come to me. Get away with me and you'll recover your life. I'll show you how to take a real rest. Walk with me and work with me—watch how I do it. Learn the unforced rhythms of grace. I won't lay anything heavy or ill-fitting on you. Keep company with me and you'll learn to live freely and lightly (Matthew 11:28-30).

Jesus knew how to live sanely and we don't. So let's turn to him as our *first* resort and not the last. Let's see how God does things and then fall into line with him.

Part 2
Recognizing Stress and Taking Action

5

Sanity Secret #1

Recognize the Warning Signals

Imagine your home smoke alarm sounded or the phone rang in the middle of the night. Would you experience some tension? If a car came careening down the road toward you or if someone shouted "Thief!" or "Watch out!" would you suddenly become alert? If you were walking home alone after dark and heard heavy footsteps approaching from behind, would you feel anxiety or trepidation? What if your doctor said you were headed for a heart attack? Would you be alarmed?

Yes! Of course you'd be concerned. You'd probably say, "I need to do something—and fast!" In all of these situations, if you didn't feel stress, you'd be at great risk. Neglecting to pay attention or choosing not to act on those warning signals would be dangerous.

Stress triggers the release of hormones and a state of mind that makes you alert to impending danger and the possibility of problems ahead, much like the red "check engine" light on your car's dashboard. When that light goes on, it's not wise to ask your mechanic to disconnect the fuse. Likewise, if you see smoke billowing from your oven, doing your favorite relaxation and deep breathing exercises might not be the best way to handle the situation. Stress has a purpose. It warns you to be alert, be ready to act appropriately, and be prepared to make changes.

Safe Stress

When the stress alarms go off, we're being prompted to change direction. If we keep doing what we're doing in spite of the sirens, the danger or calamity can stop us in our tracks and put all our dreams on hold. When stress goes undetected or is ignored, we have no way of assessing how serious a problem we have. We also have no real way of determining the best way to cope. Take note:

If God puts a warning sign in your path, pay attention!

Just after my first book was published a number of years ago, I found out this principle firsthand. After completing the initial media tour arranged by my publisher, I wanted to do so much more to get the new book into the hands of women I believed would benefit by it. So I single-handedly took on the role of publicity agent and enthusiastically organized a series of television and radio interviews, book-signing events, speaking engagements, and other media functions all over North America.

My enthusiasm occasionally exceeded logic, and although it was a fun time of celebrating my new book, the stress of a hectic schedule took its toll on my physical and emotional well-being. Occasionally appointments overlapped. And when an interview was to take place in one hour, I allotted exactly 60 minutes to drive there. With my schedule so tight, there was no cushion of time to allow for traffic jams, detours, or unforeseen delays. After keeping up this pace for a number of weeks and going home only on weekends, I started to feel the strain. I've been blessed most of my life with an abundance of energy, but now I was dragging, becoming excessively annoyed over minor frustrations, feeling achy all over, suffering with insomnia, and at times almost falling asleep while driving.

During one reprieve at home, my dentist informed me I needed to have some minor dental surgery and would require about one week to recover. I looked ahead several weeks on my calendar to find a seven-day opening and scheduled it. I knew I had overdone my life when I was back on tour and caught myself counting down the days to *dental surgery* with great excitement and anticipation: only one more month...two weeks to go...four more days to dental surgery. When I realized I was becoming exhilarated over the thought of having surgery simply because it meant I would have some time off, I was brought back to my senses and realized I'd pushed myself too far.

You've probably had the same fantasy I occasionally have—the one where you check into a hospital for a minor ailment, snuggle in a cozy hospital bed made up with clean sheets, and enjoy the bouquets of beautiful fresh flowers sent by people who love and care about you. You're served hot, nutritious meals—in bed—and have some quiet time alone to read a good novel, browse through a magazine, take a midday nap, or go to the bathroom without little (or big) hands knocking on the other side of the door. If escaping from life to spend time in a hospital bed sounds especially appealing to you, take it as a warning signal! It's time for you to make some serious lifestyle changes before the hospital scenario becomes reality...and I promise it won't be as serene as it sounds.

The first step in stress survival is to recognize the alarms that are alerting you to take action. Over the years I've discovered how to quickly recognize many of these.

Stress Symptoms Checklist

Place a check mark beside the ones that pertain to you and your life today.

____ *General discontentment*

Lacking joy in your life makes it hard to get out of bed and face another day. The psalmist asked, "Who out there has a lust for life? Can't wait each day to come upon beauty?" (Psalm 34:12). When you're stressed, you no longer hunger after life or yearn to get out there and discover its beauty. Do you remember Saturday mornings when you were a kid? You could hardly wait to get up and be on your way. You had plans and were filled with enthusiasm and anticipation for the day. It was going to be a voyage of discovery. If you don't have that kind of enthusiasm and anticipation anymore, it could be a sign you're overstressed.

____ *Physical exhaustion and fatigue*

When you're dragging around, feeling listless, and burned out, simple tasks seem overwhelming, people are annoying, and nothing is enjoyable. With your energy drained, life appears unmanageable.

____ *Prone to illness, disease, physical ailments*

Because stress plays a major role in destroying the human immune system, if you're stressed you're more likely to pick up whatever sicknesses are going around...the latest cold, sore throat, or flu. Also many major illnesses, from allergies to heart conditions, from arthritis to some forms of cancer can be related to stress.

____ *Feeling depressed*

Despair and sadness are persistent feelings of discouragement that make your problems seem insurmountable and leave you with a sense of hopelessness and powerlessness.

Caution: "Clinical depression" is caused by a physical disorder resulting in a chemical imbalance in your body. If your depression is persistent and interferes significantly with your daily life, consult your physician.

____ *Increase in body aches and pains*

You might notice more sore muscles and joints or find yourself subconsciously rubbing your neck or shoulders more often. Stress can also result in tension headaches, numbness, and feeling like pins and needles are poking you.

____ *Lack of confidence*

These are the days when you'd rather pull the covers over your head and stay in bed because you don't feel capable of tackling the life issues facing you. Waves of self-doubt intensify your problems and cause them to appear overwhelming.

____ *Increase in addictions and bad habits*

As a temporary relief from stress, many people indulge when it comes to eating, drinking, smoking, and spending. Stress can turn occasional drinkers into alcoholics, sporadic smokers into chain-smokers, and someone with a sweet tooth into a sugarholic. You may not even notice you're overindulging. And even if you do, you might go to extreme lengths to keep this self-destructive behavior from family members, friends, and colleagues. Some people become dependant upon the approval of others or they get obsessed with their work. These can also be addictions.

___ *Increase in negative thinking*

When you're having more pessimistic thoughts than positive ones, you might be asking, "What's wrong with me? It's not like me to be so negative." Whether it's pessimism, criticism, cynicism, sarcasm, or fault-finding, recognize what Zig Ziglar calls "stinkin' thinkin'" as a sign of overstress. (If you tend to be negative in general, maybe it isn't stress but a personality temperament that can be dealt with in other ways. We'll talk more about that in Part 4.)

___ *Appetite changes or eating disorders*

If you want to eat all the time or find you have no appetite at all, stress can be the cause. Whether it's eating for comfort or not wanting to eat, the key is to notice when your regular eating pattern is off schedule or off kilter.

___ *Indigestion, heartburn, nausea*

Stress puts a strain on the digestive system by encouraging the production of acids. Tension can also cause spasms in the digestive system, resulting in discomfort and stomach pain.

___ *Sleep changes or disorders*

If you have difficulty falling asleep, you wake up periodically throughout the night, you wish you could sleep all the time, or you always feel tired no matter how much sleep you get, stress during the day may be the cause. Sleep experts report that cases of insomnia and sleep deprivation are on the rise in our stress-filled culture. As a result, sleep clinics are popping up all over North America to help people find solutions.

___ *Crying comes easily*

When things get tough, it's natural to have a good cry. But when you're on the verge of tears most of the time, and they tend to spill over at the slightest comment or pressure, take it as a sign you're dealing with an overload of stress.

___ *Worry over matters you can't change*

Worry produces energy, and that energy fuels any stress you might be experiencing. When you're stressed out, you may find yourself stewing more over matters that are beyond your control. Worry is like sitting in a rocking chair. You expend a lot of energy, but you don't go anywhere.

____ *Excessive irritability over small matters*

It's normal to get annoyed when things don't go as planned. What's not so normal is exploding with fury when the toaster won't pop, the zipper won't zip, the scissors are hiding, or the flashlight won't work. (I've been told a flashlight is merely a case for holding dead batteries.) Rage is a sure sign you are way too stressed out, whether it's at home, at work, in the mall, in an airplane, or in your car. Extreme aggravation over little things and intense expressions of anger out of proportion to the situation should be seen as loud alarms letting you know your stress is out of control.

____ *No sense of humor*

One of the first things to go during high-stress times is the ability to see the funny side of life. Learning ways to have a good laugh during times of tension can alleviate a lot of pressure. When nothing seems amusing or comical anymore, and you can't remember the last time you had a side-splitting laugh, take it as a warning sign and look for something that makes you grin or laugh out loud.

____ *Nervous habits and tics*

Although these can be signs of other serious disorders, many times tics are a temporary result of overstress. They include throat clearing, nail biting, playing with or pulling the hair, touching the face, lip biting, knuckle cracking, and fist clenching. Twitches and other nervous tics can be strangely comforting in times of distress and, as a result, habit forming. They are brought on by an uncontrollable urge and tend to provide temporary relief in the moment.

____ *Inability to concentrate*

When you're stressed to the max with too many things to think about, too many items on your to-do list, and too many places to go, you may find it difficult to stay focused. If you find you must deliberately and with much effort direct your attention to something, stress could be interfering with your life.

____ *Difficulty making decisions*

Every day we're faced with myriad choices. There are more and more activities, products, services, and technology available. With everything on the increase, including stress, it can be difficult to make wise and timely decisions. When you're overwhelmed, your self-worth dissolves into self-doubt, and you tend to freeze and then procrastinate. You feel alone, afraid, and paralyzed. In some cases, this results in more stress and embarrassment.

____ *Having a "poor me" pity party*

Do you feel you are alone and the only one going through tough times while everyone else enjoys the good life? The truth is that most everyone is going through some test or trial. When you're invited to a pity party, agree to stop in for coffee if you must, but don't stay long.

____ *Poor memory*

Forgetfulness is one of the leading symptoms of stress. When your personal world is spinning out of control, your mind is overloaded with information, and you are overwhelmed with the pressures, pace, and pain of life, it's difficult to remember even the simplest things, such as your phone number or the word for dishwasher.

Chances are you've noticed at least one of these warning signs lately. If you're like most of us, you've checked off several. If you're experiencing all of them, be grateful you're reading this book right now. Offer up a prayer of thanksgiving for the flashing red warning lights and get ready. This could be the beginning of a major transition, a turning point leading you toward a significant life transformation. You don't have to live overstressed anymore!

Take Action

So what do you do when you detect a pattern of stress symptoms and their effects? Some avoid the issue altogether or try to mask the problem through unhealthy approaches. These reactions indicate your problems are becoming too much to handle. They also don't do much, if anything, to resolve the stress issue. For instance, after having an argument with your partner or your teenager, do you reach for the donuts, ice cream, cookie dough, or chocolate bar? If a friend has disappointed you or you've had a disagreement with a coworker, do you go on a shopping spree? Do you try to solve your sleeping problems using alcohol, sleep medication, or other drugs? Are you relying on drugs or caffeine to get moving in the morning? Do you avoid having lunch in the staff room so you don't have to deal with your boss or coworkers? The greater your feelings of despair or physical discomfort, the more desperate you become to relieve them one way or another, wholesome or not.

Once the stress symptoms appear, if they aren't dealt with they may remain for a long time. Imagine you are an elastic band being constantly stretched and released. For a while, you snap back into your original state, not showing any ill effects. But if the stress continues, and you are stretched to the limit again and again, you begin to wear thin. Pretty soon you become worn out and not so resilient. If you don't take action, you may snap in two. In human terms, you may burn out, become severely ill, or suffer a serious breakdown.

We all have unique breaking points. Some people can tolerate more stress than others. Only you know if stress is beginning to take a real toll in your life. Once you do, instead of giving up and passively accepting that you've finally gone over the edge, be thankful you are aware of the sirens going off. Stress symptoms are gifts that act as valuable warnings, letting you know acute trouble is brewing unless you make changes.

You may not realize how much pressure you're enduring until you become aware of the symptoms. Maybe you've been slipping up when it comes to handling crucial matters, making mistakes, misplacing important items, or missing scheduled appointments. Perhaps a severe attack of indigestion or a headache lands you in bed and lets you know your mind and body are coming under intolerable strain. Maybe an emotional outburst over something noncritical, such as a remote control that's gone missing or an avalanche tumbling from an overcrowded closet one more time, indicates you're over your stress limit.

When you're under prolonged pressure, you also can become

vulnerable to emotional symptoms, such as feeling insecure, becoming paranoid and overly guarded, or doubting the love you get from your spouse or family. Maybe you find it hard to believe your bosses or coworkers when you're praised or you become extremely suspicious of your spouse, a neighbor, or your good friend. When you're on overload for extended periods of time you may find yourself getting easily confused, messing up at ordinary daily tasks and activities, getting lost while driving in your own town, or forgetting simple things like how to spell a common word, where you keep the cutlery, or your child's name. (One toddler wore the same nightgown several times in a row, and her stressed-out mom called her Laura Ashley for 3 days.)

When you notice warning signs, heed them. Let the alarms alert you to make adjustments in your life.

When I was close to burnout, I thought the coffeemaker was broken after it brewed only a pot of hot water until I realized I'd forgotten to put coffee in the basket. After the washing machine finished its cycle, I opened the lid to find it had eaten not just the socks but everything else too. Apparently I remembered to put in the detergent and fabric softener but not the clothes. At that time, if my life were a TV show, it could have been called *Sue's Greatest Bloopers.* Once I stopped bawling, I had a good laugh at myself.

When you notice warning signs, heed them. Let the alarms alert you to make adjustments in your life. Every positive change begins with a clear decision that you are either going to start doing something or quit doing something. Improvements start when you decide to get in or get out of your situation. God created you to experience a state of harmony—mentally, physically, emotionally, and spiritually. Discomfort and lack of peace should warn you that it's time to make some positive adjustments in your lifestyle choices. So be aware. And remember: Prevention is far better than dealing with the aftermath of a crisis.

Sanity Savers & Survival Hints

- Be on the lookout for hidden or masked stress symptoms.
- When you see a negative pattern in your life, take action and make positive changes.
- Living stress free may require saying goodbye to certain behaviors, attitudes, and habits.
- You will never leave where you are until you decide where you'd rather be.
- Get a clear image in your mind of the specific results you want to achieve.
- Eliminate blaming and accept 100 percent of the responsibility for your new stress-free life.
- When God puts a warning sign in your path, pay attention.
- "We cannot do everything at once, but we can do something at once" (Calvin Coolidge).

Isolate Your Specific Stressors

What do you say when someone asks why you're feeling stressed? If you're like most of us, you may blurt out, "It's everything. Life is too crazy and frantic!" or "I don't even have the time or energy to think about it. The whole world seems to be one giant, chaotic muddle. It's all I can do to get through the day."

While those feelings are understandable, the truth is you won't be successful at dealing with stress as long as you lump it into one big fuzzy mess. Often stressors flit in and out of your mind without getting the attention and focus that enables you to take action. It's only by pinpointing exactly what's bothering you and handling one thing at a time that you'll be able to make significant and lasting changes.

It's All in Your Head

Mind Map

The simple act of putting pen to paper or sitting at your computer and inputting a list gives you something tangible to work with. Externalizing your thoughts, feelings, and ideas helps create distance and space between you and what's causing your stress. In other words, it helps you be less emotional and more objective. Doing your thinking on paper (or computer) will also help you get a better picture of the causes of the tensions and pressures currently affecting you.

Stress-free people often do their thinking on paper. One way to do that is to use a brainstorming technique known as *mind mapping.* Whether problem solving, decision making, or releasing tension blocks, a mind map provides an overall view of your life and its stressors. This is the best way to clarify exactly what you'd like to see changed. You've probably noticed the large maps placed at the entrances of amusement parks and shopping centers. If you've ever referred to one, you've noticed the arrow marked "YOU ARE HERE." The map designers know you can't find someplace else until you know where you are now. The same is true for life. You can't move to a new level of stress-free living until you understand clearly where you are and what's causing the stresses right now.

Mind mapping is a simple, fun, and quick way to create a comprehensive picture of the stressful situations you face. You'll also gain important insights into the ways you react to stress. The object is to put your life's stressors—all of them—onto one sheet of paper. You'll also identify the contributing factors and underlying factors. This allows you to see at a glance the elements of your life that cause you tension. (One workshop participant thought seeing all her stressors written in one spot would cause far too much stress. You may think so too, but trust me—it is such a beneficial exercise that you'll be thankful you pushed through.)

Creating a Mind Map

1. Gather creative tools for mind mapping: a sketchbook, spiral notebook, or large sheet of drawing paper; fluorescent markers; colored pens and pencils. On a blank sheet of paper write your name in the middle and put a circle around it. Now draw several lines out from the circle like the spokes of a wheel.
2. Label the outer end of each spoke with a stressor that affects your life. At this stage, use general terms such as Work, Home, Family, Money, Health, Relationships, and Time. List everything that comes to your mind as you pour out your impressions of what is causing you to feel so stressed. Write down the words and phrases that come to mind (or create a drawing that represents what you're feeling). Include things as

personal as issues involving intimacy and as obvious as never having enough time for yourself or being stuck in traffic. (See Figure 1.)

3. Once you're satisfied that your primary sources of stress are identified in the pattern, place a circle around each of those sources and draw more spokes branching out from each one. Label each of these spokes with the various aspects and facets of each stressor. Identify the underlying causes, the results, other people involved—whatever pops into your mind. Keep branching away from the center. The more you list, the more you'll think of.

   If you come up with another main stress category, put in an additional spoke from the center. When a particular feature of a stressor pops into your mind, insert it as another branch. Write quickly without editing and without passing judgment. By the time you've completed your mind map, the whole page will be filled with situations, relationships, feelings, and ideas that cause you stress.

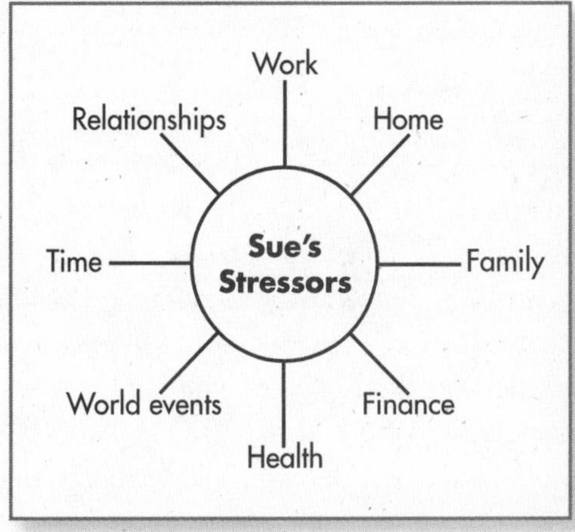

Figure 1: Basic Mind Map

4. Put your mind map away to "rest" for a couple of days to give you some time to glean further insights. Give careful thought to where to keep your mind map so it is safe and stays confidential. You want to be free to write anything you like without fear of someone else reading it.

Let me give you an example of a mind map. On one primary source of stress I've called "Work," the branches might be labeled *Boss, Coworkers,* and *Workload.* When you continue, you may work on the subcategory *Coworkers* with a branch labeled *Personality conflicts.* A branch labeled *Boss* might include *Demanding.*

Check out Figure 2. It shows these common stressors and their various aspects. Notice that the general categories are written at the end of each main spoke and then circled. More spokes come out from each of those circles, and then spokes come out of those circles, and so on. The variables of each stressor are written on the additional spokes.

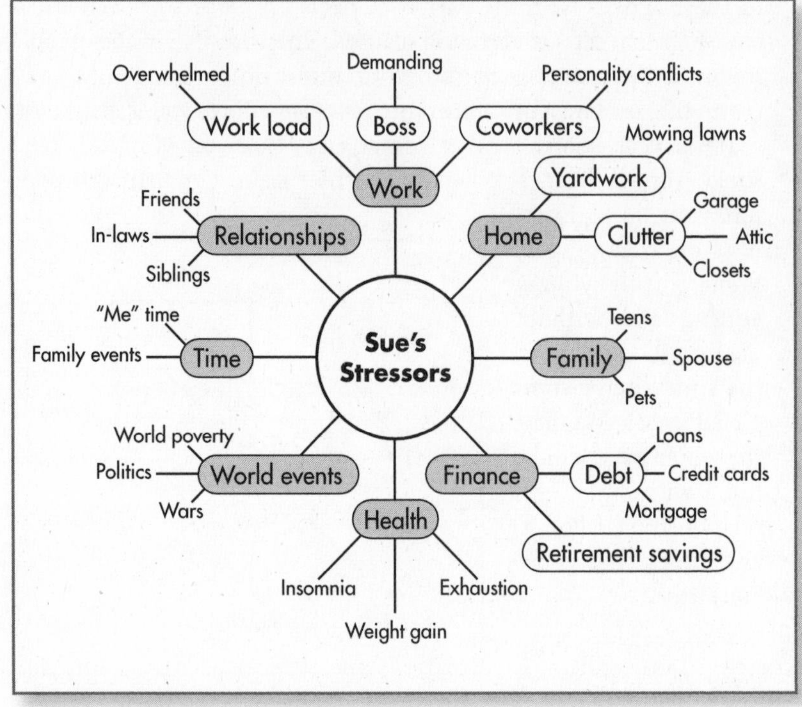

Figure 2: Detailed Mind Map

Let's say one stressor you've identified on your mind map is family stress. Various spokes might be labeled: husband, children, parents, in-laws, siblings. Your map would then be expanded with offshoots that include some of these stress-causing aspects:

- Husband—works a lot of overtime, never home, and when he is he doesn't talk; never have quality time alone together; sexual needs don't match mine; raising the kids and disciplining methods differ; finances and faith values are shaky

- Toddlers—daycare concerns; toy clutter; potty training issues; discipline
- Older children—losing shoes, clothing, homework, library books, and house keys; constantly outgrowing clothing; lots of games with dead batteries; sibling rivalry
- Teenagers—music too loud; rebellion issues; driving lessons; sharing the family vehicle; messy rooms; not doing chores; constant carpooling to sports, youth meetings, music lessons
- Parents—aging issues; the need for a home-care worker; living too far away for frequent visits; losing driver's license; need to downsize
- In-laws—preparing for long-term visit; personality clashes
- Siblings—sister makes me feel inferior; brother disagrees on everything from raising kids to family reunion details

If you work from home, a main stressor may be your workspace, which would expand to include ergonomics such as inadequate lighting, an uncomfortable desk chair, and poor air quality. Household stressors may involve living near a noisy freeway, airport, or railroad crossings; cartoons blaring from the family TV; neighborhood dogs barking; a messy house; remodeling, redecorating, or construction mess; a drawer that comes off the track every time you open it; house clutter; stacks of incoming mail; a never-diminishing pile of laundry, ironing, and mending.

Identifying stressors is the first step and creating a mind map gives you something tangible that will help you isolate the most important and frequent causes of stresses you experience. By analyzing your mind map, you can concentrate your efforts on the most serious sources and find healthy changes that will alleviate some of the stress.

For the next step, which we'll do in chapter 7, you'll need a half hour of uninterrupted time, some paper, and a pen and a marker ready. Most of all you'll need plenty of privacy.

Mind Mapping Tips

- It's best to do your mind map in one sitting, although you can add to it over time.
- Patterning with a mind map is simply a way of organizing your thoughts. There is nothing mystical or magical about mind mapping. This technique seems to mirror the way the human mind works and is based on the way your brain generates ideas.
- As you work, don't analyze. Resist the urge to scrutinize and evaluate your thoughts. You'll have a chance to examine and study them deeper later on. For now, just keep the ideas coming. And don't worry if your mind map doesn't make sense at first. It will become clearer as you go along.
- Your ideas may come slowly at first, but as you get into the flow they'll come so quickly you'll barely be able to keep up to write them down.
- If you run out of room, don't hesitate to start over with a bigger one, write smaller this time, or tape paper together to make a larger surface to work on. Or do separate mind maps for each of the main stressors you noted.
- Don't get bogged down in detail. You want a broad spectrum of wide-ranging stressful events, situations, and circumstances.
- Mind mapping externalizes the way you are affected internally by stressful events. Because of that, the ones that show up are those most bothersome to you. The most urgent and draining tension-causing situations that need immediate attention will show up in your pattern.
- Base your mind map on the present, not the past or future.
- The point of your mind map is to capture information and ideas as they are generated.
- Mind maps are as unique as fingerprints. Each pattern is only interesting to the person who created it. There's no benefit in looking at someone else's mind map. Unless you watch the layout grow or know the person well, you won't understand their thinking patterns.
- This brainstorming technique is useful anytime you want to examine information. You can use it to organize your life, set goals, or solve problems. As a sanity secret to minimize the negative effects of stress, you may want to do this exercise again in a few months to evaluate

its effectiveness. To make it more fun, clip pictures from magazines, photographs, and old greeting cards to add to your mind map.

More Quick Tips

- Using different colored pens and highlighting markers will stimulate your creativity while helping you identify various categories.
- Your goal is to turn this pattern into a "porcupine" of stressors.
- Print rather than write, so you can read the mind map more easily.
- Aside from words, you can use sketches, drawings, illustrations, scribbles, signs, symbols, images, pictures, photographs, patterns, phrases, slogans, Bible verses, and quotes.
- This is a pattern, not an outline. Expect it to be messy.
- Write whatever comes into your mind. No one is looking over your shoulder. This is between you and God.
- To help identify all aspects, consider how you spent the last couple of weeks. Remember to bear in mind things that cause stress on holidays, weekends, workdays, and vacations.
- Create as quickly as you can. As each new stressor comes to your mind, jot down one or two words or images to describe it. Very soon the crucial sources of your stress will reveal themselves and be added to the pattern. You can also come back later to add more.

Sanity Savers & Survival Hints

- Gather together a supply of creative tools for mind mapping: a sketch book, spiral notebook or large sheet of drawing paper, fluorescent markers, colored pens and pencils, a glue stick.
- Collect and use pictures you have clipped from magazines, photographs, or old greeting cards.
- Don't worry if your mind map doesn't make sense at first. It will become clear as you follow through with the exercise. Besides, it's for your eyes only.

- List everything that comes to your mind as you pour out your impressions of what is causing you to feel stressed.
- Write down all the words or phrases that come to your mind or create a drawing to represent what you're feeling.
- Include things as personal as intimate moments with your husband and as obvious as never having enough time for yourself or being stuck in traffic.
- It's best to do your mind map in one sitting, although you can continue to add to it over time.
- Putting your mind map away to "rest" for a couple of days allows you some time to glean further insights.
- The purpose of a mind map is to see what you can learn about yourself and the things that cause you to be stressed out.
- Give some thought as to where you will store your mind map. You want to feel free to write anything you like without fear of anyone else reading it.

7

Identify What You Can and Can't Control

Stress can make you feel out of control and a little dimwitted. Trust me I know. If I had any doubt, a fast-paced trip to a speaking engagement in California proved it. The insanity—that is the stress—started the night before I was to leave when I stayed up until three o'clock sorting through piles of paperwork with the hope I'd rediscover the surface of my desk, which I hadn't seen in quite some time.

There always seems to be so much to do before going away…email this…print that…file those…pay the bills…leave a message for so and so…plan a mix-and-match travel wardrobe…pack the suitcase and briefcase…leave a list of contact numbers…arrange care for the cat…remember my passport. Finally, after a couple of hours of sleep, I was ready to say goodbye to my family and drive to the airport.

Once inside the terminal, I headed toward the gate, stopping at the coffee shop, a bookstore, and the ladies' room along the way. After boarding the plane, I decided to store my brand-new leather coat in the overhead bin. That's when I realized it—I no longer had the coat! I was horrified. I'd been carrying it over my arm, along with my shoulder bag and a briefcase, and must have put it down somewhere along my route. When I felt panic starting to take over, I asked myself what I would tell my audiences to do if this happened to them. (I was on my way to present a stress survival seminar!) I'm better at helping others manage stressful situations, so I often find it works for me to imagine I'm guiding someone else through the survival steps.

The first thing I'd recommend is to "identify the specific elements that are causing stress in this situation" with the mind map technique. (No, in this case I wouldn't actually get out pen and paper, but I'd do it mentally. Eventually you'll find you can envision a mind map.) In my case, there were several aspects causing stress: the coat is brand-new; I paid a lot of money for it; by now, it may have been stolen; it will have to be replaced; I'll have no coat to wear when I arrive; the plane is taking off in a few minutes so there's not much time to search for it; I feel like an idiot for losing it.

I didn't quit there. After completing this step, I quickly moved to the next one: "Determine what elements I can and can't control." This powerful sanity secret may sound simple, but it is considered by many stress experts to be the primary skill and foundation of stress survival. Knowing the difference between what you can control and what is beyond your control is the main cornerstone in minimizing the effects of stress on your health, your well-being, your relationships, your job, your ability to cope, your enjoyment of life, and your sanity. Either you can do something about a situation or you can't. To deal successfully with stress and tension, learn the difference and don't spend a lot of time focusing on what you can't control. Knowing how to differentiate between the two is a tool that can transform your outlook and heart rate! So I mentally made my list with two columns:

Can't Control List

- The plane will take off shortly.
- I must be on it.
- The coat is missing.
- It may have been stolen.
- I may never see it again.

- I will be embarrassed over losing the coat.
- Replacing the coat will be costly.

Can Control List

- Notify the flight attendant about my dilemma and see if he has any suggestions.
- Ask if I may get off the plane for five minutes to retrace my steps.
- Have attendant radio security to pick me up in a cart and drive me around the airport.
- Ask if the airline would hold the plane for a few extra minutes.
- Pray that God protects my coat and leads me to it.
- Call my insurance company when I return home to see if the coat is covered in my policy.
- Shop for a new coat and get on with my life.
- Forgive myself for being too rushed and not concentrating on what I was doing.
- Ask for divine wisdom in finding ways to slow down and be mindful in the future.
- Pray that no one on the flight will be in my audience tomorrow!

While all this was going on, I was also tempted to verbally beat myself up about losing the coat. I don't know about you, but I've always carried around a special invisible baseball bat for occasions like this. I use it to whack myself over the head a few times while repeating such non-nurturing affirmations as "Loser! How could I be so stupid? What a dumb thing to do. I can't remember anything. This confirms it—I'm an idiot. I'm so careless I'd lose my head if it weren't attached. There's no hope for me." Does this sound familiar? I have a solution to that!

Instead of beating yourself up this way, realistically consider the worst-case scenario. If the most horrible thing did happen, is it a life or death situation? Will it matter one year from now? Does it really matter in the light of eternity? If not, it probably isn't worth losing your sanity over. Chances are it's probably not the worst thing that's ever happened to you or the worst that could happen in the future. Ask yourself a few questions: "What about this situation is within my control?" "What's beyond my control and not worth worrying over?" "What did I learn from this situation?" "What would I do differently next time?" Then do what you can and close the door on the past. You can't go back and change anything, so do what you can and release the rest.

Are there people in your life who would gladly take the bat from you and give you a few whacks over the head (as though you don't do a good enough job yourself)? They add to your misery with their comments: "How could you do something like this? Was your head in the clouds? I can't believe you could be such a dummy." When that happens, be prepared to say the same thing you tell yourself: "I can't go back and change it...if I could, I would. So here's what I've learned, and this is what I will do differently if it ever happens again. In the meantime, here is what I *can* control."

What happened with my coat? As it turned out, I was able to get off the plane, was escorted around the airport in a cart until we discovered my coat at the security check, and then was taken back to the gate. Apparently I'd placed it on the conveyor belt and, after passing everything through the scanner, I picked up only my purse and briefcase. Thankfully the staff had kept it there, recognized me when we pulled up, and began waving the coat in the air. I was able to get back on the plane in time for take off. I spent my flight time thanking God for his goodness and answered prayer.

The Impact of Control

Control is a crucial element in human nature. We don't like ourselves or our lives very much when we feel out of control. Even though so many things are beyond our sphere of influence, there are areas we can orchestrate. To see what an impact the element of control makes in our lives, consider this interesting university experiment.

Two groups of people in separate rooms were given difficult puzzles to solve. To add to the challenge, there was a time limit. As well, a recording of loud, distracting noises was playing in the background—doors slamming, bells ringing, children yelling, babies crying, and horns honking. Does that sound a bit like your life? A crisis to handle, time pressures, due dates, and deadlines to contend with, along with lots of noises and interruptions that frustrate your efforts.

Choice, not chance, governs our future.

The only difference between the two groups was that one was given a device to shut off the noises, which would make it easier to buckle down and tackle the task. But there was a catch—they were told only to use the device if the noises became unbearable and they felt pushed to the brink. They promised to go as long as possible without using it.

At the end of the experiment, the results were interesting. The group that didn't have the device failed. Not only did they not complete the task on time, they said it was not humanly possible with all that noise. The other group completed the puzzle perfectly and on time. But can you guess the most interesting part? They never turned off the noise! Simply knowing it was within their control to do so was enough to overcome the pressures and get the job done. Isn't human nature interesting?

We crave the element of control over our stressors. But here's the truth: There is only one thing over which God has given each of us total control in this lifetime. That is our power to choose. Each and every day we make choices, and those choices determine the outcomes. Choice, not chance, governs our future. Remember the Serenity Prayer by Reinhold Niebuhr?

> God, grant me the patience to accept that which I cannot change, the strength to change that which I need to change, and above all, the wisdom to know the difference.

Here's an exercise you can use as a follow-up to your mind map. Take a large sheet of blank paper and divide it down the middle into two columns. Label them: *Can Control* and *Can't Control.* Now go back and examine each of the items you identified on your mind map and begin transferring those elements into the appropriate columns. This step gives you a clear picture of where you want to direct your energy. By focusing on those aspects you can control and learning to cope with what you can't control, you'll save yourself a lot of frustration, misery, and anxiety.

Stressful events don't always have fairy-tale endings like my leather coat experience, yet the bottom line to avoid a lot of unnecessary tension and unhealthy stress is to ask, "What about this situation can I control?" and "What is beyond my control?" When you consider what you can do about the situation right now, it may not seem to be much, but it just might be the first step in a significant and far-reaching solution. Whether or not I found my coat, I would always know I'd done all I could to correct the situation.

In the midst of your particular stressful situation, once you put pen to paper you'll find there are many things you can control. You can ask for help, write a letter, make a phone call, gather information, make inquiries, check out your options, research on the internet, move from the neighborhood or city, quit the job, apply for a transfer, declare bankruptcy, talk to the person, admit your mistake, ask for forgiveness, go back to school, have the operation, report to the police, seek legal advice, take a course, read the manual, do it, discard it, delegate it, file it, organize it, pay it, fix it, refinish it, repair it, mend it, clean it, buy a new or used one, start a new tradition or end an old one, learn from your mistake, pay the price, start over, see every day as a new beginning, pray and trust God, leave your cares at his feet knowing you'll receive his incredible peace and wisdom.

For all those things that are beyond your control, we're going to explore some coping mechanisms so you can keep or regain your sanity.

Sanity Savers & Survival Hints

- Keep asking, "What about this stressor is within my control?"
- Make a list of things you can control on a daily basis, including how you spend your time and your money, what you do about your health, how much TV you watch, how long you talk on the phone, which books you read, what people you associate with, which goals you set for yourself.

- Make a list of things beyond your control, including other people's attitudes, beliefs, value systems and behaviors; weather conditions; traffic; government decisions; work politics; high prices of fuel and groceries; lines at checkout counters.
- The bottom line is always "What *can* I do about this situation?"
- "What can't be cured must be endured" (author unknown).
- "Be anxious for nothing, but in everything by prayer and supplication, with thanksgiving, let your requests be made known to God" (Philippians 4:6 NKJV).
- One thing you can always do that is within your control is to pray and ask God to intervene in a situation.
- Remind yourself that God is in complete control and you are not. He knows the future even though you don't. Pray the prayer that never fails: "Your will be done, Lord." Jesus asked, "Which of you by worrying can add one cubit to his stature?" (Matthew 6:27).

8

Sanity Secret #4

Develop Coping Mechanisms

During a raging storm one winter night at the Buffalo, New York airport, a number of flights had to be cancelled. A long line of passengers waited, hoping they'd be rebooked on other flights. The gate agent was doing his best to deal with everyone's needs and concerns. While most passengers waited patiently, one woman pushed her way past all the rest and demanded to be put on the very next flight because she had a very important appointment (unlike the rest of the travelers, who apparently liked to hang around airports). The agent explained that he would do what he could since there were lots of people ahead of her. She kept arguing her case and finally, in exasperation, hollered in a very arrogant manner, "Sir, do you have any idea who I am?" At that moment the agent picked up his microphone and announced, "May I have your attention, folks! Is there anyone here who recognizes this lady? She can't remember who she is." Now I'm not sure it was the best coping mechanism for all the parties involved, but it probably worked for the airline agent.

When we're caught in the midst of a stormy situation that clearly falls into the "can't control" category, we need a reservoir of strategies available that will help us stay calm, get control over our emotions, and maybe even defuse the situation. Humor is one of the best coping mechanisms we can use to tolerate the intolerable, yet it is often the first thing to go in a frustrating situation.

Sometimes we just have to laugh! There are many situations and people over which we will have little or no control—a nasty boss, a grouchy spouse (a good friend told me sometimes she wakes up grouchy, sometimes she lets him sleep!), heavy traffic, unpleasant or severe weather conditions, company policies, politics, government decisions, and people's attitudes and behaviors to name a few. When I have to deal with an irritable person, I imagine that he (or she) has stubbed his toe or is suffering from a severe case of hemorrhoids and tell myself, *It's no wonder he's acting this way!* If someone cuts me off in traffic, I *choose* to imagine it may have been someone's 85-year-old grandfather, and he's losing his license so he's having one last joy ride. He probably didn't even realize he cut me off, bless his heart. (I know this one's a bit of a stretch, but you get to tell yourself anything you want, so you might as well say something that will release your stress, add a bit of humor, and avoid telling yourself things that could trigger a heart attack.)

Coping mechanisms are powerful sanity keepers. They guide us into a place of composure so we can relax our bodies, renew our energy, and intensify our problem-solving capabilities in even the most difficult situations. There are times when we simply need a quick and immediate release from unexpected stress, a crisis, or sudden pressure. The following simple practices can make it possible to stay calm in the midst of a difficult, worrisome, frustrating, or demanding situation.

10 Instant Relaxers

1. *Close your eyes for a few moments.* The simple act of shutting your eyes (not when driving in heavy traffic, please!) has been known to encourage the type of brainwaves that promote detachment, self-control, and relaxation. When you close yourself off in this way and deliberately take a step back, you'll begin to feel more objective and find your mind in tune with fresh, new ways of dealing with the situation. You can enhance the benefits by resting your fingers or palms gently over your eyes, exerting a slight pressure on them, or lightly massaging the muscles around your eyes and eyebrows. Go ahead—try it now!

2. *Speak calmly to yourself.* Every word you hear is internalized, even

the ones you speak to yourself. When you are tense, your self-talk is anxious or fretful. But each word is like a seed planted, and those seeds influence your responses by growing what you've planted. God's law says you will reap what you sow. You've been given full control over which seeds you plant through your power to choose. With practice, you can train yourself to sow the seeds you want to grow through your choice of words, giving clear direction to your body, mind, and emotions in stressful situations. Keep repeating these helpful "seeds" to yourself: "My mind, body, and emotions are now calm," "I am at peace," "I am relaxing and releasing all tension," "I thank God for giving me this remarkable gift to stay calm," and "This too shall pass."

3. *Breathe deeply.* Many people who are under stress often forget to breathe. Although God has given us two lungs with amazing air capacity, when we do breathe, most of us use only a fraction of lung space, and we pay a price for it. Watch a newborn baby and learn the proper way to breathe. Infants naturally breathe deeply, all the way into their bellies. Their tummies move up and down with each breath. Over time we've learned shallow breathing from the chest, which is common when we're sick or sleeping. When we master diaphragmatic breathing—from the gut—again, we notice our stomachs moving in and out. For most women, this is hard to do since we've been conditioned from an early age to hold in our tummies. But the body, especially the brain and nervous system, thrives on abundant oxygen. A good dose into your lower lung cavities will decrease blood pressure and relieve the stress you're experiencing.

4. *Sigh.* You can relieve a lot of body tension by taking in a deep breath and releasing it with a long, deep sigh. If possible, get away by yourself in another room, outdoors, or in your car and let it out freely and loudly. You may find you occasionally sigh or groan quite naturally when you're in a stressful situation. Doing it purposefully can alleviate much mental and emotional tension. Along with a sigh, try yawning. It stretches and relaxes facial muscles, promotes healthy breathing, and relaxes the whole body. Making yourself yawn a couple of times is therapeutic. Since it's contagious, you can have fun watching others around you start to yawn too. (I imagine you're probably yawning right now!)

5. *Still your body.* When things get out of control, we tend to get physically jittery, restless, and agitated. Nervous tics such as touching the face, playing with the hair, rubbing the thumbs and index fingers together, or nail biting are augmented and exaggerated. By firmly settling your body and consciously focusing on the stillness, you can relax and detach from the pressures that are bothering you. You will also be conserving valuable energy that would be wasted on fidgeting and squirming and put it to better use doing creative problem solving.

6. *Create a little distance.* In some tense situations, it may be necessary to temporarily get away from the stressful location. A change of scenery and a chance to be by yourself can help you collect your thoughts, clear your mind, alter your perspective, and determine how best to deal with the root of the stress. If you have time and can manage it, take a drive in the country. Put on your favorite music and enjoy the landscape. A change really is as good as a rest. You may gain a fresh perspective and a new outlook concerning your situation.

7. *Sip a steamy cup of tea.* Whenever there was tension brewing in our home, my mother would also be brewing—a pot of tea, that is. Often when we would hear her put the kettle on to boil, we were aware something major was happening. Later, once I lived on my own, even if I wasn't under any pressure, Mom would call and gently persuade, "Have a cup of tea, dear. You'll feel better." I'd say, "Mom, I feel just fine." She'd respond, "I know, but after a cup of tea, you'll feel even better!" She was usually right. These days I tell my daughters that if Grandma were here, she would recommend some tea. Now they tell me the same thing! Simply holding a warm cup of tea can be enough to ease your mind, soothe your emotions, and calm your body. Warmth is a great relaxant. Drinking tea is equally beneficial, especially if it's an herbal variety. So put the two together, and you're sure to get great results. Perhaps because we associate having a cup of tea with taking a break, it also encourages us to slow down, relax, and recuperate.

8. *Make sure there is a buffer in your schedule.* When I'm traveling and need to change planes, I've discovered the airlines know they need

to allow more than a few minutes for passengers to make our way to the connecting flight. In the same way, when we have a frenzied schedule full of ongoing appointments we can build in buffers between them. Even a few minutes can be a great coping mechanism and help you to recover and de-stress so you're ready for the next event.

9. *Look your best to feel your best.* When I haven't invested the time or effort to look my best for myself, whether it's getting my hair styled, having a facial, getting a manicure, or wearing something I find attractive, I am more likely to experience the negative effects of stress. It's easy to get into the rut of being careless with our appearance when we're always short of time and running behind schedule. Whether you stay up late to take a fragrant bubble bath or get up early to spend a few extra minutes styling your hair or putting on some makeup, perfume, and a fresh outfit, you'll feel better when you like what you see in the mirror.

10. *Be tuned in to your monthly cycle.* Keep track of your emotions for a month or two. Record them, along with your menstrual cycle, on a calendar or in a journal. Try to pinpoint when you're likely to be experiencing PMS. When you know your hormones will be raging, be selective about what activities you schedule at that time and who you spend time around. To cope best, especially when you don't have much choice, be sure to get plenty of rest, cut back on sugar and caffeine, and get extra exercise.

7 Quick Rechargers

Now that you're equipped with some sanity keepers for relaxation, here are some five-minute energizers that will help you cope by uplifting and recharging your mind and body during stress and strain. Relying on these as permanent stress solutions may not give you long-term benefits, such as the sanity savers we'll get to in other chapters, but there are times when you need an instant boost to get you through.

1. *Benefit from the miraculous energizing properties of water.* Hold your hands under warm, running water while giving them a deep massage for several minutes. You'll feel the stress being drawn right out of your body. Then briskly dry off with a towel and lather on some rich hand lotion.

Splash cold water on your face and pat dry. Take a moment to slowly drink some cool water to cleanse and refresh your body. The sound of water is soothing too. Whenever possible, spend some time listening to a babbling brook, a fountain, rain falling on the roof, or water bouncing from your umbrella.

2. *Think energy.* If you were to drag yourself around, shuffling your feet with a slumped-over posture, thinking thoughts of weakness and powerlessness, you would soon start to feel very lethargic. Physical acts and feelings often go together. Actors use this principle all the time. When they need to experience a certain emotion, they first focus their thoughts and start moving like a person experiencing exactly that, and very soon after, the feelings follow. Try standing tall and walking with purpose while envisioning yourself brimming with vibrant vitality. The energy will follow.

3. *Do some simple stretches and energy shakes.* When you need to be recharged in a hurry, try this quick energizer. Stretch your arms straight out in front of you, make a fist and squeeze tight. Now open and close them a few times. Then shake your hands from the wrists. Move them vigorously and keep it up for a few minutes. Hold your hands over your head and keep stretching up. Squeeze your fists shut and open them again. Do the energy shake again. Gently lower your arms as you continue shaking. Do this as often as necessary during a tense and stressful day.

Flex your feet in much the same way. Sit down with your legs outstretched. As you breathe in, tense the muscles of your feet as tightly as you can. Let the tension go and stretch your legs as you breathe out. Feel the stress being released from your entire body.

For neck tension, do a few shoulder shrugs by taking a deep breath and raising your shoulders up toward your ears. Hold for a moment as you hold your breath. Then breathe out, letting go of the tension you've created. Repeat this a few times. Since most of the tension in the body settles in the shoulders and neck, you can release stress through your body by relaxing these areas.

4. *Smile!* Smiling is a natural energizer. God so miraculously designed

our bodies that when we smile the muscles in our faces send messages to the brain letting it know how we are feeling. Regardless of what emotions we're experiencing, the brain accepts the smile message that we must be happy and releases chemicals and neurotransmitters (some are more powerful than morphine!), which flow through our bloodstream and in a short time we start to feel happy.

Some people I know use this technique to fight emotional depression as well as physical pain—backaches, sore muscles, headaches, stiff joints, and other ailments. Experiment by forcing a smile first thing in the morning before you get out of bed. Enhance your efforts by repeating, "This is the day the Lord has made. I will rejoice and be glad in it!" and "The joy of the Lord is my strength." Smile at yourself in the mirror, and you will generate a rich supply of energy.

5. *Get outdoors and grab a few quick breaths of fresh air.* Okay, so the air isn't as fresh as it once was, but it can still be a powerful energizer and a wonderful tonic. The next time you're under pressure, get out into nature, breathe in deeply, and imagine your lungs expanding and filling with pure, nourishing air. Breathing is the key to life and very closely related to our energy level and state of mind. When we're tense, we breathe incorrectly. Then we have an imbalance in the oxygen and carbon monoxide levels circulating around the body. Toxins aren't breathed out properly and leave us tired and susceptible to illness—the last thing we need during times of stress.

6. *Take a brisk walk.* Not only does walking stimulate your body and increase your energy, it can put a tangible physical distance between you and your stressors. Furthermore, it creates a mental distance that helps you detach and forget for a while. That's when new and creative solutions often come. Be prepared with a pen and paper to jot down those ideas. They come like butterflies, landing for a moment and then vanishing.

7. *Make your own music.* Singing, whistling, or humming can give a boost to the thyroid gland, which plays a role in controlling your energy level. Making music can inspire your mind and provide your physical body with renewed strength.

When you feel under excess pressure, take time out for your favorite relaxation activity, whether it's playing a musical instrument, reading a novel, dancing to lively music, baking, or browsing through photographs of happy times. Even if it's the last thing you feel like doing in the stress of the moment, your mind associates the activity with peace and relaxation so you'll soon start to feel peaceful.

Aside from these instant relaxers and rechargers for relieving the stress of the moment, most coping mechanisms can be worked into your daily schedule to be practiced on a regular basis. They'll fortify you for those stressful experiences that are beyond your control. Take a few minutes to think about what would make you feel relaxed and sane when there is insanity all around you. Is it getting out your art supplies and painting a picture? Maybe it's taking a warm bath or working in your garden. It might be browsing through a new magazine or sipping a cup of your favorite coffee or tea. Start your own list of coping mechanisms, of whatever makes you feel calm and peaceful, and keep it handy for tough times.

Sanity Savers & Survival Hints

- If your cup is running over, maybe it's time to turn off the tap.
- Recapture your childhood and become an expert at play. Blow bubbles in the backyard, make a sand castle at the beach or snow angels in wintertime, take your umbrella and walk in the rain, jump in mud puddles.
- Plan fun activities: watch cartoons, see a fireworks display, escape to a matinee, eat warm cookies with cold milk.
- Avoid foods that lower your resistance to stress—coffee, caffeinated tea, colas, chocolate, sugar.
- Be silly. Wear Groucho Marx glasses, a red clown nose, or a funny hat for your family or out in public—and act completely normal.
- Lighten up and have a good laugh at yourself when you've messed up.
- Remind yourself that "this too shall pass." Everything on this earth is

temporary; nothing is permanent. I love the Bible verses that say, "And it came to pass," and I add, "Not to stay!"

- Don't let what you can't do stop you from what you can do.
- When you're facing a situation clearly beyond your control, ask for help.
- The best coping method of all is to turn to God. He is always available to listen and act on your behalf. Help is closer than you think—just pray!
- "You don't have what you want because you don't ask God for it" (James 4:2 NLT).

9

Sanity Secret #5

Be a Creative Problem-Solver

For stressors beyond your control, the best secret is to have the predetermined coping mechanisms we covered in chapter 8 at your fingertips. When something is within your control, be prepared by being solution oriented rather than problem minded. If something stresses you, it is a problem. There are *always* a host of possible solutions or answers for each problem, even though the answer might be "no" or "not that way" or "not now."

Expectations play a huge role in your outcomes. If you anticipate problems with no answers, that's what you'll get. When you seek and watch for solutions, they'll become apparent. The choice is yours because people generally see what we're tuned in to and what we expect. I remember driving my new navy-blue convertible around town, believing it was one of a kind in my area. It wasn't long before I started to notice plenty of others—the same make, model, and color! What happened? Did a voice boom from the heavens saying, "You can bring out all the others now that she has one"? Where were all those navy-blue convertibles before? They were there all the time, of course. It's just that I didn't notice them until I got one of my own. My focus had changed. Likewise, whether you look for problems or solutions, you'll notice what you focus on. Maybe someone you know has shaved off a beard or mustache (a man, hopefully!) and plays this little game with you: "Notice anything different?" You probably think, "You're not wearing your glasses" or "You've parted your hair on the other side." Chances are you don't even notice the missing facial hair because we tend to see more with our brains than our eyes. So start expecting answers and solutions to your problems, and that is what you'll find.

The main goal of problem solving is to develop creative solutions to your stressor rather than react to it out of past programming. If you keep doing what you've always done, you'll keep getting more of what you've always had. Rather than worrying and fretting about your problems like you may have done in the past, there are two sets of skills you can develop: rational problem solving and insightful problem solving. With rational problem solving you use logical brainstorming and analytical reasoning. Insightful problem solving involves inner wisdom, perception, and discernment, allowing you to think outside the box, break through the ways you've normally viewed your problem, and open up to innovative ideas for resolving your stressor. Deep inside you almost always have the right answers. You usually know what is best for you. Let's take a look at both problem-solving skills.

Rational Problem Solving

- Analyze the stressor so you can go beyond symptoms and isolate the underlying causes.
- List what you'd rather see happen or need more or less of that is within your control.
- Brainstorm your options and alternatives. Be open to all possibilities and write them down, even if some don't seem feasible.
- Pray over your list. Listen to God and reflect on the options he gives to determine the most hopeful and promising choice. (One woman wanted more peace in her marriage. She saw her options as leaving the relationship; trying to change her spouse; or getting involved in a personal interest, such as becoming a member of a singing group, joining a bowling league, taking art classes, and going to plays with friends. She chose the last option and saved her marriage.)

- Develop an action plan with specific goals and logical steps to achieve it. The more explicit you are, the more likely you are to achieve your goal.
- Evaluate your goal and adjust your action steps when you run into roadblocks. Mid-course corrections are to be expected. (Airline pilots say airplanes are off course more than on track.)
- Reward yourself for your efforts. Achieving a goal deserves recognition and acknowledgment.

Insightful Problem Solving

- Set the tone by quieting your mind, wearing something comfortable, sitting in a sunny spot, playing some inspirational music in the background, having a cup of coffee or tea, making a fire in the fireplace, or lighting some candles.
- Get your journal out and describe the stressor you're facing. This is important. Ask yourself questions using the five "W's"—who, what, when, where, and why—to get you going. Brain research has taught us that when our brain hears a question, it immediately goes to work to find an answer.
- Be sure to ask the right questions: "What can be done?" or "What is within my control?" Often we don't get the results we're looking for because we ask the *wrong* questions: "Why am I so stupid?" "Why am I always late?" "What's wrong with me?" "Why does everything happen to me?" "How could he act like such a jerk?" "Who are these kids, and why are they calling me mom?"
- Pour your heart out. As you identify your particular concern and insights come, fill in the details. At this point don't analyze, criticize, or edit. Just note whatever comes out.
- Spend time in solitude, silence, and prayer. Listen for God's voice giving you ideas, insights, wisdom, and divine guidance. Write them down.

- Thank God in advance for his divine help and insightful answers.

When one woman's boss asked if she would quickly organize the storage room before the president of the company stopped by, she knew she had only a few minutes to get the job done. So she prayed and asked God for divine guidance and a creative solution. Shortly afterward, the two gentlemen made their way down the hall toward the room. They noticed the door was shut and there was a sign on it. When they got close, they could see that it said "Women." Now that's creative problem solving! Sometimes I wonder if we spend a lot more time and effort on problems than is necessary.

People Problems

When it comes to problem relationships, you may find that when you start to see your own stressors solved, those people you felt needed to be "fixed" will start changing in ways of their own too. One woman I know bought herself a television so she and her hubby wouldn't argue anymore about who got the remote control. These days he would rather have her with him, so he is satisfied to share control of the TV. Now they watch a mixture of programs they both enjoy. But this wouldn't have happened if she hadn't taken steps to solve her own stressor.

There was a time when I wished my husband, Cliff, would attend more concerts, theater, and ballet with me. I longed to have picnics by the lake, take long country hikes, and go on evening strolls too. But those weren't activities that interested him. Rather than crying the blues or telling him, "If you loved me you would go with me," I decided to make plans to go alone. On one occasion I said to Cliff, "I have two tickets to the ballet. I'd love it if you would accompany me, but I can ask a friend, my sister, or my daughter." Another time I said, "I've got a picnic lunch packed and in the car. If you'd care to join me, that would be great. Otherwise I can enjoy it on my own." In both cases, he chose to join me without voicing objections. Naturally I had to be prepared for a possible no response, and I needed to be sure I would really enjoy the ballet or a picnic in the park without him.

Part of my stress solution occurred to me when I came to the conclusion that if a picnic was what mattered to me, I should be able to get pleasure from it with or without his company. If going to the ballet was a de-stressor for me, I would enjoy it as much with a family member, friend, or by myself. Now I love it when Cliff comes along, and I love it when I go alone. Either way I enjoy myself. As long as I show up, I'll have fun! However, if spending time with my hubby is what I want more than anything else, I can spend it with him doing something we both enjoy or go along on an activity he prefers.

❊ ❊ ❊

Do what you can, with what you have, where you are.
THEODORE ROOSEVELT

Problem solving is often a matter of setting up routines so you aren't repeatedly dealing with the same stressful issues or wasting time or energy recycling identical arguments day after day. Creative solutions, whether rational or insightful, start with a notepad, a pen, and a cup of coffee or tea.

Sanity Savers & Survival Hints

- Whenever you face a problem, get a clear image in your mind of your desired outcome and your ideal future success.
- Focus on your potential not your limitations. Think about possible answers rather than the difficulties.
- Instead of telling God about your big problem, tell the problem about your big God!
- Look for the good. Assume there is a hidden treasure inside each problem.
- Often when God wants to give us a gift, it comes wrapped in hardship or adversity. If you look for the hidden gem, you will always find it.
- Success has been described as "a series of wonderful opportunities brilliantly disguised as impossible situations."

- "You can pray for anything, and if you have faith, you will receive it" (Matthew 21:22 NLT).
- Seek the lesson in each adversity. Situations come to help us learn something, become better, and/or grow.
- Whatever you're facing at the moment, know that it is exactly the right situation you need to conquer to ultimately achieve a stress-free state.
- Choose to be optimistic. A positive mental outlook is indispensable to handling stress.
- Think and talk about the solution, not the obstacle or setback.

10

Sanity Secret #6

Problem Solving in Action

Let's look at some illustrations of creative problem solving to help you pinpoint recurring challenges that cause you stress. Use these examples to resolve your own stressors. Implement one or two solutions at a time. Before you know it, some issues will no longer be major sources of stress, conflicts will be worked out, and peace will replace frustration.

Personal Growth & Relationship Stressors

Problem: You want to make changes and improvements, but hardly have time to read the self-help books you're interested in, including the one you have in your hand.

Creative solution: Take a book with you when you have an appointment or are meeting someone for lunch and read while you're waiting. Before bed read several pages of a novel or one chapter of an inspirational book. Get up a bit earlier than usual and spend quiet time with a cup of coffee or tea and a book that lifts your spirits. Listen to inspiring motivational programs and audiobooks while you're in your car. While everyone else watches TV, do some reading.

Problem: Personal fitness and exercise are the first things to be put on the back burner when your schedule gets hectic.

Creative solution: Remind yourself that your health is top priority, and you won't be able to enjoy your life, spend quality time with others, or fulfill your purpose on earth if you fail to look after yourself first. If you like working out at a gym, join one you feel most comfortable in that is conveniently close to your home or office. Arrange to take an exercise class you can attend three times each week, either at a club or with friends at someone's home. Purchase a couple of exercise DVDs and some hand weights you can use to work out at home. Walk around your neighborhood several times a week with a girlfriend (provides accountability and company). Do something you really enjoy so you are more likely to stay committed. Get into the habit of taking your vitamins at the same time each day, preferably at breakfast, and keep them easily accessible.

Problem: Eating snacks and junk food is putting on the pounds or making you feel lethargic.

Creative solution: Watch for signs that you're eating because of stress rather than hunger. Feeling hungry for a while won't harm you. Have healthy snacks prepared in advance—celery and carrot sticks with low-fat dip, hardboiled eggs, skim-milk cheese, salsa with whole-grain crackers, multigrain bagels, fresh fruit, yogurt. When you get a craving for an unwholesome snack, drink a big glass of water before giving in. Sometimes we mistake thirst for hunger. Besides, the water is good for you… and it will fill you up.

Problem: You have so much to do that you don't know where to begin.

Creative solution: Sit down with a cup of herbal tea or coffee and put pen to paper (or sit at your computer). Start by making a Master List of everything you need and want to do at some point in the near future. Prioritize each item. Make your Daily Action Plans from this list. Work on only the top priority goals and activities. Keep asking, "Is this the best use of my time right now?" and "Is there a better way to get this accomplished?"

Problem: You keep putting off getting together with friends, waiting for "leftover" time.

Creative solution: Recognize there will never be spare time. For high-priority activities you must *make* time. Create a list of favorite people you'd like to catch up with, and plan to see one a week even if only for coffee. (They don't have to know they are on your hit list!) In the meantime send emails or cards so they know you're thinking of them. Be sure to arrange the time together.

Problem: You feel like a complete failure. Discouragement is something you struggle with daily. You never seem to have enough energy to get things done, and you slip up so often your life feels like it's spinning out of control.

Every day is a new beginning and a chance to start over.

Creative solution: Beating up yourself only produces more problems and difficulties. Set some short-term goals, and every day work toward one or two. Take some time to list the things you're doing right. Keep a victory journal! Acknowledge your achievements and accomplishments, no matter how trivial they may seem. Remind yourself that everyone makes mistakes. Learn from them and move on. Every day is a new beginning and a chance to start over.

Problem: You're caught in the trap of worrying regularly about a lot of things you can't do anything about. Whether it's your son late getting home from his part-time job, your spouse who seems disinterested in your relationship lately, a child who isn't fitting in at school, or the lab test results you haven't received yet, you find yourself fretting, fuming, and fussing most of the time.

Creative solution: Accept that you'll always be faced with concerns and issues beyond your control. While it's tempting to agonize, you use up a lot of energy without changing a thing. It's far better to turn worry energy into prayer power. Take your concerns to God, who cares about *every* need you have. You can trust him with the fears and longings of your heart. Ask him for help.

Problem: Conflicts with your spouse are always present and troublesome. Either your hubby seems distant, you rarely agree on important matters, or you often feel you fall to the bottom of his list of priorities.

Creative solution: Remember you and your husband have differing views and priorities based on upbringing, personal preferences, unique character traits, and past experiences. As well, you are probably at different stages in your personal and spiritual growth. Besides, it's futile to try to change another person. It's better to stop expecting something of someone that he is not giving or maybe isn't capable of giving. Take your concerns to your heavenly Father.

Problem: You're a single mother and have to be mom, dad, and sole provider, which is taking its toll on you and your children.

Creative solution: Be faithful to yourself when it comes to healthy self-care. Take time to nurture yourself without guilt. Staying fit and healthy is one of the nicest things you can do for your children. Get in the habit of doing tasks and activities as a family—yard work and household chores, bike rides, working out at the gym, walking the dog. Learn basic repair skills together to cut back on costs while spending time together, such as taking night courses in mechanics, gardening, or computer technology. Take up a sport or interesting hobby you all enjoy. At the same time, be sure to set some goals for yourself that are separate from your family goals.

Time & Scheduling Stressors

Problem: You're always running late, especially in the morning.

Creative solution: Start by determining the time you want to arrive at your destination and then work backward. Figure out how many tasks you need to complete first, approximately how long each one will take, and what time you have to start or set your alarm to make it all fit. Be sure to build in a cushion of extra time to allow for unexpected events—traffic jams, accidents, emergencies, crises. When you're ahead of schedule, don't make the mistake of thinking you can fit an extra activity or two into that time slot or you'll be running behind again.

Problem: Heavy traffic causes your stress level to rise.

Creative solution: Whenever possible, avoid driving and running errands during rush hour or at lunchtime. Do your shopping just after stores open or right before they close. You can shop for many items on the internet. When you're stuck in traffic, listen to soothing music or motivational messages, plan your shopping list, mentally work on a project coming due, count your blessings, talk to God and pray for loved ones, or dream about future goals.

Problem: You're always writing the same things: checklists for travel and suitcase packing, contents of diaper bag or briefcase, bookwork or tax papers, grocery lists, medical emergency information, babysitter instructions, and so on.

Creative solution: Prepare forms on your computer for each of these lists and print out as many copies as you need at a time. If you don't use a computer, type or write your lists and have photocopies made at a local print center.

Problem: When you're going someplace for the first time, you get frustrated because you waste a lot of time trying to find the place: driving in circles, retracing your steps, stopping to ask for help. You end up calling to say you'll be late.

Creative solution: Before you leave, call ahead to get exact directions. I do this as a backup even though I use map programs and have a GPS. Write down the exact address and phone number to carry with you. Keep an assortment of maps in the glove compartment of your vehicle. Use the internet to print maps and directions. If you're going somewhere you'll visit again, write out the directions and draw a map on the back of a Rolodex card, put the name, address, and phone number on the front, and file it for future use.

Problem: You use up your entire lunch hour going to the post office or standing in line at the bank.

Creative solution: Create a small mail center at home and avoid the line at the post office. Have on hand stamps of various denominations, assorted envelopes, padded mailers, boxes in various sizes, adhesive labels and black markers to cover old information on boxes, shipping tape, a small scale, and a postal rate chart. This way you can simply drop off packages on your way to or from work.

Have a set time once a week when you go to the bank or do your banking over the internet. Arrange automatic deposits, withdrawals, and payments whenever possible.

Problem: You spend valuable time repacking the same toiletry items every time you travel.

Creative solution: Buy travel-size items for all your toiletries or transfer product from regular sizes into small travel bottles. Keep duplicates of everything you'll need in your overnight bag. You're ready to go!

Problem: You waste time searching for things you use often.

Creative solution: Check your prime storage space to be sure you aren't filling it with items you use only occasionally. Switch things around so items you use frequently are readily available. I now have two drawers for cooking utensils—one for most often used ones and a second one for least used.

Problem: Your family is always running out of basic essentials such as toilet tissue, hand soap, laundry detergent, and cleaning supplies.

Creative solution: Print a form listing the materials you use in your home: cleaning supplies, paper goods, personal products. You may have separate lists for office supply, hardware, and drugstores. Make it a rule in your home that whoever notices the product is getting low marks it on the list. When shopping, buy in bulk.

Problem: When you're preparing to give a gift, you spend a lot of time running around to purchase wrapping paper, bows, and tape.

Creative solution: Assemble a wrapping station in your home. Use a drawer or a large plastic bin that fits under the bed. Keep it stocked with a variety of wrapping paper, gift bags, ribbon, bows, tape, scissors, cards and tags, and even a selection of greeting cards and small gift items for hosts or last-minute occasions.

Problem: Running errands always takes longer than it should because you retrace your steps and have to go back to get what you forgot.

Creative solution: Make a comprehensive list before you leave home. Plan your route efficiently so you don't backtrack or waste time and fuel. In addition, run your errands at a time of day when most others don't.

Household & Family Stressors

Problem: You often run late in the mornings because you and/or the children can't decide what to wear.

Creative solution: Before going to bed at night, decide what you'll wear the next day and have your children do the same. Lay out each outfit. Consider accessories and shoes as well. This is a good time to check for missing buttons, drooping hems, and stains.

Problem: You keep losing instructions, directions, articles, recipes, and household tips you want to save for reference.

Creative solution: When you come across information you want to refer to later, clip or tear it out and place it in a file or large envelope. When you have time, create a file for it or glue small clippings to index cards and place them in a file box. You may also use a three-hole punch and store them in a binder with dividers.

Problem: You have clutter piling up everywhere, taking up space and making it difficult to find things.

Creative solution: Find a local charity drop-off box and set a goal to donate items every month. Keep bags or boxes handy for putting in items you no longer need or use. Rather than one major spring clean-up, do a little all year long. Think about having a garage sale or organize a large neighborhood sale.

Problem: Junk mail, magazines, catalogs, and newspapers pile up for weeks before they get sorted or read.

Creative solution: Develop the routine of putting each day's paper in the recycle bin before retiring for the night. Use a stacking tray to create a family mail center. Personalize a shelf for each individual and use one for magazines and catalogs. Always discard the last catalog when the new one arrives. When browsing through magazines, use sticky notes to mark the articles you're interested in. Carry the magazines with you in a reading file for times when you have to wait. Recycle once you are done. Purchase cardboard magazine holders for those issues you want to keep and store on a bookshelf.

Problem: Your family loses track of crucial items: car and house keys, sunglasses, cell phones, gloves, and important papers.

Creative solution: Place a basket for each family member on a shelf by your entrance door. When people arrive home, have them place important items in the basket right away. Keep an extra house key hidden outside and a spare car key in your wallet or date book. Create a lost-and-found basket in the front hall closet. When someone finds sports equipment, clothing, or toys lying around, this is where they should be placed. Let everyone know where to look when something is missing.

Problem: Your schedules are so hectic it seems you're always in the car on the way to the next appointment or practice.

Creative solution: Use the time in the car to catch up with one another or play some fun games. When our kids were young, we would play the Alphabet Memory Game. One person starts with the letter A and says, "I was on my way to the ball game (beach, picnic), and I took an apple." The next person must repeat the statement with "apple" and add a baseball bat, beach ball, or other B word. Play continues until you've reached the end of the alphabet. Or use the time to have everyone dream aloud something they'd like to see happening in their lives five years from now. Start a fun tradition when music lessons or soccer practice is over: go out for an ice cream cone or frozen yogurt, play a game of Pictionary once you're home, or read aloud one chapter of a book before bed.

Problem: When you need to take something with you, you often leave without it and have to go back to get it or you beat yourself up for forgetting.

Creative solution: Put a sticky note on the exit door as a reminder. If you're taking something bulky, put it in a bag or box and place it in front of the door so you can't leave without moving it. If it's on a hanger, hook it over the doorframe so it's blocking your way out.

Problem: When you arrive home with packages and parcels, you have to make several trips into the house.

Creative solution: On the way out the door, grab a large canvas tote bag to take with you. Once you arrive home, load it with all your purchases, small bags, library books, and other odds and ends you've picked up and carry them all into the house at once. If you have a long walkway, keep a little wagon close to where you park your car and load it up. The next time you go out to your car, take the wagon so it will be ready for next time.

Problem: Taking a vacation causes so many hassles you wonder if it's worthwhile going away.

Creative solution: Once you determine where you're going, create a to-do list and a packing list. Begin to lay out everything you'll need—passport, mix-and-match wardrobe, toiletries in plastic bags, camera, cell phone charger, carry-on bag for travel games, magazines and books, and a file for paperwork including your itinerary (leave a copy at home), confirmation numbers, and directions. Take a plastic bag for dirty laundry and an empty suitcase for souvenirs and gifts.

Book your flights, hotels, and rental cars early. Surf the Net and check with your hotel for specific travel tips, tourist sites, and directions. Get maps or invest in a GPS. Don't overload your itinerary. Take lots of photos for great memories.

Make arrangements for your mail pickup, plants, yard and pet care. Leave your house clean and tidy with the laundry and dishes done, beds made, and garbage removed. When you get back, your home will be a welcome haven.

Problem: Thanksgiving, Christmas, Easter, and other holidays are so stressful you wish you could hide until they're over.

Creative solution: Call a family meeting and decide what's important to all of you. Scale back or eliminate those areas that aren't critical. Create joyful, rich holidays with some new traditions and easier rituals. Lower your decorating, cleaning, and cooking expectations. Get rid of unrealistic standards by keeping things simple. Have a potluck dinner instead of cooking everything yourself. Cut back on gift giving by setting a $10 limit; see how ingenious and creative everyone can be. Set a holiday budget that is reasonable. Limit the number of events you'll attend. Look for ways to help others. Going against the grain takes more creativity and energy, but the results are well worth it.

Financial Stressors

Problem: You always run out of cash so you're continually running to the bank or ATM.

Creative solution: Limit your trips to the ATM and bank to once a week. Based on recent weeks, budget how much you should need. Keep the cash in an envelope and make a note on the outside each time you take some out so you'll have a written record of your spending. You can put your receipts in the same envelope or designate a separate one.

Problem: You often miss your due date when paying bills and end up with penalty fees and late charges.

Creative solution: Get in the routine of paying bills in the middle of the month or at the end, or pay them as they come in. Most banks make it possible to pay bills through an automatic draft from your account or you may be able to set up automatic payments online.

Problem: You frequently pay late fees on videos, DVDs, and library books.

Creative solution: Place a basket beside the exit door. Label it "Returns." Immediately after watching, place DVDs back in the case and put them into the basket. Do the same with library books. Next time you go out, return the items.

Problem: You need to increase your income to pay off debts.

Creative solution: Make appointments with a financial planner and your bank manager or loan officer. Find ways to consolidate loans and credit-card debt. Consider getting a part-time job or turning a hobby into a small business. Make the most of the money you do have by cutting back and going bare bones with living expenses. Make your own pizza instead of ordering in, rent a movie rather than going to the theater, take a bag lunch and Thermos of coffee to work, and have your clothes altered or mended. Sell the extra refrigerator in the garage or the TV you don't use. Have a garage sale.

Mealtime & Food Stressors

Problem: When it comes to family meals, food preparation, and other household duties, you're the one doing all or most of the work.

Creative solution: Establish a household rule that the spouse or family members who didn't cook or help prepare the meal are responsible for cleaning up—washing dishes, taking out the garbage, and sweeping the floor. Follow through with all the housework. Everyone contributes to the mess, so everyone helps clean up. With kids, stand firm and let them know they do not get privileges—playing computer games, talking on the phone, spending time with friends, watching TV—until responsibilities are fulfilled.

Problem: There are never enough clean dishes or the sink is always full of dirty ones with dried-on food.

Creative Solution: Get in the habit of cleaning dishes right after eating. When it's not possible, at least rinse them or let them soak in a sink filled with hot, soapy water. If you wash dishes by hand, do them with a family member. Use the time to reconnect with your hubby and talk about goals and priorities or catch up with a child's activities, perhaps even broaching a difficult subject. If you're alone, light some candles and listen to your favorite music or an audiobook. Use the time to dream about your future, plan your next vacation or romantic rendezvous with your husband, or imagine yourself as being successful in a particular pursuit—a weight-loss effort, a project at work, or a tennis tournament. If you have a dishwasher, start it right after dinner. That way you can unload it, put the dishes away, and set the breakfast table before bedtime. Give yourself permission to use paper plates and cups now and then.

Problem: Breakfast time is chaotic and anything but the peaceful, relaxed, composed start to the day you want it to be.

Creative solution: Make as many preparations as possible the night before. Set the table. Put out the vitamins, cereals, bread, toaster, and jam—anything that will contribute to an easy-to-prepare, healthy morning meal. Pack the day's lunches while you're cleaning up after dinner the evening before. Say grace together before breakfast, and teach your kids to offer thanks on their own. Before everyone leaves, take time for a "minute prayer." Often we don't pray with loved ones because everyone is rushed, but in one minute you can bless them and ask God for protection for the day.

Problem: When cooking, you have to make last-minute trips to the store for missing ingredients.

Creative solution: Plan your menus in advance and write them out. As you do, look up recipes you'll be using and list all the ingredients. Take this list with you when you do your weekly shopping. It also helps to keep your pantry well stocked, replenishing it regularly.

Problem: Grocery shopping takes up so much time.

Creative solution: Shop during off-peak hours when stores are less crowded. Buy in volume once a month at bulk stores and wholesale clubs. Keep your pantry stocked with staples—pasta, canned soups, juices, tuna, peanut butter, jam, sauces, baked beans, canned tomatoes, herbs and spices, coffee and tea, mayonnaise, relish, mustard, ketchup, vegetable oil, pickles, baking ingredients. Visit the grocery store weekly for fresh produce, dairy products, breads, and other incidentals. Write your shopping list so it corresponds with the grocery store aisles. If you have teenagers, delegate the shopping to them (be specific about brands).

Problem: You buy chocolate at the store and have to get it home in a hot car.

Creative Solution: Forget taking it home. Eat it in the parking lot. (If you get melted chocolate all over your hands, you're eating it way too slowly!) Remember, money talks but chocolate sings!

Okay, so maybe that last one is a bit of a stretch. Whatever problems you face, focus on solutions rather than past issues. Instead of worrying about how you got into this stressful mess, concentrate on where you want to be and what you'd rather do. Everyone is creative, and when you give yourself time to think, you'll come up with the best solutions for you. Solutions are inherently positive whereas problems are inherently negative. It takes faith to believe solutions will come. As soon as you focus on finding answers and then they come, your faith will build. As you open the door, God will provide the way.

The First Resort

Over the years I've had some great thoughts as to how God could solve my problems. At times I've even listed my solutions for him: make my spouse as romantic as the ones in romance novels, take away the struggles my kids are going through, change my grouchy boss' heart, cure my dad of cancer, build my international speaking business and take it to the next level. While some of the things on my list happened, many of them didn't. At one time I might have felt God let me down when that occurred. Now I see that I was using prayer as a way to control God...as if that were possible.

As a last resort, when all else failed and nothing was going as planned, I would go to him spent and worn out. But now I come to him differently—totally surrendered and as the *first* resort and not the last! Rather than telling God what to do, I bring my prayer requests, leave them at his feet, and remember his promise to me: "I know what I'm doing. I have it all planned out—plans to take care of you, not abandon you, plans to give you the future you hope for" (Jeremiah 29:11). Then I pray the prayer that never fails: "Your will be done, Lord."

> Have you ever come on anything quite like this extravagant generosity of God, this deep, deep wisdom? It's way over our heads. We'll never figure it out.
>
> > Is there anyone around who can explain God? Anyone smart enough to tell him what to do? Anyone who has done him such a huge favor that God has to ask his advice?
> >
> > Everything comes from him. Everything happens through him. Everything ends up in him (Romans 11:33-36).
>
> If you make yourselves at home with me and my words are at home in you, you can be sure that whatever you ask will be listened to and acted upon (John 15:7).

PART 3
Keeping Your Sanity

11 Sanity Secret #7

Practice Healthy Self-Care

When You Need Pampering and Nurturing

Does this sound familiar?

Your schedule is overloaded, a project deadline is coming up, you just agreed to head up the planning committee for your boss' retirement party, and you keep saying, "Once I get through all this, I'm going to take a rest."

or

You're fighting a cold, you feel worn out no matter how much sleep you get, and you can't remember the last time you took an entire day off. You won't take a break because everything depends on you being available to people who are counting on you.

or

You're carpooling the kids, it's pouring rain, you're stuck in a traffic jam with a splitting headache, and what you really long to do is get home, change into your pajamas, and curl up with a steamy cup of cocoa and a good movie.

or

> You had a miserable day at work, there's nothing good on TV, you don't have the energy to read, and the only messages on the answering machine are your friend canceling tomorrow's lunch date and someone asking you to volunteer for another community fund-raiser.
>
> or
>
> You feel lonely even though you have a partner or lots of friends and family. You're fighting depression, and you feel even worse after talking with someone you had hoped would perk you up.

So what do you do next?

- Complain to your mother, who will give you a dozen reasons why this could be happening to you and twice as many suggestions for pulling yourself together.
- Buy a bucket of chocolate chip cookie dough and devour the whole thing while watching *Wheel of Fortune* and *American Idol*.
- Go to bed, pull the covers over your head, and stay there for three weeks.
- Read *Sanity Secrets for Stressed-Out Women: Energize and Renew Your Life.*

Every week I hear from women who say they are frustrated, frazzled, frayed, and worn out. Whether it's trying to keep up with the laundry; controlling paper clutter; going to work every day; operating a business from home; coping with toddlers or teens; caring for aging parents; being available for spouses, coworkers, employees, and friends; or being overly involved in church, community, and other volunteer endeavors, women are running out of steam. They want to know how to feel better so they can—you guessed it!—continue *giving*. With little or no personal time left, these women just keep giving and giving...and eventually find they're attempting to function on empty. They've either forgotten to care for themselves or feel guilty about doing it.

Self is not a nasty four-letter word! Too often we're satisfied to take the burned toast and give up our favorite TV show so someone else in the family can get what he or she wants. We need to give ourselves permission to be nurtured occasionally too. Looking after ourselves is not only a good idea, it's vital. Healthy self-care is essential for our survival. We know how to take care of others. We do it every day. But how often do we nurture ourselves? By taking care of our personal needs, we can continue giving to others out of abundance instead of lack.

Looking after you is truthfully one of the kindest things you can do for those you love and care about.

Women are the nurturers of this world. It seems to be or is assumed to be our innate gifting. Amazingly, we're able to find the time, energy, and money to help someone in need. But when our personal needs go unmet and our tanks beg to be refueled, our bodies get stressed and we react negatively to situations because of our emotional emptiness. Then the very people we desire to nurture feel guilty for needing us in the first place. Add to that the hormonal crazies we often undergo during PMS, pregnancy, and menopause, and it's no wonder we're sometimes not in condition to keep nurturing. Our bodies wear down, our minds race in turmoil, our emotions are erratic, and our spirits become discouraged.

One principal sanity secret for stress-free living is to nurture yourself first. I call this *healthy self-care.* Don't feel self-centered. Taking time to care for yourself must be high on your list of what's important. You may have to cut back on some activities that are not filling your tank. When you do, people may try to send you on a little guilt trip to persuade you to say yes to things that are not priorities to you. Don't feel guilty about not doing something because it's what someone else wants of you. Remind yourself that when you say *yes* to one thing, you're saying *no* to something else. And that something else may be your sanity!

Looking after you is truthfully one of the kindest things you can do for those you love and care about. Think about it: You aren't capable of or qualified to look after someone over the long haul until you take care of yourself. In the airplane survival procedure you're told that if an oxygen mask drops down, place it on yourself first so you are equipped to care for others. Yet so often our main impulse is to look after everyone else first and leave our own needs to the end.

Sadly, even once we decide to care for ourselves, personal renewal is usually what falls to the bottom of our to-do list. We may even take on a martyr mindset, playing sacrificial victim as we suffer for the cause. But when we neglect self-care, all other areas of our lives will pay the price. It is impossible to handle everything we're responsible for if we're physically exhausted, emotionally frazzled, and spiritually empty. We enter into a vicious cycle and a no-win situation.

The next time you're tempted to think your own needs don't matter, remember that you are the hub—the nucleus—of many aspects in your life. Your family, friends, and coworkers don't need to deal with one more cranky, irritable, tired, and resentful person. They are looking to you as someone who provides solid support, offers calm guidance, and gives joyfully out of an abundant heart. You can only do this when you have stable and strong inner resources. When you've kept your reservoir full, you will feel happy, content, energetic, enthusiastic, and prepared to enrich other people's lives. So let's explore ways to nurture *you* so you can become the woman you've always known you could be.

The Beauty of Harmony

No matter how many roles you have—wife, mother, sister, daughter, friend, aunt, grandmother, employee, employer, career professional, business owner, volunteer—you have only one life. Harmony helps you be sure that the many different aspects of life—physical, emotional, mental, spiritual—are in correct relationship to each other. As long as each component gets the attention it deserves (no more, no less), you will be prepared and available to enhance the lives of others. And you'll be able to meet the demands of your life with all the energy you need. Here are 12 sanity secrets for achieving harmony.

1. *Take care of your body.* Without your health, all else is meaningless...if not impossible. By caring for yourself regularly, your physical body will more likely be prepared to function effectively. When you don't provide your body with proper sleep, exercise, rest, and nutritious fuel, you are constantly tired and will feel overwhelmed and overloaded.

2. *Expand your mind.* Keep up ongoing learning and lifelong education.

By stimulating your mind with new information through reading good books and taking classes, you'll keep your mind brimming with ideas and problem-solving abilities. When you neglect to do this, your mind goes stale, and you risk becoming predictable and monotonous—in person and in life.

3. *Develop your spiritual nature.* Deep down you are aware that you're more than the body you dwell in. Your spirit needs attention and growth too, although it's not always as apparent as the other facets of our being. If I could not draw on God's wisdom, strength, and power daily, I'm certain I would crumble. I've become so aware that I simply don't have all it takes to run my life, my career, and my ministry by myself.

God's Word reminds us, "'[It's] not by might nor by power, but by my Spirit,' says the Lord Almighty" (Zechariah 4:6 NIV).

4. *Recognize what depletes and refills you emotionally.* There are some situations, circumstances, and people that drain your energy. There are also some that replenish you. When your emotional energy reserves have been drained, you lose perspective and become dangerously weak. Your problems appear overwhelming and your strength is sapped. Life seems out of control. By replenishing your energy supply and avoiding or limiting those elements that drain you, you become emotionally resilient and can face your problems with strength, hope, and positive expectations. Become aware of what refuels you.

5. *Plan time to play.* Sometimes adults become so grown up we lose our sense of adventure and become too serious. We need to recapture our childlike senses of awe and wonder. We need to have leisure activities: fun personal times as well as time with family and friends. Schedule play dates into your weekly calendar to balance heavy matters. A friend of mine was going through a dreadfully difficult and complex time in her marriage and business, so I invited her to have lunch with me. I told her there was one catch. Since it was my treat, I insisted we go to the playground first and use the equipment before going to lunch. She reluctantly agreed and soon we were using the teeter-totter, the swings, and the slide—while dressed in our business suits and high heels. She said she hadn't laughed so hard

in years, and we never did get lunch! The power of play is without doubt one of life's priceless pleasures.

6. *Pamper yourself with a spa treatment.* Get a massage, facial, scalp treatment, pedicure, or manicure...or all five! You'll be relaxed and energized!

There's a local spa I visit that offers the opportunity to use all the facilities without booking a pampering treatment. For a small fee, robe, slippers, and locker are provided. I can enjoy the outdoor hot springs, indoor whirlpool, swimming pool, fitness room, sauna, and steam room. There is a cozy fireplace area where I can curl up with a book, snooze, or order room service. Lemon ice water, herbal teas, and fresh fruit are also included in the cost. Check to see if there are similar services in your area. Other times you can create a spa at home. Turn your bathroom into a soothing sanctuary with scented candles, an array of luxurious bath products, and a terry cloth-covered inflatable bath pillow. Soak in a bubble bath sweetened with scented bath salts and add some soothing classical background music and a steamy cup of herbal tea or glass of flavored sparkling mineral water. Relax and let the water wash over you. Bask in the candlelight and stay as long as you need to wash away all your stress. When you're ready, have someone bring you an oversized, fluffy towel that's been warmed in the dryer, dry off, lather on some silky body lotion, and put on a pair of silk pajamas or a cozy terrycloth robe. You might want to give yourself a mini-massage with some lavender oil. Apply a small amount to your hands and rub them together until they are warm. Start by massaging your forehead, cheekbones, and throat. Move on to your hands and fingers, and finish with a foot massage.

7. *Take a fantasy vacation.* When you've got the "kids drive me nuts, the washing machine's broken, I banged my knee, just ate a whole bag of cookies, and might as well curl up and watch television" blues, it's a good time to take an imaginary trip. You'll save money and your sanity! Amazing as it sounds, going to your favorite "mental Shangri-la" can be nearly as beneficial as a real trip.

If you've ever awakened from a nightmare with your body trembling and your heart pounding, you were responding solely to what was happening in your mind. A fantasy trip works like that only in reverse. Experience all the *positive* results of getting away on vacation—feeling calm, relaxed, energized, and refreshed. Pick a favorite vacation spot from your youth, an actual place you've vacationed as an adult, or someplace you dream of visiting...a sandy beach on a Caribbean island, a cottage by a lake, a log cabin in the woods, or a mountain chalet.

To add to your fantasy experience, visit the library for books about where you would go on a real vacation. Log on to websites that allow you to visit places you may not have a chance to see otherwise—the Louvre in Paris or a waterhole in Africa. Collect travel brochures and guidebooks about places that interest you. Gather magazines and other media, a sheet of poster board, a pair of scissors, and a glue stick and make a dream vacation collage. Borrow or rent travel videos of your favorite fantasy spots. After you watch them, you'll be able to really visit them in your mind.

Ask, "If I have just one day to do anything and be anywhere, what would I do and where would I do it?" My favorite imaginary vacation is to rent a beach house with Cliff, stock it with plenty of fresh fruit, homemade crusty breads, and old cheeses, English breakfast tea from Herrods, Mozart serenades on CD, and lots of Belgian chocolate. We'd do nothing but sleep in, read, play in the ocean, nap, munch on snacks, take long strolls in the moonlight, and be together. When you look at your dream vacation, consider which elements you could incorporate into your life right now. Expand your horizons. Whenever you can, go on a real retreat—alone or with family or friends.

8. *Let nature nurture you.* When I'm completely overwhelmed with life, I'm drawn to nature. Some of my most deeply nurturing experiences have taken place outdoors. As I wander through the backwoods behind our home, I find it so easy to commune with God. Yes, I know he is everywhere, but he seems especially close here. If I walk long enough through the countryside, I feel calm and slow my pace. The purity of nature has a way of cleansing me, washing away my tension and stress. Regardless of where you live or work, there are wonderful places to enjoy nature nearby, even for city dwellers. When you pine for the tranquility of nature, follow your instincts. Walk barefoot on a beach; tour a greenhouse, garden center, or florist shop; visit an aviary or butterfly conservatory; or camp

out under the stars and moonlight. Experience how the sights, sounds, scents, and textures of nature have a way of reviving your soul. Whether it's a picnic in the park or a wilderness trip, get outdoors as often as you can to enjoy the glorious scenery, gaze on a magnificent landscape, and drink in the beauty and power of God's incredible creation.

9. *Spend quiet time in a special place.* Choose a spot that refreshes and inspires you—your bedroom, a den, a guest room, a cottage. Crawl into bed with a pile of fluffy pillows or hide under cozy covers on a comfy couch. This is a healthy way to pamper your body, mind, and spirit back into harmony. Give yourself permission to hide out for an afternoon or a day and do whatever you like—immerse yourself in a good novel, watch movies, sleep, listen to your favorite music, eat comfort food, browse through magazines, or a combination of all these—without guilt. Tell yourself the world is not going to end if you take some nurturing time for yourself.

At one time if I indulged in a day or even an hour like this, I'd cancel most of the benefits by feeling guilty. My inner critic would say, "You lazy slob. Snoozing in the middle of the day. Everyone else is out there getting things done, but not you. You're going downhill fast. How low will you sink?" I had to remind myself frequently that I'd be better off later, be more efficient and effective at work, be a more creative problem solver, and be a more enjoyable person to be around by taking time out.

Don't wait until you are so burned out you can barely keep going. When you find yourself saying, "If I can just make it over this next hurdle" or "Once I finish this project I'll take some time out," create a warm, safe haven *now* instead of waiting. Unplug the phone, wrap up in a comfy quilt, and indulge.

10. *Dress for comfort.* Have you ever thought about what it would be like if you dressed to feel good rather than to look thin or project the right image? Imagine how you'd feel if you opened your closet to find only clothes that are comfortable, fit you perfectly, and make you feel good when you wear them.

Considering the extraordinary amount of attention given to women's fashion, it's no wonder we attempt to squeeze our body parts into uncomfortable clothes that tug, choke, pull, pinch, bind, and hike up or down.

Undergarments that are too tight and waistbands that dig in are bound to make a difference in our facial expressions, attitudes, demeanor, and performances. They make us crabby and short-tempered and leave red indents all over our bodies when we get undressed at night.

Magazine articles, catalogs, and commercials bombard us with techniques that promise to help us look ten pounds thinner, but rarely do we hear how to dress comfortably. "How do I look?" has always been the question rather than "How do I feel?" Dressing for comfort doesn't mean looking like a slob, wearing shabby, scuffed, tattered items from the back of your closet.

When you purchase new clothes, shop with comfort in mind: flannel pajamas you'd wear 24 hours a day if you could get away with it, cotton-knit sweaters, fleece-lined sweatshirts, cuddly bathrobes, downy slippers, loose-fitting jeans, oversized shirts, cozy socks, and the soft cotton undies that make you feel like you're on vacation. Go through your closet, take inventory, and make a list of what you need to fill in the gaps. Include what you'd like to wear when relaxing in the evenings, running errands, going to the park with the kids, having Saturday morning breakfast with your hubby, or hanging out with a friend. Create a visual collage of your new wardrobe by clipping pictures from catalogs and magazines. Paste them in a notebook along with your list and carry it with you when you shop. Getting rid of your uncomfortable clothes gives you the freedom to invite and enjoy comfort into your life.

11. *Treat yourself to comfort food.* Undeniably food can provide the peace we long for when we are stressed, albeit only temporarily. The flip side is that polishing off an entire bag of Oreos between the grocery store and home (making it necessary to stop off at a Dumpster to dispose of the evidence) also brings guilt, a big dose of self-hatred, an onslaught of self-punishing exercises, and weight gain. When our inner critics flood our minds with condemnation about our irresponsibility, some of us have been known to throw the remainder of a dozen donuts into a roadside garbage can as we're traveling in a last-ditch attempt to prevent ourselves from finishing them off. Then we go home and force ourselves into neck-to-knee body shapers and clothes that are too tight—constant reminders that we've behaved badly and must be reprimanded.

When eaten in moderation, food can be used for comfort without becoming a harmful, sedating influence. What comes to mind when you think of comfort food? Baked macaroni-and-cheese casserole? Peanut butter cookies warm from the oven? Chocolate milk, butterscotch pudding, or tomato soup with grilled cheese sandwiches? Lemon meringue pie or vanilla fudge? I think of spaghetti and meatballs, chocolate brownies, toast and jelly, and hot cocoa topped with marshmallows. Often comfort foods are familiar ones we had as children. They're the ones we reach for when we feel overstressed, overextended, and underappreciated. If you fuel your body regularly with balanced nutrition, you'll be able to tolerate a little fat and sugar now and then.

12. *Surround yourself with comfort symbols.* Your home and workplace should be nurturing, comforting havens where you enjoy spending time. If your workplace depresses you, turn it into a space you'll find refreshing and inspiring. If there are times you don't want to go home because it's not a pleasant place to be, take a few steps to transform it into a cozy refuge and a safe sanctuary.

Remember to appeal to all five senses. Surround yourself with colors, fabrics, textures, artwork, photographs, potpourri, candles, and accessories that represent comfort. If you can paint your office, keep in mind that tints of red are thought to stimulate creativity and shades of blue decrease tension. Being in a room painted in colors you like will greatly enhance your performance and productivity. At home, paint walls in shades that calm you and select furnishings in styles you find comforting and that urge you to curl up and rest.

To encourage relaxation at home, drape a cotton comforter, patchwork quilt, or fuzzy blanket over furniture and add a few fluffy cushions. Place your favorite books, photographs, and magazines around the room. Add houseplants or a vase of your favorite flowers to brighten any room and bring the outdoors inside. When the weather is chilly, make a fire in the fireplace. If you don't have one, arrange and light votive candles on a metal tray for a similar effect.

When I'm preparing myself for a day of writing, there are comfort rituals I set in place to create an inspiring atmosphere. I have discovered that wearing a cozy robe or silk lounging pajamas and being wrapped in the quilt handmade by my mom keep me comfy and help me perform at my best. A vanilla-scented candle flickering nearby, a steamy pot of cranberry tea or freshly brewed Swiss Almond coffee served in my favorite china mug, and some Bach serenades or Chopin waltzes playing softly in the background set the stage for me.

Whether it's comfort clothing, comfort surroundings, or comfort food, I'm sure we can all perform at peak levels when we are snug and relaxed.

Healthy self-care requires an investment of time, effort, and serious planning. If you're still not convinced you have time to nurture yourself back into balance or pamper yourself into wellness, consider this: It's been said that in a lifetime, the average North American will...

- watch 1700 hours of TV each year
- spend time learning how to operate 20,000 different gadgets, appliances, and machines, from DVD players and clock radios to electric knives, washing machines, coffeemakers, blow dryers, computers, and car options
- spend 5 years waiting in line, 3 years in meetings, 2 years calling someone who isn't there, 1 year searching through clutter for misplaced items, 8 months opening junk mail, and 6 months waiting in traffic for the lights to turn

If we can find time to do all that, surely we can take the time to get refreshed and recharge our lives.

Sanity Savers & Survival Hints

- List your favorite simple indulgences and treat yourself to something you love to do on a regular basis—go to a movie, stroll outdoors, spend an afternoon reading.
- Put nurturing time in your schedule.

- Say no to requests that intrude on your nurturing time. Learn to ignore interruptions, turn off the phone, and don't wear a watch.
- Start a journal and make entries every day or so. Sit quietly and write about what is on your mind. Note your thoughts and feelings, list the people and situations you want to pray about, and write down all you're grateful for. You'll be amazed at the insights God can reveal to you in these times of quiet solitude.
- Let others take care of themselves. Sometimes we do more caretaking than is necessary.
- Learn to delegate, and don't put pressure on yourself to make things perfect.
- Exercise *your* way. Choose exercise you enjoy and something that makes you feel good about yourself. Some people put themselves through torture to get fit. If you hate going to the gym, don't do it. Choose a sport you enjoy. Take up dance, join a water aerobics class, or play badminton or tennis. Exercise is not about punitively trying to create an ideal body. It's about becoming and staying healthy.
- Take time off. Book vacations at regular intervals during the year. Pay attention to when you feel stressed and take a long weekend. Time spent relaxing will go a long way toward a happier, more energized you.

Rethink Life Balance

When Life Seems Out of Whack

The challenge of work–life balance is without question one of the most significant struggles faced by women today. I've surveyed thousands of my readers and audience members about their greatest personal and professional stressors, life balance is always at or near the top. Without the right balance of family, work, personal, and leisure time, we begin to begrudge our commitments and responsibilities. We feel worn out and used up, and there is no joy in our lives.

You may be familiar with the Wallenda family. They were possibly the world's most well-known balance experts. For years German acrobat Karl Wallenda and his family astounded audiences with high-wire feats, including their most memorable: the great pyramid—three tiers made of seven people. Balance in this sense implies precise and simultaneous poise, focus, stability, and strength.

Once reached, balance may give the impression of ease. Have you ever noticed how those high-wire performers look so composed? They may sit or stand on the wire nearly motionless, but that doesn't mean they're resting. No, the hard part is scarcely over. Once perfect balance is attained, it must be sustained. Every fiber of each performer's being is completely consumed with maintaining perfect balance. Is that what we really want? Extreme concentrated exertion with no room for error?

When our lives become complex and rigid, our stress increases. So what's the cure? As a former *accomplishment addict,* my ultimate dream was always to achieve that kind of balance—an elusive state in which every cog in every wheel fits perfectly and moves smoothly and efficiently. I knew if I could just achieve this, I could add yet another tier of goals and projects. Once that tier was balanced, I could add another…and another. Balance like this, I believed, would result in a never-ending reserve of time and energy, along with the enduring and loyal cooperation of others.

Flexibility. These days I know that kind of balance is not for me, especially if I have to climb up to that high wire wearing tights or one of those skimpy little outfits. The truth is that balance without flexibility is stressful and doesn't allow for the detours and surprises God gives us. We live in a crazy, unbalanced world. Our lives are rarely in perfect balance. The desire to balance personal, family, home, and work demands has long been a juggling act. Between the long hours, daily commutes, meetings, job challenges, family schedules, relationship issues, personal commitments, and unexpected dilemmas, there's little time left for personal needs. It's not surprising we feel overloaded, burned out, and weary.

Then there's the matter of getting our bodies, minds, and spirits in balance. When any one of these is out of whack, everything suffers. We go through life like a three-legged stool with one leg cracked, ready to give and topple over any minute. When we're out of balance, we feel drained and nothing is fun anymore, even when we do manage to fit in a time-out.

> Measure balance by what energizes you versus what drains you.

Still, leading a rich, well-rounded life is essential to our sanity, inner peace, and enjoyment of life. In that sense true balance isn't necessarily what you do, but how you view life. We tend to aim toward balancing two aspects of our lives: doing and not doing, working and not working, accomplishing and not accomplishing. We think if we could separate the doing from the not doing, and attain equal amounts of both, we'd be on our way to balanced living.

A better way would be to measure balance by the activities that leave us energized versus those that drain our energy. It's not a chore if you're washing dishes or making the bed while having meaningful interactions with your spouse. It wouldn't be a bothersome task to drive your kids to the soccer game while catching up on all that's happening in their world. Maybe you're stimulated when working on an article you're submitting to be published or energized staying up late to prepare a gourmet dish for a dinner party tomorrow evening. Work that is rewarding and allows you to fulfill your true values and highest ideals is great. With that as part of your balance, life is pleasurable, and you'll feel energetic.

Stephanie is a woman who is balanced, energized, and enjoying her life most of the time. But it wasn't always this way. For years she tried to find balance by blocking her time into isolated boxes. Each box was solely dedicated to a particular aspect of her life: family, home, work, or personal obligations. She admits that she felt perturbed and unfulfilled most of the time, no matter how the boxes were arranged.

As an entrepreneur who travels much of the time, she has an unpredictable schedule and little routine to her days. In the past, not only was her personal time often nonexistent, but she depleted a great deal of her energy feeling guilty and thinking about what she should be doing in one box while still inside another. No matter what she was involved in, she felt she should be doing something else. All the shoulds weighed her down, and every activity took on a negative feeling, even though much of what she was involved in could have been pleasant, rewarding, and enjoyable.

Eventually she started paying attention to the emotions she was experiencing. Realizing that negative self-judgment was not helping her performance or making her happy, she started eliminating "should" and "shouldn't" from her vocabulary. She substituted "I choose to" instead. Rather than telling herself, "I should visit Aunt Mary" she substituted "I choose to visit Aunt Mary even though my schedule is tight because I want her to know how much she is loved and appreciated" or "I choose not to visit Aunt Mary right now because it would put me under extreme pressure while I'm trying to meet my project deadline. I may be in a better position next week." That simple change means she can view either option as something she freely chose. And remember, in chapter 7 we discovered that choosing makes us feel like we have more control. By choosing, Stephanie can give 100 percent to every activity. She releases the false guilt about what she's doing—or not doing—at any given moment.

So start catching yourself whenever you say "I must," "I have to," or "I have no option." The truth is, you really don't *have* to do anything. You don't even *have* to get out of bed in the morning. After a few days, I'm sure someone would come looking for you. Nor do you *have* to go to work every day. There is government assistance available should you quit. If you choose not to raise your children, there are agencies that will take them and place them in other homes. You don't *have* to pay your taxes. You can go to jail instead. Get the point? There are always alternatives. It's just that you may not like the options or consequences. In essence, you do what you do because the benefits usually outweigh the cost.

Obvious enough, isn't it? Life is about setting priorities and making trade-offs. That's what we do. But in our all-or-nothing culture, choosing to limit our priorities or go against the mainstream is often seen as failure. We strive for achievement everywhere all the time. Then we feel guilty and more stressed when inevitably we fall short. Trying to perfectly balance our work and personal life all the time is a losing proposition. There are some smarter ways to stay sane while juggling life and work responsibilities for the long run. The key secret is flexibility.

10 Simple Rules to Take Back Your Life

1. *Stop trying to be CEO—Chief Everything Officer.* You don't have to be in charge of everybody and everything at all times. When you believe you do, you allow your commitments and daily events to take control of your life and rob you of joy, peace, and energy. If you're going through a particularly demanding time, grab as much help as you can get. Companies now provide a multitude of ready-made meals and partly prepared dishes to help at mealtimes. Today there are a host of technological miracles to simplify your life, from internet shopping to the microwave oven. Get good at delegating, hiring, and asking for help. Let the neighbor's kid wash the car, your sister babysit, and your mother-in-law iron her son's shirts if that's what they offer to do. You can do the same for them if the situations were reversed. If you can afford it, pay someone to clean your house. Practice saying no when another obligation would add to an

already overloaded schedule. You don't have to be "Manager of the Universe." Remind yourself that if you weren't here, life would go on.

2. *Change the way you talk to yourself about your busyness.* Repeat to yourself, "There is no hurry," "I have more than enough time," "Everything is unfolding just as it should," and "God is in control of events in my life." Just speaking these things will probably make you let out a big sigh of relief! When I was writing my last book, I felt I was seriously falling behind schedule and might not meet my deadline. While making the bed one morning, I started talking it over with God. I confessed my panicky feelings. I heard God say in a comforting voice that came from deep inside me, "All is as it should be." Then I heard it a second time. Although it wasn't an actual audible voice, my entire body calmed down, along with my thoughts and emotions. I started saying those words to myself anytime I felt anxious about my deadline. Each time I did so, I felt the assurance from my heavenly Father that the book would get finished exactly when it needed to be. And it did!

3. *Lower your standards.* Stressed-out women are often slaves to their own ideals. When a report is due, you may be tempted to do one that is twice as long as necessary and hand it in a day before it is required. When you're volunteering at a fund-raising event, you're the first one to arrive and the last one to leave. Be lenient with yourself. Don't worry if you can't bake cookies every time you're asked to, the bed doesn't get made every morning, or the towels stay in the dryer for a couple of days. Remember, when you're busy it's better to let your standards slip than your relationships. Any meal tastes better when it's eaten together, even if it doesn't happen until late in the evening. Besides, you can't see the clutter and dust by candlelight! Relax your personal standards. Chances are no one will even notice or care as much as you do.

4. *Escape the superwoman trap.* Through the media we're constantly being bombarded with unrealistic standards by which we measure our worth, happiness, and success. On TV and in the movies we're presented with images of women who pack way more into their lives than is feasible. Then we're lured into attempting too much and feel like failures when we

discover we can't accomplish every goal. Superwoman doesn't exist. If she does, she's usually driven to perform and will eventually burn out. If she's you, let her off the hook!

5. *Stick with what you're good at.* According to the "Pareto Principle," also known as the 80/20 rule, 80 percent of the value of your daily tasks and activities comes from only 20 percent of the items on your to-do list. That means only 20 percent of the value comes from 80 percent of the items. If a task or activity can wait until later, or someone else can do it, then you shouldn't be doing it. Here are some examples of how the Pareto Principle works:

- 20 percent of volunteers contribute 80 percent of the volunteer hours
- 20 percent of products sold account for 80 percent of the profit
- 20 percent of committee members perform 80 percent of the tasks
- 20 percent of telephone callers make 80 percent of all the calls to your home or work
- 20 percent of your favorite restaurants is where 80 percent of eating out is done
- 20 percent of the church membership donate 80 percent of the budget

Always focus on the best and cut out the rest!

6. *Accept your life stage.* There are chapters in your life when you will devote a large part of your time and energy to specific people or projects. You may have to put some elements of your life on hold while you look after other areas. You might not be able to continue sewing your own fashions or decorating your home while you raise toddlers. For a season, you may have to say no to chairing the women's networking committee in favor of carpooling teenagers or taking your aging parents to doctors' appointments. When you've just started to build a business, you may not have much of a social life. But these things will come full circle, and you

can resume those activities later on. Simply accepting where you are and knowing this is a phase will help you feel less stressed. Although there may be very little you can do to change your circumstances in times like these, you can plan something to look forward to once the tide turns.

7. *Expand your timetable.* If it's not possible to fit everything into one week, consider altering your schedule. While raising two daughters, Cliff and I realized we weren't spending a lot of time together. We decided to have a weekly date: a romantic evening by the fireplace playing Backgammon, a candlelight dinner in a fancy restaurant, or a long country walk. It worked for a while, but because of constantly shifting schedules, we changed it to a monthly date rather than stressing about missing an occasional week. It may not have been ideal, but it was more realistic and less likely to fail. When we could, we fit in additional dates in-between—bonuses! Some people think it's far too formal to schedule time together as a couple, but sometimes making an appointment to see your partner or to spend intimate time together is the only way to make it happen. The method may not be the most romantic, but the outcome sure can be.

8. *Think quality not quantity.* While it's become a cliché, it is true that if you only have a short period of time to play with, make every second count. Plan times when you and your spouse and/or the kids can talk as well as times when you can crash together on the sofa, eat popcorn, and watch a good movie. During the day take advantage of a quick phone call, a text message, or a 20-minute meeting over coffee. You may even want to arrange having a coffee break with a friend over the phone. Just plan ahead so each of you can be prepared to enjoy a favorite drink while chatting. If you can give your husband, kids, or friends 100 percent of your attention, even for brief periods, it goes a lot further than compromising and giving them hurried, stressful times simply because you think you should.

9. *Rethink your purpose.* Balance is helpful but it shouldn't be your life goal. Rather, it's a way of describing an outcome. Seeking to attain perfect balance is frustrating because it's an intangible that changes all the time.

Determine your highest values and then set concrete objectives in the areas that are most meaningful to you.

10. *Consider your priorities.* If you still feel your life is out of whack, take a long, hard look at what's important to you. Sit quietly with a pen and journal and write out your top ten priorities in life. Does your list include your relationship with God? With your spouse? Your children? Other family members and friends? How about your health and wellness? Perhaps you've included financial freedom, spiritual growth, and contributions to charities. Are there activities in your life you should seriously consider dropping, at least for the time being? Sacrificing something you enjoy doing is always difficult, but are you willing to risk your health and relationships if you don't? Use your list to provide focus and keep you on track.

Sanity Secrets & Survival Hints

- Achieving a "balanced" life will take some planning and effort, but it will give you more energy and time to focus on things that are truly valuable to you.
- Ask God for divine insights. He delights in turning chaos into order and transforming weaknesses into strengths.
- A sense of balance can make the difference between merely surviving and really living.
- There is no time like the present!
- Living a balanced life is not an end to itself. Decide which activities are right for you.
- Balance is the key to functioning effectively and bringing more joy into your life.
- To put everything back into perspective, read what God says in the book of Job, chapter 38.
- Create a Daily Balance Kit. I don't know who originally created this list, but it's worthwhile:

- a *toothpick* to remind you to pick out the good qualities in others
- a *rubber band* to remind you to be flexible; life may not go the way you want, but it will work out
- a *Band-Aid* to remind you to heal hurt feelings...whether yours or someone else's
- a *pencil* to remind you to list your blessings every day
- an *eraser* to remind you that everyone makes mistakes, and that's okay
- *chewing gum* to remind you to stick with it and you can accomplish anything
- a *mint* to remind you that you are worth a mint
- a *Hershey's Kiss* to remind you that everyone needs a kiss or hug every day
- a *tea bag* to remind you to relax daily and go over your list of blessings

13

Simplify Your Life

When Things Are Complicated

There's nothing that quite compares with the feeling I get when I allow myself to simplify parts of my complicated life. Whether it's scaling down on unnecessary possessions, letting go of clutter, cutting back on responsibilities, pruning away obligations, or minimizing the longings in my life, simplification produces an invigorating sensation much like skinny-dipping in a crisp, cold lake: exhilarating and a little scary at the same time.

At one time or another most of us have felt our lives are too busy. We wear too many hats, rush too many places, and own too much stuff. If you're drowning under a sea of family responsibilities, work pressures, social obligations, community commitments, car repairs, unpaid bills, and yard work, maybe it's time to uncomplicate your life. Simplification means reorganizing your routines and your possessions to focus on what is truly meaningful. It's minimizing the chaos and being purposeful with your time, your belongings, and your actions. It's not always easy to do, but the rewards are great. You'll need courage and fortitude to pare away parts of your life you no longer need, but you'll feel much lighter!

There's a big difference between your needs and your wants. To start pruning, determine what you must have and what you'd like to keep.

Then let the rest go. The following three questions will help you rank your daily activities, make decisions about material belongings, determine your highest priorities, and set future goals.

- What will this mean to me next week?
- What will this mean to me in ten years?
- What will this mean to me in light of eternity?

Focusing on the answers to these questions will keep everything in perspective. Integrate them into your regular thought patterns. The next time you're unsure about eliminating an obligation, adding one more commitment, or making a purchase, ask, "Will this be important to me down the road?" If it will, take it seriously. If not, let it go.

Simplification minimizes the unnecessary and focuses on using your choices to promote your priorities and values.

❋ ❋ ❋

Nothing is better than simplicity.
WALT WHITMAN

Some people sabotage their success by subconsciously bringing about more stress. Making life complex and difficult is one way to avoid pleasures you feel you don't deserve. When you do happen upon joy and contentment, do you often hold back from experiencing the full deal because you're entering unfamiliar territory? Complicating things is one way to get back into your comfort zone, which includes your established chaotic habits. To change these destructive patterns that keep you stuck takes conscious effort and a willingness to tune in to your thoughts.

Be Here Now

❋ ❋ ❋

In the present moment, there is no stress.
STEPHAN RECHTSCHAFFEN

Maybe you've noticed. Stressed-out women tend not to live in the moment. They hold off being happy. They believe joy, contentment, satisfaction, and peace will come once certain conditions are met. They say, I'll be happy when…I'm married, get divorced, move to a bigger house, buy a newer car, finish my project, get control of the clutter, have children, and so forth. Then, I'll *really* be happy when the baby sleeps through the night, has all her teeth, finishes his shots, gets potty trained. Or, I'll be happy when the kids go to school, grow up, leave home; when I get a better job; when I have a different boss; get out of debt; pay off the mortgage; retire. And then? When I retire I'll do all the things I never got around to doing: take up oil painting, learn to play the piano, write a book, go for more walks, visit with friends more often, travel the world.

When we're stressed to the max, we tend to put off living until circumstances are ideal. It's like we're waiting to hear God's voice boom down from the heavens saying, "Your life is now perfect. You may go ahead and start enjoying it!"

In our pursuit of a happy, healthy future, we often forget the present moment. A bumper sticker I saw reminded me to "Be Here Now." How often are we somewhere…and yet someplace else in our thoughts? We're in the shower first thing in the morning, but in our minds we're already battling the cares and concerns of the day, or dealing with worries of yesterday, or fighting fears of tomorrow. We never fully enjoy the benefits of warm water streaming over our bodies, miraculously energizing and calming us at the same time. Water has incredible invigorating, soothing, and stimulating properties that we miss when we aren't in the present moment. The next time you shower, feel every drop of water as it bounces against your skin and flows around your body. Relish the experience. It may be the first time you've been present in the shower for a long, long time. When your mind drifts off and you think about the kids, your bank account, your full schedule, and all the things that need to be done, gently bring it back to the water trickling and spraying over your body. Experience refreshment and new energy!

> One of the most powerful sanity secrets is to be fully present and attentive to the situation you're in.

"Be here now" involves being "mindful." Decide now to go through your day being fully aware of what you're doing and how you're feeling. Approach each activity with your full attention. Bless the moment you're in and quit waiting to have everything in perfect order before you live fully. Face it—you will never be completely caught up anyway. One time I was hard at work in my office and thought, *What am I doing? Work, work, work. I should get my hubby and children and take them to the country for a picnic.* So I did. But when we were having a picnic I thought, *What am I doing here with all that work back at the office?*

You might be very good at turning yourself *on* to get more work done, but more importantly, can you turn yourself *off*? Do you make the switch between home and work and back again? Can you be fully where you are so you can experience high levels of engagement? One of the most powerful sanity secrets to maintaining life and work balance is to be fully present and attentive to whatever situation you're in. Don't put your happiness on hold waiting for a better time. Life is not a dress rehearsal... and it shouldn't be a stress rehearsal either. When you are working, work. When you are playing, play. When you are resting, rest. Get good with finding your personal on/off switch.

When we start living in the moment and stop longing for what we don't have, there are endless possibilities to enjoying our existence each and every day. Look for them. Be on the alert for innocent pleasures and simple delights. Life's little diversions too often get lost in our hectic days.

Gratitude—Too Blessed to Be Stressed

❁ ❁ ❁

Not that I speak of want, for I have learned to be content
in whatever circumstances I am.
PHILIPPIANS 4:11 NASB

Complex lives can alter our perspective by giving us tunnel vision. When we're stressed with the intricacy of our situation, it's as though we have blinders on and notice only the burdens, difficulties, setbacks, and troubles. All the good around us is blocked out. It is easy—and common—during times of stress to allow the trials and obstacles to build up and quash the blessings. As a result, our perceived needs, high expectations, and unrealistic demands outweigh our apparent resources to deal with them.

There is one remedy that works to simplify things every time: an attitude of gratitude. Count your blessings! You'll be amazed at what thankfulness can do. When we're grateful, our whole focus changes from what is wrong, what we don't have, and what we think we need to what is already good around us. Start a gratitude journal. Make a list of the blessings in your life—from yesterday, last week, and last month. If none come to mind, ask:

- Can I see, smell, hear, taste, or feel?
- Can I breathe, move, stand, walk, or talk?
- Do I have hot water for a shower?
- Has anyone told me he or she cares about me?
- Do I have clothes to wear?
- Do I have a bed to sleep in?
- Has my car been running smoothly? (If not, can I afford to get it repaired?)
- Has a coworker, boss, or customer ever complimented me?
- Is my roof free from leaks? (If not, is it leaking in only three spots?)
- Have I made progress on a project?
- Has my child come home with a good grade (or simply come home)?
- Was I able to rescue the Sunday roast from the floor before the dog got it?

Begin making a conscious note of every blessing you experience. Even though you acknowledge you're stressed, you can also recognize, appreciate, and rejoice that you are blessed. Aside from material goods, blessings also include character strengths, talents, God-given gifts, attributes, abilities, and skills. Acknowledge all that you are and all you have. Your spouse, family, relatives, friendships, and other relationships are blessings too.

Count them all and shout to the rooftops, "I'm glad to be alive!" Identify every source of pleasure and comfort you enjoy. Don't overlook anything. Write out a list and post it on the refrigerator. Refer to your list when you feel stressed.

If you're still having a hard time counting your blessings, be thankful you don't have a hangnail, an ingrown toenail, a splinter, or a paper cut. We aren't usually appreciative of these things until we have to deal with them. When I ended up in the hospital recently with a vitamin pill stuck in my throat, I became very thankful, once it was removed, that I could swallow. I admit the ability to swallow wasn't something I thought of very often, and it wasn't on my gratitude list—but it is now!

❊ ❊ ❊

"It's snowing still," said Eeyore gloomily.
"And freezing. However," he said, brightening up a little,
"we haven't had an earthquake lately."
THE HOUSE AT POOH CORNER

Knowing our blessings sparks energy and inspiration. Recognizing our blessings can put our burdens into perspective, making them less threatening and easier to cope with. Gratitude and inner peace seem to go hand in hand. Focusing on our blessings generates a feeling of simple abundance. Thinking grateful thoughts reminds us that our lives are already filled with so much of what we want and need.

> If you've lost all your marvels, discover how to be awestruck again.

Our outlook colors everything in our lives. The enemy (the devil) wants to bring us down, to make us feel burdened and overwhelmed. Recognizing God's blessings builds us up and sets us free. Choosing to look for the good is a sanity secret that will make a huge difference in your ability to live stress free in spite of any difficulties. Choose what you will dwell on—burdens or blessings. I choose blessings!

❊ ❊ ❊

How the good God loves those
who appreciate the value of his gifts.
JULIE BILLIART

Each morning spend a little time focusing on all you're grateful for as you contemplate the day's priorities. Let trivial matters fall by the wayside. Go to that place where time stands still. Putter, dawdle, or dillydally a while. Think about times when you have been so engrossed in a project or hobby or other interest that you didn't notice the passing of time. When you were a kid, you knew how to live simply. You took time to daydream. Your mother probably called it "La La Land," but it was a place where you could be completely absorbed with a kite, a balloon, an airplane, or a bird. If you've lost all your marvels, discover how to be awestruck again.

Sanity Savers & Survival Hints

Take a break! Simplify by taking a complete break from what you've been doing. The secret is to make the change as different from what you've been working on as possible. You can alter your body position, activity level, location, and the senses you usually use. If you've been doing left-brain logical work, switch to right-brain creative activity. If you've been on your feet, sit down for a while. If you've been at your desk for a long time, get up and move. Here are 14 other quick breaks to simplify your life:

- listen to soothing music
- take a power nap
- eat an uncommon healthy snack, such as mango, papaya, feta cheese, a pomegranate, almonds
- invite someone special to meet you for coffee or tea
- do a series of slow stretches
- browse through a magazine or your favorite photo albums
- take a drive in the country—roll the windows down and sing loudly
- ask a friend to meet you for a picnic and swap bag lunches

- spritz the air with lavender fragrance
- do some artwork or a relaxing craft project
- play a musical instrument
- arrange with a friend or coworker to have a coffee break over the phone
- do a crossword, jigsaw, or number puzzle
- visit a library or church and sit quietly inside

Get Out of the Fast Lane

When Life Is Speeding Past

An amusing wall plaque in the kitchen of my grandparents' cottage read, "The hurrier I go, the behinder I get." Although the poor grammar makes me smile, as a little girl with all the time in the world, the axiom really didn't have much impact. But when my adult world went whirling out of control on the spin cycle of life, those words came back with great meaning. Buried under an avalanche of responsibilities, duties, tasks, and activities, the more I rushed around and the faster I tried to get things done, the less I accomplished. My frustrations led to misunderstandings, mistakes, and oversights, causing me to fall even further behind. For years I fell into the 24/7 trap—at times working around the clock in an effort to get everything done while patching up blunders and trying to stay sane. Eventually my dissatisfaction sent me on a quest to discover a better way. What I found was there's more to life than increasing your speed. Besides, it's possible to achieve more by doing less. Here are two simple ways to slow down the clamor and commotion.

Unplug Your World

When my friend was feeling completely fed up with her life and yearning to exchange modern technology for a little bit of nature, her husband took her camping for the first time. At every opportunity he passed along outdoor survival wisdom. One day they got lost hiking in the deep woods. He tried the usual tactics to determine direction—moss on the trees (there was none) and the position of the sun (it was an overcast day). Just as she was beginning to panic, he spotted a small cabin off in the distance. He pulled out his binoculars, studied the cabin, turned around, and led them right back to their camp. She was impressed. When she asked how he did it, he replied. "Simple! In this part of the country, all the TV satellite dishes point south."

❊ ❊ ❊

For fast-acting relief, try slowing down!
LILY TOMLIN

Modern technology can come in handy—in more ways than one. I can't imagine going back to the days before computers, TV—satellite or cable—GPS, DVDs, CDs, and iPods. The downside is that it keeps us constantly connected to the world or the workplace. To slow our pace, there comes a time when we need a complete break from electronics.

Can you remember the days when no one carried a cell phone during a peaceful stroll through the neighborhood or on the beach? One morning I was taking my usual walk by the lake and passed a young mother strolling with her small child. He was chattering away at her side, pointing out a sailboat in the distance, wild ducks and geese along the shore, fluffy white clouds above, and the big red-and-white lighthouse at the end of the pier. I could hear her speaking and thought how wonderful it was to see these two having such a great conversation. As I got closer though, I could clearly see the mom was talking on her cell phone, oblivious to the squeals of delight coming from her young son. When he asked to stop for a drink, she clumsily lifted him up to the water fountain with her one free hand without missing a beat in her phone conversation. While the little one seemed unaware that his mom was not part of his conversation, I couldn't help but think about all this mother was missing. This moment in time was a wonder she would never experience.

In your quest to slow down you may have difficulty separating technology from your personal life. We say family and other relationships come first, but we have to do more than pay lip service to this ideal. Let others know you honor them by the little things you do. Here are some helpful guidelines.

- When it's mealtime, establish that no one answers the phone.
- When you spend time with the kids or grandkids, don't take work to read. Pay attention to them by remaining present. Make a conscious effort to be mindful and stay in the moment.
- Use your laptop or BlackBerry for working when you're on the road or away from the office, not for checking email when you're out for a romantic dinner, having lunch with a friend, or visiting your parents or grandparents.
- When you go for a walk, keep the cell phone for emergencies only.

We persist in believing that all our gizmos and gadgets are making life better, despite evidence to the contrary. They often fill our days with more haste and insanity, keeping us stressed and isolated from what contributes most to a healthy life: balance.

More than 200 years ago poet William Wordsworth made the statement, "The world is too much with us." When the world is too much with us, priorities become distorted and values become skewed. Perhaps slowing down for a weekend, or even one day, by avoiding the trappings of modern technology would do us good. Think about it. From the time we crawl out of bed in the morning until we collapse back in it at night, we hear timers on stoves; buzzers on washing machines; beepers on pagers, email, answering machines, watches; and the ringing of telephones relentlessly reminding us that someone wants our attention or something needs to be looked after.

Just for a day turn off the ringer on the phone. Let voicemail take the calls. Don't set your alarm or wear your watch. Pay no attention to time. Forget checking your email. In fact, don't even turn on your computer. Leave the television, radio, and DVD player turned off too. You may even want to go so far as to turn off the lights and enjoy some candlelight.

It's not easy to slow down when we're immersed in all the paraphernalia of modern technology. A friend sent me the following list from an unknown author.

You know you're living in the 21st century when...

1. You accidentally enter your password on the microwave.
2. You haven't played solitaire with real cards in years.
3. You have a list of 15 phone numbers to reach your family of 3.
4. You email the person who works at the desk next to you.
5. Your reason for not staying in touch with friends and family is that they don't have email addresses.
6. You pull up in your own driveway and use your cell phone to see if anyone is home to help you carry in the groceries.
7. Every commercial on television has a website at the bottom of the screen.
8. Leaving the house without your cell phone, which you didn't have the first 20 or 30 (or 50) years of your life, is now a cause for panic, and you turn around to get it.
10. You get up in the morning and go online before getting your coffee.
11. You start tilting your head sideways to smile. :-)
12. You're reading this and nodding and laughing.
13. Even worse, you were too rushed to notice there was no #9 on this list.
14. You actually went back up to check that there wasn't a #9 on this list, and now U R laughing at yourself!

The Power of a Positive No

When it comes to slowing down, you can't say yes to every request. One time I was invited to speak at an engagement on the same day as my three-year-old granddaughter's first tap dance recital. When I realized the dilemma, I can't tell you how difficult it was to look in those big brown eyes...and tell my client I wouldn't be able to make it. Usually we have a hard time saying no because we fear hurting a relationship, losing a deal, or not being liked or accepted. But there are times when no is the only answer if we want to keep our sanity. If I'm asked to make a casserole or dessert for a church fundraiser, I find a way to do it. Cooking and baking have long been favorite hobbies of mine that help me unwind and relax. But if I'm asked to do something that's not relaxing for me and my schedule is already packed, I say no. Knowing what drains us and what energizes us is key to saying a "positive no."

I read a story the other day about a little girl who was asked to say a blessing over the food at a dinner party. When she said she wasn't sure what to pray, her mom suggested, "Why don't you just say what you've heard me pray before?" The girl quickly bowed her head and prayed loudly, "Lord, why did I ever invite all these people for supper tonight?"

How often do you get yourself into a position where you regret having taken on so much? Saying no isn't an easy thing to do, and sometimes the people we need to say no to is us!

❊ ❊ ❊

I can only please one person per day. Today is not your day.
Tomorrow isn't looking good either.
T-SHIRT SLOGAN

Saying no doesn't come easy to me. One Sunday morning after church I asked a family we know if they'd like to come for lunch the following week. I thought it would be fun to throw some hot dogs on the barbecue, open a bag of chips, and later enjoy ice cream cones while taking a stroll by the lake. During the week I started thinking about some other friends I could invite. It wasn't long before my guest list was up to 24 people. For some reason, it didn't seem right to serve hot dogs, so the hot dogs soon became steaks, the potato chips turned into potato salad, and dessert went from simple ice cream cones to homemade pies.

But it doesn't end there (I'm ashamed to admit). Next I checked out the patio furniture, and it looked a bit worn. I decided to perk it up with some paint and new cushions. The gardens needed to be freshened up with some serious weeding and a few new plants. After remembering our guests would be using the spare bathroom near the patio, I noticed it was in desperate need of an update. So after choosing wallpaper and paint, along with new accessories, work was clearly cut out for me.

On the day before my not-so-simple lunch, I was up to my ears in baking, cooking, redecorating, and cleaning. When I noticed my hubby slipping out the door to indulge in his hobby—drag racing—I asked him where he thought he was going since all these people were coming. He replied very sincerely, "Honey, I'm going to do what I planned to do all along." When I objected and complained about all that had to be accomplished, he told me, "I never would have done this to myself." Oh, how true. While his comment may have stung for a moment, the sad truth is that he was right. I *had* set myself up.

When we take on more than we can handle and expect others to jump onboard with our craziness, we're setting ourselves up for a lot of frustration. Why is it that for some of us "enough" is never enough? Rather than slowing down, we have an irresistible urge to go one step further.

Here's another perfect example. For years a group of our friends took turns getting together in each other's homes for an evening of fun, games, and snacks. Over time, simple munchies turned into a sit-down, late-night luncheon, and eventually became a full-fledged three-course meal. Each hostess started getting out her fine china, crystal, and silverware. The table was set with linens, candles, and fresh flowers. Soon the trend of getting together for games and snacks fell by the wayside. As more and more women took part-time jobs or full-time careers, most found there just wasn't the time to put on such extravagant meals.

I missed getting together so much that I decided to start a new trend. When I mentioned to one friend that I was thinking of inviting people for a simple snack of toast and tea, she gasped in disbelief but said she wanted to be there to see how it turned out. We sat around our bare kitchen table with paper plates, napkins, and mugs. The toaster was set up at one end. There was a loaf of crusty white bread and one of whole wheat, jars of jam, jelly, and peanut butter, and a large steaming pot of tea. As guests called their requests to Cliff, he would pop the bread in the toaster and pass it down the table when it was ready. We drank hot tea, ate toast laden with jelly, laughed a lot, and enjoyed each other's company.

When my friend saw how easy it was, she gladly volunteered to have the next gathering at her home. She also served white and whole wheat toast with tea, as well as bagels and cream cheese. The next hostess to follow suit offered all that plus fresh-baked muffins with a variety of homemade jams. Soon there were nut breads and cinnamon buns and sour-cream coffee cakes. The concept spread and grew, and before we knew it, tables were being set with linens and silver, candles and fresh flowers. Out came the china and crystal, and you guessed it...we ended up back where we started.

Why is it that we women have such a need to do more? We do it to ourselves. I'm learning that the person I need to say no to more than anyone else is me!

> It's not only okay to say no to yourself and others, it's imperative if we want a stress-free life.

We do go overboard when it comes to serving guests. And sometimes we do much more caretaking of our family members and friends than is necessary or even expected. To keep our sanity, we need to let others take care of themselves. We need to be responsible practically and emotionally. That means we don't have to be a maid to our families or therapists to our best friends. We don't rescue our sisters or brothers from their latest crises or try to be all things to people at work, in the church, in the organizations where we are members, or at clubs where we volunteer. We are entitled to say no, do less, or even not get involved in the first place. People pleasers seldom lead balanced lives because their time is being controlled by everyone else's plans. And women tend to be people pleasers.

Beyond that, slowing down requires delegation. Once we delegate a task, the truly hard part is resisting the urge to go back and fine-tune what the other person has done...or even to do it all over again to *our* satisfaction. If your child makes the bed and it's a little messy, let it go. When someone else folds the laundry, accept it as is. With all my traveling, I'm blessed to have a hubby who will occasionally do the laundry. From time to time wet items even make it into the dryer. Every now and then towels may get folded and put away in the linen closet. The trouble is, when I get home and notice the towels have been placed in backward, I'm likely to lose it. (I'm sure you know what I mean by backward. That's when the rough edges are facing out rather than the round, smooth folded edges we like to see when we open the linen closet.) Now I know I should be thankful the towels made it this far, but it's so hard not to point out this grave error, especially when there is a 50–50 chance of getting it right. Yes, when it comes to my perfectionist tendencies, I am learning very slowly to slow down by looking the other way.

It's not only okay to say no to yourself and others, it's imperative if we want a stress-free life. When someone asks you to bring cookies to the parent–teacher meetings and you're already feeling overloaded, say, "Normally I'd be glad to help, but I already have more than enough projects going right now." If you've been approached to head a committee for a retirement party or run for office in a women's networking organization, and your schedule is full, a graceful response that allows you to say no with diplomacy is "I appreciate the invitation to be involved. However it's not going to work for me at this time." Leave it at that. The problem with adding an explanation is that usually our reasons don't sound good enough and so we start to embellish them to support our position. This is also known as lying. Or the other person counters or offers to take care of the excuse we've given...and then we're stuck doing the job or admitting we just didn't want to take on the project in the first place.

Learn to say no to the telephone too. The phone can be our best friend or our worst enemy. A number of years ago, when I was having a meeting with a client in her home office, the phone rang every few minutes. She didn't pick it up. I encouraged her to feel free to answer it, and I will never forget her reply. She said, "I put that device in here for my convenience. I never allow it to interrupt a meeting." Today people constantly chat on cell phones in public places so this attitude is getting rare. We allow the phone to run our lives. Here are some simple ways to control phone use.

- Break the "must answer the phone anytime it rings" habit. That's why we have voicemail and answering machines. Return calls at your convenience.
- Respect other people by not talking on the phone during

mealtimes, at a restaurant, or anytime you're involved in a face-to-face conversation.

- Don't feel bad about screening your calls with caller ID. It was invented for busy, stressed-out people. Answer only those calls you want or need to take.
- Set limits on your phone time. Take calls only at certain times of day. Keep a watch or timer handy.
- When you take or make a call, let the other person know how much time you have to talk.
- If you're asked to hold, say no and offer to call back or have the caller get back to you.
- If you must take another call requiring you to put someone else on hold, let the first caller know upfront you're expecting another phone call you need to take. Give them the option of holding or calling back later when this happens.
- Set your cell phone or pager on vibrate instead of ring. Don't allow it to interrupt what you're accomplishing at the moment—unless you have prearranged to have a client or family member check in with you at a certain time.
- Call long-winded friends or family members first thing in the day, just before meal times, or at the end of the day. This provides boundaries for how long you can talk.
- Call chatty business associates or clients close to quitting time or on Friday afternoon.
- Let nonstop talkers know you only have five minutes or schedule a time when you can talk longer. Courteously and thoughtfully guide them to the point of the call.
- Use a cordless phone or headset so you can move around and do other things while you talk.
- Cut solicitors short by saying, "Thank you for calling, but I'm not interested and I never do business over the phone. Please take my name and number off your list."
- Write frequently called numbers on a Rolodex card.

Highlight any other numbers you plan to look up in the phone directory more than once, so they will be easy to spot next time.

- Avoid playing "phone tag" by making appointments for important phone calls. Think of them as face-to-face meetings and treat them like one. Mark them on your calendar with the phone number and make notes about what you'll talk about. Be prepared before the call with any information you'll need.
- Use email rather than the phone. It's faster and you can send or reply to emails at a time that suits you.
- If you do get stuck waiting on hold, clean out your purse or wallet, organize a drawer, update your shopping list, file your nails, dust a piece of furniture, clean your eyeglasses, purge some files, or straighten your desk.

If saying no to others or yourself is difficult, remind yourself there are only 24 hours in a day and 168 hours in a week. If you sleep the recommended 8 hours a night, you're left with 112 hours a week. If you work a 40-hour week, you're down to 72 hours per week. Now everything else has to be squeezed into those 72 hours. At some point you have to get good at saying no so you won't burn out. This is a practical way to promote slowing down and refusing "offers."

In our world many things have a sense of urgency about them—deserved or not. While we may not be able to change that, we can control whether or not we allow the clamor to affect our private lives. Plan to escape for a day and take time to muse, ponder, contemplate, and reflect on what real stress-free living is all about. Practice saying no!

Sanity Savers & Survival Hints

- Remind yourself that there's more to life than increasing its speed.
- Pray the following prayer. I'm not sure who wrote it, but it's so powerful.

Slow me down, Lord. Ease the pounding of my heart by quieting my mind. Steady my hurried pace with a vision of the eternal reach of time. Give me, amidst the confusion of my day, the calmness of the everlasting hills. Break the tension of my nerves with the soothing music of the singing streams that live in my memory. Help me know the magical restoring power of sleep.

Teach me the art of taking minute vacations, of slowing down to look at a flower, chat with an old friend, make a new friend, pet a stray dog, watch a spider build a web, smile at a child, or read from a good book. Remind me each day that the race is not always to the swift, and that there is more to life than increasing its speed. Let me look upward into the towering oak and know that it grew great and strong because it grew slowly and well.

15

Sanity Secret #11

Get Off the 24/7 Merry-Go-Round

When You Need More Time

If you're like most of us, you often catch yourself saying, "If only there were more hours in a day," "I can't seem to get caught up," or my all-time favorite, "Here it is, the end of the day, and I haven't even begun what I planned to do." Everywhere I go women tell me they'd appreciate even one more hour in their day.

You've probably had days when you feel closer to the end of your rope than the end of your to-do list. Whether you're juggling a marriage, home, children, full-time career, part-time job, home business, or all of these, managing time is tricky. Even women who are super-organized sometimes end up transferring today's to-do items to tomorrow's list. With interruptions, emergencies, and changed plans, it's impossible to always stick to our daily goals—no matter how prepared we are. In spite of our best intentions, a work meeting goes on longer than expected, the dentist is behind schedule, an injured child needs to be rushed to the hospital, the dog throws up on the carpet, a shopping trip takes longer because someone with too many items is in the "8 items or less" express lane, and there's a traffic jam on the way home.

❀ ❀ ❀

God placed me on this earth to
accomplish a certain number of things.
Right now I am so far behind I will never die!
AUTHOR UNKNOWN

As much as we'd appreciate having one more hour in our day, I wonder how much that would really help. We'd probably just fill the extra hour with more activities. Effective time management is not about cramming more into our day. It's about using the time we have the most beneficially to reach our personal, family, and work goals. Since 24 hours a day is what God established, I believe there are ways to do less and achieve more.

No Time: The Crisis of Modern Life

Recently I used a time log to find out where my time was going. I recorded every activity over a period of several days. What I discovered was that there were a lot of "time leaks," amounting to more than a couple of hours each day. These were interruptions that could have been avoided or shortened, time spent waiting for an appointment or being placed on hold on the phone, opening junk mail, reading emails, or shuffling paperwork from pile to pile before making a decision about each piece. Not to mention the computer games, the television, and idle chatter.

Naturally we'd accomplish a great deal more if we could have that lost time back in one solid chunk. But in short spurts scattered here and there, can those minutes really make a difference? Yes! The number of jobs we can do when we have just a few minutes might surprise you. When there's a commercial on TV, dinner is in the oven, the chiropractor is behind schedule, you're on hold on the phone, or you need a short escape from the project you're working on, here are some things you can accomplish:

- clean out one drawer
- declutter one shelf of a cupboard or closet
- organize your purse, wallet, or briefcase
- file your nails, remove old polish, or apply a fresh clearcoat

- mend a hem, sew on a button, or tidy your sewing kit
- pay a bill
- file important papers
- write a thank-you note
- clean one shelf of the fridge
- clean the inside of the microwave
- purge one file folder
- sort and fold laundry
- purge a basket of magazines and catalogs, tossing the old ones
- empty a wastebasket
- dust one or two pieces of furniture
- scan junk mail
- make a shopping list or purge your coupon file
- unload the dishwasher
- feed and water the pets or plants
- purge and update your Rolodex file or address directory
- refill your business card holder
- sort through the mail and place interesting pieces in your reading file
- refill the paper in the printer
- clean your glasses
- work on tomorrow's to-do list

Do you ever look at remarkably efficient, organized, stress-free women and wonder how they do it? Do you wonder if they have a magic wand that gives them more of that crucial commodity called time?

I've found there really isn't one simple trick to get more out of time.

One thing I've noticed busy women have in common is they take advantage of being able to multitask.

Two-Timing Tasks

Some stress experts don't believe in multitasking. They prefer to stay focused on one matter at a time and strongly recommend that we do the same. This way of thinking could stem from problems they've run into as a result of attempting to give several projects equal mental attention or from times when they wore themselves out trying to do two or more things at once.

Chances are, though, that these judgments regarding multitasking stem from some fundamental differences between male and female brains. Men tend to focus on one thing at a time. Women tend to multitask. I think it all started with the caveman. Imagine what it was like back then. Men were the hunters, and women were the nurturers. While the men went out in packs to hunt for meat to bring home to the tribe, the women stayed home and raised the children; kept the cave in order; gathered fruits, nuts, and seeds; and carried out their daily activities within a communal society of other women.

In their biological role of hunter, the men discovered one valuable rule: Stay focused. When hunting for food, a hunter's life is often on the line, as well as the survival of the tribe. Imagine what would happen if a man on the chase were easily distracted? What if the women were there and wanted to discuss the details of the hunt? "Sweetheart, why is that woolly mammoth making its way over here so quickly?" "How do you like my new hunting outfit? I hope it doesn't make my rear look big." "Can we stop for a potty break soon?" "I'd love coffee!"

> Women understand that successful multitasking involves combining noncrucial jobs that don't require deep concentration.

Men know that when hunting for food, they need to be stealthy—silent, furtive, and extremely cautious. (I occasionally get to see my husband like this when we're driving on the highway, and he's taken on the mission of getting the driver in front of us to move into the slow lane where he belongs. In a stealth-like manner he flashes the high beams and may even honk the horn. His focus remains fixed.) A man on the hunt knows not to take his mind off the target for a second. If he does, the target could get away or eat him. In either case, he's not taking dinner home to the tribe. It's crucial for him to set his sights on the prey and concentrate. One thing he would never do while stalking is talk. I've learned to not ask where my hubby's mind is when I'm chatting away in the car, thinking we're having a meaningful conversation, and I suddenly notice he's concentrating on his "target."

Now the cavewoman's nature was totally different. She was at home disciplining and educating the kids, cooking the meals, laundering the loincloths, gathering the grains, and sweeping out the cave...all at the same time. Because we're social beings, we'd also be communing with the other women of the village. It's our nature to join forces, team up, and work closely with one another. And this doesn't disturb our ability to get everything done.

Women understand that successful multitasking involves combining noncrucial jobs that don't require deep concentration. We're quite good at it. The problem comes when we overdo, piling on more and more tasks without giving thought to how crucial they are or how multitasking will affect our ability or our sanity in the long run.

Let's look at some creative ideas and projects that can be done simultaneously without getting messed up or burning the house down. (I nearly burned down the house while multitasking. I learned some valuable strategies, including always setting the timer when using the stove or oven.)

- Anytime you walk through the house, pick up something as you go and put it where it belongs.
- Never go upstairs empty-handed. Take along something that belongs up there.
- If it's okay with the family member or friend, put the groceries away, unload the dishwasher, fold laundry, or have a coffee break while you chat on the phone with him or her.
- While you prepare dinner, check the pantry and make your shopping list.

- While doing household chores, clean up as you work.
- Start a load of laundry before tackling another task. When you stop for a coffee break, move the clothes from the washer to the dryer. Have your kids do the same when they do homework and stop for a snack.
- Give yourself a manicure while you watch the news or between tasks while working at the computer. Nail polish has time to dry fully, and you can be fairly certain you won't wreck your manicure while simply watching TV or inputting.
- During TV commercials, pick up clutter; see how many dishes you can wash, dry, or put away; or how much clean laundry you can fold.
- As you unload the dishwasher, set the table for the next meal.
- Clean out a drawer while waiting for the water to boil or the coffee to brew.
- Listen to a book on CD while driving or stuck in traffic.
- When you arrive early or have to wait at an appointment, write a note to someone or read from your reading file.
- Use long drives to catch up with your husband. Ask what he's been thinking about lately, what he enjoys most, what's challenging for him, and if there are ways you can be an encouragement.
- When you're the passenger, read interesting stories or articles out loud to someone in the car. My husband is not a big reader, but he sure enjoys it when I read on our car trips. As an added benefit, it opens the door to interesting discussions.
- Take your child along when you walk the dog or run errands. Use the time to initiate meaningful conversations. My mom refused to get a dishwasher because she found that doing dishes together was when she got to hear

about her kids' greatest dreams and biggest fears, as well as what they were doing and who they were involved with.

- Before you run errands, determine your route and consider what else you might pick up or drop off along the way.
- Hang garments in the bathroom while you shower to steam out any wrinkles.
- Fold laundry and sort socks while watching TV. This is a great job for your kids!
- Read a book, catalog, or magazine while you're on exercise equipment.
- Order library books online while you check your email.

Doubling up on noncrucial tasks and activities can free up more time to spend having fun and doing other things we want to focus on. A good way to get started is to make a list of tasks that can be done at the same time. Post it in clear view and refer to it often. Remember to praise and reward yourself and others every time you or they multitask effectively.

Prioritize Activities

Always focus on top priority tasks and activities. Too often we run out of time or energy because we've been spending it on low-priority items. When we want to determine our top priorities, there are two elements to consider:

1. *Level of importance:* How critical is this? If it is done, what benefits will I reap? If it doesn't get done, what will it cost?
2. *Level of urgency:* Is there a time frame? Do I have a due date or deadline to meet?

The tasks and activities rating the highest in both of these considerations determine which ones you tackle before the others. If something you plan to do is high in importance, meaning the rewards for completing it are great or the cost of not doing it is huge, then it will be at the top of your To-Do List. If the level of urgency is high, meaning it must be completed within a certain time frame, it will be foremost on your list as well.

These are fairly obvious conclusions. The problem comes when an item is high in urgency but not in importance. The mail is delivered or the phone rings, and you're tempted to stop everything to take care of it. These activities may have a *sense* of urgency, but usually the result of not doing these tasks immediately is not critical (unless it is an emergency phone call, in which case you can use Caller ID or listen to the voice mail message).

Likewise, when an activity is high in importance but not in urgency, we are tempted to put it off because there is no definite time limit. Even though we realize our health, relationships, spiritual growth, personal goals, financial concerns, home or car repairs, and anything that requires upkeep and maintenance are important, they often fall to the bottom of our To-Do list. Although we understand the cost if we don't look after it, or the rewards if we do, without a cut-off date and that sense of urgency that lets us know it's top priority, we tend to procrastinate.

❊ ❊ ❊

It is not enough if you are busy.
The question is, "What are you busy about?"
HENRY DAVID THOREAU

One way to avoid a crisis is to put items of high importance on your To-Do List even though they have no time frame. Try giving yourself fake deadlines. Make up due dates. By doing this, you can prevent these tasks from turning into a crisis. If your doctor said, "You need to get healthy by Friday," you probably already have a crisis on your hands. When your bank manager says you need to make some serious changes in your finances within the next ten days, you might be facing an emergency.

While we were raising children, Cliff and I had a weekly date night marked on our calendars. Every Friday we would spend time together doing something fun. Sometimes it would be dinner in a fancy restaurant and an evening of live theater, other times we'd go for a stroll and grab a hamburger at an outdoor stand, or we'd stay home to roast hot dogs and marshmallows in the fireplace, followed by a game of Backgammon. It didn't matter what we did, as long as it was time together doing something we both enjoyed. Our relationship was a top priority, and we created a time frame to take care of it.

When I was working in sales and my daughters were in their teens, I would come home at suppertime to find the girls alone and eating sugary snack foods or watching TV programs I wasn't fond of. So I decided to make a date with my girls every weekday right after they stepped off the school bus. I would simply let my afternoon clients know I had another appointment (which was true!) so I could make sure I got home in plenty of time. The girls and I would spend that time having a snack together, talking about our day, doing some homework or baking, and then preparing dinner together. It became a time we all looked forward to as we created some fond memories. With a little planning and effort, you can be sure to get your top-priority activities looked after even if you can't get everything done.

Schedule Your Days

Do you ever get up in the morning and think, *I've got so much to do I don't know where to start?* In my effort to live effectively and efficiently—to control and not be controlled by daily demands and expectations—I've come up with something that revolutionized my time-keeping habits. Although I've always been a list maker (I love checking things off), I now separate my To-Do List from my Daily Action Plan. They are two individual time effectiveness tools. I used to make a killer To-Do List that realistically couldn't be accomplished in a lifetime. I'd go to bed each night feeling disappointed for not completing more items. Now with two lists, I can check off everything I plan to do in a day. Here's how it works.

1. Make a Master List of your to-do items that are ongoing. Itemize everything that has to be done by you or someone else.
2. Create a Daily Action Plan consisting of items taken from the Master List in order of priority.

To do this, purchase two inexpensive, spiral-bound notebooks. As activities and tasks come to mind, add them to the Master List, put the due date next to them, and assign a priority to each one based on the levels of importance and urgency. The second notebook is for Daily Activities, and it will contain only the top-priority items taken from the Master List that must be done *today.* This way all top-priority tasks and activities get taken care of, appointments are kept, deadlines are met, and you get to check off all the items. The next day you go back and transfer more items from the Master List to your Daily Activities List. Of course, new activities and tasks are being added to the Master List too, so priorities may change. You might want to write your lists in pencil or create a computer file.

❋ ❋ ❋

Your goal is to maximize your time so you can work toward your ultimate purpose in life.

An alternative to making a list in a notebook is to create a "Flexible List" with sticky notes. Write one task or activity on each note and mount all of them inside a blank file folder. This way you can toss out, add, or reshuffle the notes on a daily basis. This method also works well when you're managing a large project, organizing a party or family reunion, or planning a vacation.

Sanity Savers & Survival Hints

- Pay attention to your inner body clock. Are you a morning, afternoon, or evening person? Do the high-energy tasks during your peak energy hours and the low-energy activities when your energy is at a naturally low level.
- "Every minute is a golden one for him who has the vision to recognize it as such" (Henry Miller).
- Build in enjoyable escapes and book some creative time-outs from your stressful activities.
- Take advantage of "wasted time," such as when you're forced to stand

in line, stop in traffic, or wait in the dentist's office. Organize your thoughts, goals, dreams, and plans.

- "I, Wisdom, will make the hours of your day more profitable and the years of your life more fruitful" (Proverbs 9:11 TLB).
- Quit saying "I'm too busy" and "I don't have enough time." Words are powerful seeds, and you will *always* reap what you sow.
- Don't let what you can't do stop you from what you can do. Even small changes can make a big difference. Build in a cushion for the unanticipated and emergencies.
- "Lost time is like a run in a stocking. It always gets worse" (Anne Morrow Lindbergh).
- "There is a time for everything, and a season for every activity under heaven" (Ecclesiastes 3:1 NIV).
- A clear sense of direction and a plan can open up more stress-free hours in your day.
- "We can make our plans, but the final outcome is in God's hands" (Proverbs 16:1 TLB).

16

Sanity Secret #12

Conquer Procrastination

When You Dread Beginning

Do you put off tasks you don't want to do or don't like to do? Do you say, "I'll just get to it later when I have extra time"? Even after you've made a decision to start, is there part of you that still holds back? Procrastination can be a major cause of stress, and often it's because we never have leftover or extra time.

Occasionally procrastination can be good for us, like the other day when I put off having a second hot fudge sundae. Likewise, if you're trying to quit smoking or cut back on caffeine or sweets, delaying gratification may be the best answer. But most of the time procrastination is the biggest time thief in our day. We all do it though. The trouble is we decide to put off something but our minds never let us off the hook and nag us relentlessly. Or, when we finally do get around to tackling the task, we don't do it as well as we should because we're rushed and working under the pressure of a deadline.

It's human nature to procrastinate. But if putting off a job is a *consistent* pattern for you that interferes with accomplishing important tasks or living stress free, it may signal an internal conflict. Some of us are so afraid of failure that we'd rather not try to do something than make an attempt and fail. Other times we think we need more time than we do, the thought of the activity overwhelms us, we'd rather be doing something else, or we hope the need to do the task will go away.

So why are you putting things off?

- If you think doing things at the last minute is good because "the adrenalin rush helps you and you thrive under pressure," consider whether the stress is keeping you from doing your best work because of panic regarding the deadline.
- If you're afraid of doing a poor job so you don't even get started, remember that your true goal is to do your best—not to achieve perfection.
- If you just can't seem to fit certain jobs into your schedule, or they're something you dread facing, determine your priorities and count the cost of not doing them.

Don't Wait Another Minute

* * *

Endings are better than beginnings.
ECCLESIASTES 7:8

Are you are a good starter but not a good finisher? How can you alleviate this problem? Try one or two of these ideas to get going on a task you've been putting off. Remember, time is being used up in your daily account whether you spend it effectively or not. Each new day you're given 24 hours, or 1440 minutes, or 84,600 seconds, which disappear at the end of the day. Leftover time can't be rolled over and minutes or hours frittered away can't be salvaged. So make the most of your time. Small accomplishments can add up to big results at the end of the day.

Procrastination Prescriptions

- Follow the 15-minute rule. Identify one project you can finish, set a timer, and get going. Spend 15 minutes every day on a task you've been putting off. Before you know it, you'll have the dreaded task completed.

- Make a log and keep track of how long projects take. It's usually less than you think, and that will be good motivation for next time.
- Use the salami technique when tasks seem overwhelming. Pick one large task you've put on the back burner and break it down into manageable, bite-size pieces, like you would slice a stick of salami.
- Bypass your mind and all the excuses it conjures up. We can fall prey to the *paralysis of analysis.* Just do the task. Often it takes the same amount of energy to feel bad about not doing something as it does to get the job done.
- Focus on the beginning of the task rather than the end. Looking ahead to the finish can make tasks daunting. Do the first part of the task—address the envelope, prepare the outline for the report—anything that gets you unstuck and moving.
- Do the worst part first. In any task there is usually one nasty aspect you dread. Get it over with or it will haunt you and drain your energy. The rest will seem easy.
- Give yourself a sense of urgency with a bogus deadline. Often tasks don't get completed because there's no cut-off date. According to Parkinson's Law, work always expands to fill the time allotted.
- Commit to getting the job done by telling someone else what your deadline is. Go public by asking someone to hold you accountable. You'll also have a built-in support system.
- Create a balance sheet and weigh the pros and cons of starting or putting off the task.
- Know your inner body clock. When possible, plan your day according to your most productive time. Are you a morning, afternoon, or evening person? Plan the most difficult or unpleasant activities during those times when you have the most energy and are least likely to procrastinate.
- To focus on your goal, write reminders and post them in different places (i.e., the mirror, the refrigerator, the front door). The more you remind yourself of the desired outcome and visualize how you will benefit from finishing, the more likely you will follow through.
- Reduce distractions and interruptions. When you have something that needs to be done, you need to close the door, turn off the TV, silence the

ringer on the phone, and not answer the doorbell. Remove whatever distracts you from doing the job at hand.

- Eat healthy food, exercise, and get enough sleep. Exercising creates more energy, and you'll be less likely to procrastinate. Eat foods that are fresh and raw as much as possible instead of sugars and caffeine. This will provide a steady release of energy instead of a short boost. Getting at least eight hours of sleep will energize you…and you'll be able to maintain more energy during the day.
- Get organized. Disorganization causes chaos and is very distracting. When you're organized, you are better able to focus on a task rather than the clutter. Have all the necessary equipment and supplies on hand before you begin work. If you're planning to declutter the basement, have lots of garbage bags and empty boxes. Buy some shelving units and an assortment of clear plastic storage bins. Keep your receipts and return any you don't use.
- Don't let mistakes hold you back. If you demand perfection from yourself, you're probably going to put off beginning something until the perfect moment. Nothing is perfect, so it's not going to happen. Realize that perfection is impossible to obtain. Do your best and acknowledge what you've accomplished.
- Create a mental picture of the completed project. Keep in mind how good it's going to feel when the project is finished. Remember this feeling when beginning a new project.
- Avoid overextending yourself. Evaluate your obligations and then prioritize them. Is there anything you can omit, delegate, or move to a different time frame? Set realistic goals. Make a list each day of the tasks you need to complete in order of their importance. Finish each task before starting the next one.
- Make the task at hand as pleasurable as possible. When you're doing a job, ask, "Is there a fun way to do this?" Make a game out of it. Be creative. Put on some peppy music that makes you want to move. Ask someone you have fun with to help. Give yourself points or prizes as you do the task.
- Plan for setbacks. Some are bound to happen. Planning will prevent you from slowing down when there is a delay. Don't give up.
- Consider penalizing yourself if you haven't completed a task. For

example, skip a television show or a stop at your favorite coffee shop if you don't complete a job on schedule. You probably won't want that to happen again, and you'll strive to get the good feeling that comes with completing a chore.

- Reward yourself when you've completed a boring or unpleasant task... and even when you've achieved a small task on time. If you know a Starbucks coffee or other treat is waiting for you when you succeed, you'll be more motivated to get the job done. The more positive reinforcement, the less likely you will procrastinate.
- Focus on what you have done rather than on what is left.

Sanity Savers & Survival Hints

If you wait for perfect conditions, you will
never get anything done.
ECCLESIASTES 11:4 TLB

- One key to conquering procrastination is to start. Do something *now.* If you have a thank-you note to send, address and stamp the envelope. If you have a bill to pay, get out your checkbook and pen. If you have to make a phone call, look up the number and dial.
- For five minutes do something—anything—you've been putting off: dust some furniture, clean a drawer, purge your wallet or handbag, organize your desktop.
- Finish some endeavor you've started but not completed—a craft, an art project, household repairs, mending or sewing, decorating, landscaping.
- Buy something to make the task more exciting. If you're planning to spend the day in the kitchen cooking and freezing a week's worth of meals, buy that saucepan you've been considering, a unique cheese grater or garlic press, or a bright, cheery apron..

- Make a list and check off items periodically throughout the day. Soon accomplishment will be more appealing than procrastination.
- "Until you value yourself, you will not value your time; until you value your time, you will not do anything with it" (M. Scott Peck).
- Reward yourself for a job well done with a healthy treat.
- "Nothing is so fatiguing as the hanging on of an uncompleted task" (William James).

17 Sanity Secret #13

Clear Out the Clutter

When You're Drowning in Stuff

By nature I'm not an organized person, but I can't stand clutter either. At one time I took my need to be organized to extremes and drove nearly everyone around me crazy with my perfectionist tendencies. With my desire to have everything absolutely neat, I would beg, "Please don't sit against that cushion. I just fluffed it" and "I hope you won't walk on the carpet. I just vacuumed and you'll disturb the nap." A concerned friend finally told me she didn't think it was the nap that was disturbed!

At that time conditions in my life were so out of control that I felt the need to have power over something. My marriage was in trouble, my health was going downhill, and my finances were suffering. But having everything in its place was something I could do successfully.

I'm much more relaxed these days. Although I'm no longer a fanatical perfectionist, I do know there's a big difference between being organized and being clean and tidy. If you called to say you were coming over to visit in a few minutes, I can get neat in a hurry. All I have to do is open a drawer or find a big box, and with one swipe I'd have it neat. Run a mop over the floor, and use a feather duster on the furniture, and things look fairly clean and presentable. But I still wouldn't necessarily be organized. I'd still have the mess and the stress.

Being organized means you can put your hands on any item when you need it. It means you have orderly systems and structures in place to store items you want and need for easy retrieval. You don't have to wade through piles of stuff to find something.

The main cause for disorganization is clutter. When we have too many possessions, we trip over them and have to keep sorting through them to find what we need. Getting rid of "mess stress" involves major decluttering. The problem is many people have a bit of "pack rat" in them—the impulse to gather and store. Why do we hoard? According to behavioral experts, hoarders are often highly intelligent and creative. (I don't know about you, but that definitely makes me feel better.) They see more connections between things, which leads them to value items more than other people. Creative people can imagine uses for almost anything in the future...and sometimes their imaginations run away with them. We can come up with all kinds of excuses for holding on to things. Do you rationalize clutter with any of these?

- If I get rid of it, I'll need it for sure.
- I'm going to get in shape and then it will fit again.
- I may need to use the old blender for spare parts to repair the new one.
- My kids may want this antique typewriter or answering machine someday.
- I'm saving these fabric odds and ends to make a quilt or doll clothes.
- Soon you won't be able to get your hands on one of these.
- I paid good money for that.
- It's too good to give away.
- I may use these various wallpaper scraps to create a patchwork motif in a room.
- It was a gift from someone special.

If some of these statements sound familiar, you may be a clutter bug. I'd like to tell you my excuse...that the reason I struggle with being organized is because I'm one of those creative free spirits. While that may be true, it's not a valid excuse for disorganization. Besides, no matter how creative I am, I've found I can be even more inspired, innovative, and imaginative once I'm organized.

When you decide at last to get rid of the things you're holding on to, you will experience incredible freedom. Henry David Thoreau once said that if he was cleaning and came across an item he didn't use or need, he'd toss it rather than fool with it or try to find a place for it. This philosophy—dealing with the item immediately—is a good approach. Here's someone who had time to wander in the woods, write books, and philosophize about life, becoming one of the most-often-quoted theorists of our time. What do the rest of us do? Instead of purging and tossing some of what we've accumulated, we go out and buy larger filing cabinets, additional stackable trays, elaborate closet organizers, backyard sheds, or rent storage units. We add on rooms or garages to our homes and build bigger houses with basements and attics.

One friend told me recently he spent the whole day looking for something in his big garage. The lawn mower? The trimmer? No, the car! Professional organizers estimate that many of us spend nearly an hour each day looking for things we've misplaced. Some people live in such large houses and own so much stuff they often have to spend days searching for their children. Most of us spend our time, not wandering joyfully in nature, but cleaning, dusting, rearranging, keeping track of, stepping over, pushing aside, piling, and insuring all our belongings. When we're not doing that, we're selling them off at garage sales or working overtime to buy more.

> With every item you buy, get rid of two similar items via the recycle bin, someone who needs it, a charity, or the trash.

We can't resist the late-night commercials that convince us to buy the latest gadget that promises to make our lives easier, which it does a couple of times the first year. Then what happens? The shiny new gizmo makes our lives miserable because we have to do something with it. It needs to be stored, cleaned, or repaired. We feel too guilty to get rid of it because we paid good money for it. There are the pasta machines, the juicers, and the bread makers, for instance. In this day and age, everyone has time to use at least one of these, right? Who are we kidding? When was the last time you used yours? Maybe you could be using that storage space for something you do use regularly.

Then there's food clutter. You buy a whole jar of a specialty spice for one ethnic dinner or a gourmet ingredient that goes in only one recipe and you never use it again. Our kitchen cabinets and pantries are out of control. Most of us are not even able to find the lids for the 20 or more food-storage containers we own.

And what about the exercise machines? Everyone has at least one of these sitting somewhere in a back room or basement keeping all the spiders in shape. Equipment and programs look really appealing in those TV commercials, when someone else is doing the sweating. At first we go wild, believing we will somehow resemble the people in the commercials. Then we realize why we don't. It's because, aside from the treadmill, what we really need is the stair-climber, bike, rower, and ski machine. Unlike everyone else, we will really use ours. Honest! The truth is we thought the fat would just disappear, but the only thing that disappeared was our money and space.

When purchasing anything new in the future, use this rule of thumb: If it's not something you would save if your house were burning down, don't buy it. Here's another good rule that works when purchasing something you really do need: One in, one out. Better yet, one in, two out! With every item you buy, get rid of two similar items via the recycle bin, someone who needs it, a charity, or the trash.

To prevent a build up of jars, bottles, and tubes in your bathroom or kitchen, get in the habit of using up what you have in your cupboard before opening any new product. Whether it's skin care, hair care, makeup, shower gel, bubble bath, lotions, creams or ointment, tea, coffee, cereal, spices, baking ingredients, or condiments, you'll be surprised at how much still remains in the bottom of those containers. (Be sure to check the "best before" date on the package before using it.) It's very tempting to start the nice-looking new one when you bring it home from the store rather than finishing what's left in the old container. Then the old one gets shoved into the back of the cupboard or wastefully thrown away.

When it comes to cosmetics, I like to make it a contest to see how much more I can get out of those partially used containers before opening the new one. A simple lip brush can allow you to use one tube of lipstick or concealing cream for another month or so!

Clutter has become a fixed and inevitable part of our lives. It extends into every facet of our existence. The size of our homes has increased, yet we have a storage crisis. We spend billions of dollars each year on organizational products. Most new homes have multicar garages. Many homes now have a "transition room," a place to channel any belongings with no permanent spot of their own. According to one survey, some women are so fed up with clutter they'd rather clean out a closet than lose weight. And many of them say they would get more satisfaction from organizing a closet than from making love. We are desperate to become clutter free. Let's face it, half the clothes we have in our closet haven't fit since 1992. But we're saving them just in case the miracle diet works or our grandchildren take a sudden liking to retro styles.

> If you're tired of sorting through all the stuff to find what you want, get rid of some of it.

Decluttering is one of the best sanity secrets when it comes to creating more time and less stress in life. It's one of your most worthwhile activities and takes less time to do than you might think. Being organized truly saves you time, energy, and frustration and brings satisfaction and great rewards. If you're drowning in clutter, maybe it's time to make space for what matters most. Whether your clutter is a stack of papers—flyers, magazines, catalogs—or miscellaneous items—clothing, sports equipment, toys, games, kitchen gadgets—it's possible to shrink those piles (without Preparation H!). If you're tired of sorting through all the stuff to find what you want, get rid of some of it. It's very simple. Minimize, pare down, and purge.

For those items you do want to keep but find they're always in disarray, designate a place for them and be sure to put them there. The motto most of us learned as kids is a good reminder: A place for everything, and everything in its place. One main cause for disorganization and missing items is they have no permanent residence.

In my home we used to waste time looking for sunglasses, gloves, and cell phones. One day I placed small wicker baskets on a shelf by the back door. We started putting those items in there when we arrived home.

It's also the place where we put outgoing mail, discount coupons, library books and DVD rentals to return, and anything else we need to remember to take with us the next time we go out. Problem solved!

Paper Clutter

In most homes and offices, the biggest source of disorganization is paper clutter. You may remember this lie we were sold a number of years ago: Computers will decrease our paper use. The truth is that computers have generated ten times more paper clutter than before! Does your in-basket look more like a wastebasket? Are you drowning in the paper flood that pours into your home every day? You know, those piles that collect on *clutter magnets* around your house—desktops, tables, and countertops. Paper clutter includes everything from the endless stream of incoming sales mail (catalogs, flyers, advertisements) to business material (bills, receipts, warranties, bank statements, insurance renewals, medical information, school papers).

How you deal with that paper determines whether you live in an atmosphere of chaos and clutter or calm and in control. Along with clutter comes frustration, tension, pressure, and conflict. The never-ending paper flood gets us down. We usually leave papers lying around without filing them away for several reasons:

- *Out of sight, out of mind:* "If I put them away, I'll never remember to do them."
- *The black hole mentality:* "If I file something, it will mysteriously fall into some dark abyss and I will never see it again."
- *Indecision.* "I don't really know where it goes so I'll add it to a pile."
- *Temporary holding areas.* "I'll just put it here for now until I can decide where it really goes."

Here are some ways to gain control of your vital paper information and clear out the piles of clutter:

- Don't put it down; put it away. Handle papers only once.

- Before filing a task, an appointment, or an event paper, place a note on your Daily Action Planner saying what it is, where the notice is filed, and the date it needs to be done.
- Open mail by the wastebasket and recycle bin. Get rid of envelopes and enclosures right away.
- Make a decision about each piece of paper using the 3 Ds: do it, delegate it, or discard it. If it's a bill that needs to be paid, pay it. If it's correspondence that needs an answer, send a reply. If someone else can handle it, pass it on.
- Have a central filing system set up for all important paperwork: medical reports, insurance papers, home and car care information, and anything you have to refer to on occasion.
- Color-code your hanging files and folders so you can place several categories in one file drawer. Various groupings of different colors will be easily recognizable.
- Don't pile it; file it.

A Decluttering System

Set aside 30 minutes each day for the next six weeks. Use a timer and only work until it goes off. Gather four boxes, a clipboard, and a pen. Label the boxes: Throw Away, Give Away, Reroute, and Store. Pick one clutter problem area to tackle. Place each item you pick up in its respective box:

- *Throw Away*—Anything that is broken, outdated, or of no use to anyone. Work fast. No rescuing or reconsidering! Seal the box when it's full and don't peek inside again. If you're not sure about an item, create a "slush box," place the item in it, date it, and check again in six weeks. You may be free to let go of it by then. Recycle everything you can!
- *Give Away*—Items you no longer use but are in good condition to pass along, bless, and bring joy to others. They can be dropped off at church or shelter. Use the

one-year guideline. If you haven't used it or worn it in a year, you're probably not going to.

- *Reroute*—Anything that is in good condition but belongs in another spot. Give photos and other memorabilia to a grandchild or other relative who is compiling a family scrapbook.
- *Store*—Items in good repair you want to keep but aren't used or referred to regularly. Allow one "Memory Treasure Chest box" for each family member to store mementos and memorabilia. When it's full, each person must decide which items go and which stay. For large items, such as science fair projects or fishing trophies, take a picture of the person with the item instead of storing it.
- Use the clipboard and pen to list any areas in that space that needs to be cleaned or repaired. Come back to do those chores later rather than taking up valuable decluttering time. It's too easy to get caught up in cleaning and lose the decluttering momentum.

To declutter your desk, table, or countertop, set aside a couple of hours or an afternoon. Look at your piles and make some decisions. There are different types of piles people have. There are anthill piles that pop up here and there. Then there are piles that turn in to "the blob" and eventually spread all over the entire surface. Some people have piles all lined up and overlapping, similar to a deck of cards when playing solitaire. You never want to have a pile of anything on any work surface. Use storage areas.

Start by gathering everything into one big pile. (I know this is scary, but trust me—it works!) This may be difficult for you because right now, even though it isn't organized, you probably know generally where everything is and can put your hands on it—the fourth pile, 15 pieces down. But you're running the risk of misplacing something or overlooking an important deadline.

Begin working at your big pile by removing the larger pieces—directories, magazines, books, catalogs. Divide what's left into four piles: Urgent, Ongoing Tasks, Messages, and Trivia.

- The Urgent pile contains all items that must be attended to right away or they'll turn into a crisis. Hopefully you don't have too many of these lying around.
- The Ongoing Tasks pile is for activities that need to be done regularly—bills that need to be paid, daily plans, and goals for the future.
- The Messages pile is for phone messages, mail, meeting memos, and any correspondence that needs a reply.
- The Trivia pile is for junk mail, memos about events long past, coupons that are outdated, and duplicates of other information. According to organization experts, 80 percent of what is currently in your piles is trivia. You can get rid of a big chunk right away! If you're not comfortable throwing a few of the items away, place them in a slush file to be checked in a few weeks so you can reconsider. For the rest of the items in this pile, recycle.

Now you have three piles left. Place each paper in its own file folder, either an existing one or one you will create now. Go through the stack and note each to-do item on your Daily Action Planner before filing it away. To keep your work surfaces uncluttered, handle incoming paper by making a decision instead of starting a new pile.

You can use this system for cleaning and organizing your closets too. Empty the entire closet, place everything on the bed, and vacuum the closet. Next, sort the contents into four piles: keep, give away, throw away, and mend/clean. Put all those pieces you wear regularly and are clean and in good repair back in the closet. But arrange them in order of style and color: business, casual, and formal wear.

Storage & Space Management

Rather than keeping things where you think they *should* go, store them where they are most convenient. Storage doesn't have to be conventional; it just has to work for you. There are some items you can keep in the same place where you use them:

- I keep a tube of moisturizing foot cream in my hosiery

drawer. That way it's handy to lather on just before putting on socks or pantyhose in the morning and again before going to bed at night before donning a cozy pair of cotton socks.

- Furniture polish and a dust rag can be kept in a drawer in each room so they are within easy reach for quick touch-ups between cleaning days.
- Keep shoe polish in the hall closet for a speedy retouch before going out the door.
- Keep a lint roller, a can of anti-static spray, and an envelope filled with store coupons in the glove compartment of the car.

Always store like items together: cooking utensils, coffee equipment and supplies, laundry items, sewing and mending materials, athletic gear, gardening tools, picnicking paraphernalia, and travel supplies.

Things needed at the same time should be in the same place. For instance, have a spot designated for stationery items, including note cards, writing paper, envelopes, stamps, return labels, pens, pencils, hi-light markers, sticky notes, stapler, staple remover, and ruler. Correspondence will be so much simpler!

To save time and energy by not hunting for things before leaving the house, keep decorative wicker baskets labeled for each member of the household on a shelf near the main door. Use them for sunglasses, cell phones, gloves, and any other items needed on the way out.

Store frequently used items in several places—pens, pencils, sticky tape, masking tape, shipping tape, scissors, rulers, stapler—so they are handy when and where you need them. Keep a notepad and pen to create shopping lists in the bathroom, office, and kitchen. Have duplicates of cleaning supplies in the kitchen and all bathrooms so you don't have to cart them from room to room. Keep separate ongoing lists for items you need to purchase from the hardware store, drugstore, department store, and grocery store.

Little Things Make a Big Difference

Does getting rid of clutter and organizing your life sound overwhelming?

If so, I have great news for you. Being organized doesn't require you to perform time-consuming, complicated systems. It is not rocket science. It's not something that's going to take you years of soul-searching to start. It's not something only a few can achieve. Just a few small organizing tips applied with a positive attitude can help you be more organized today than you were yesterday. Here are a few hints to help you arrange time to read your latest library book or watch a special on TV.

- When preparing meals, clean up as you go, washing by hand or putting appropriate items into the dishwasher. Put away ingredients that need to be stored in the refrigerator or pantry immediately after you use them.
- Set out the next day's clothes the night before. This way you don't waste valuable time in the morning looking for the right thing to wear. If you can, choose the entire week's worth of clothes for the little ones who can dress themselves or have them choose. No more morning arguments over what to wear.
- Fill up your gas tank when it hits the quarter-of-a-tank level. In case of a delay in traffic, you won't have to worry about running out of fuel.
- Have a routine each week for the days you do errands and shop. You'll save fuel since you won't be constantly running to the store for forgotten items. Be sure to use shopping lists and take coupons if you use them.
- Put perishable groceries directly in the refrigerator instead of setting them on the counter first. Wash and cut fruits and veggies before putting them away. Enlist the kids to put away the canned goods.
- Cook some meats ahead of time and store in the freezer. For those too-busy nights you can get a healthy dinner on the table in a jiffy.
- Pick a regular day each week to pay your bills and do other desk-related chores. If you don't have bills that week, work on your budget or bank statement. With

multiple users of debit cards, even a bit of disorganization can lead to expensive overdraft charges.

- If you're comfortable having bills paid online, sign up for this service. Mark your calendar on what particular day the bills will be paid so you can keep track of what's happening.

- When making appointments, mark your calendar right away, including contact information. If something changes or you have questions, you'll have the information you need handy.

- Have the family work on planning the weekly agenda so there is no one left in the rain waiting for a ride. Arrange carpools with other family members and friends when possible.

- Color-code your family. Have one color for each family member for towels, toothbrushes, hair-care items, file folders, stackable trays, backdoor baskets, hampers, laundry baskets, and more. This saves a lot of time by preventing confusion.

- Have a place for tote bags with items that are needed every day for work, school, and activities. Fill them with needed items so you can just "grab and go":

    - *Library/DVD Bag*—When books are read and DVDs have been watched, everyone places them into this bag to be returned.

    - *Dancing/Music Lessons/Sports Bag*—Include all the gear, clothes, books, instruments, sheet music, and other necessities.

    - *Overnight Bag*—Store an extra toothbrush, hairbrush, underwear, pajamas, slippers, socks, small toiletries, a travel hair dryer, slippers, a wrinkle-free outfit for the next day and socks. Do this for the kids too, so if Grandma and Grandpa invite your little ones for an overnight they can be ready in no time.

- *Dry Cleaners Bag*—Have everyone put their clothing inside when they need them dry cleaned. Upon returning, place the ticket stub for pick-up in the backdoor basket.

You Know You're in an Organized Home When...

How often do you wonder if you're making any progress in your organizing journey? Many times we fail to recognize how much progress we've really made. At times it's measured in baby steps, at other times it can be measured in leaps and bounds. If you have put forth any effort at all, you're making progress! Here are some easy ways to tell when you're getting an organized home.

- You can direct someone to something and he or she finds it! How often in the past have you given up searching for something because even Sherlock Holmes couldn't find it? We've all been there.
- You know what is on hand for quick meal planning. Have you stood in front of the open refrigerator trying to figure out what to prepare for supper? When you have a plan, you'll be able to put together a nutritious, delicious meal because you have a handy inventory of your freezer and your pantry contents.
- You don't have to wonder who has to be where and when. Maybe like me you've taken the wrong child to the wrong activity at the wrong time. Whether we have one child or many children, it's a challenge making sure everyone is at the right place at the right time. By having a central calendar with everyone's activities clearly noted and color-coded, you'll know at a glance when someone has to be somewhere.
- You can entertain without two month's notice. It's not only possible, but when you're organized, it's a pleasant and enjoyable experience. You'll know where your serving pieces are, have the menu prepared, and be able to relax and enjoy your guests.

- You no longer suffer from chaos. You have everything in its own place. Drop-in guests no longer generate a "drop down, shut the lights off, and hide so they think we're not home" response.
- Clean up takes a few minutes here and there in an organized home. By establishing routines, you keep up with the housework and maintain a clean house.
- Your working surfaces stay clear. You no longer have piles toppling over because you have the filing, recycling, and other clutter solutions in place.
- You can move freely from room to room in the dark. There is no need to put nightlights in every available outlet to avoid injuries. Sounds silly, I know, but how many times have you found things with your toe or your shin or your knee? When everything has a place and is in its place, you can move about freely—even in the dark.
- You have time to enjoy hobbies and other activities that renew, refresh, and invigorate you. In an organized home you have time to nurture yourself.
- Your entire family can get ready and out the door in less than an hour every day because lunches are made, backpacks are ready, permission slips are signed, clothing is laid out, and the breakfast table was set the night before (unless you have pets).
- You know what you have and where to find it. You don't have to run out at the last minute to buy a tool or ingredient because you can't find the one you know you have somewhere. You'll not only have what you need, but you'll know exactly where it is.
- Putting groceries away doesn't involve an entire afternoon of "finding room." You have an organized pantry, and it's simply a matter of putting the groceries in their place, freeing up your afternoon for a good book, fun and games with the family, or some very important me time.

- You no longer have to pay late fees for video rentals or fines for overdue library books. You have a basket or a box of some kind that is specifically used for rental returns. This basket keeps your returns near the door so you can grab them to return the next time you or someone goes out.
- Getting dressed for work or school is no longer an agonizing decision or an aerobic exercise. In an organized home, the clothing is always in the closet, hung up neatly, and arranged either by outfit or with like things.
- Preparing for taxes no longer involves a month-long search for all the paperwork. You have an accordion file set up with general categories, such as receipts for deductions, income statements, expenses, and tax records, where each piece of paper that is relevant to taxes has been stored. When tax time rolls around, it's simply a matter of grabbing the file to get started.

✻ ✻ ✻

Everything should be done in a fitting and orderly way.
1 Corinthians 14:40 NIV

If you practice some or all of these ideas you will find the extra time to do those things you really enjoy. By decluttering, you'll feel more in control. And letting go frees you up to receive. The Bible says to clear out the old to make room for the new (Leviticus 26:10). (I'm not suggesting you get rid of everything. Keep the first-aid kit and your computer!) Refuse to saddle yourself with unnecessary junk. Life is full of things for you. You don't need to grasp every scrap to satisfy yourself. God promised to provide all you need...and he will! Disorganization can trap you into living a life filled with stress, frustration, and chaos. It can rob you of precious time you should be spending enjoying life. By clearing out clutter and overcoming disorganization, you can be set free to live the kind of life you've always dreamed of.

Sanity Savers & Survival Hints

- Your environment, cluttered or not, influences your outlook and your outcomes.
- When decluttering ask, "What would I save if the house was on fire?"
- When you buy one new item, discard an old one.
- To find your keys in your handbag, place them on a colorful bungee-type cord with a hook on one end. Attach the other end to the zipper pull inside your purse. This way you can grab the cord and reel in your keys.
- Create a central phone messaging system. Buy a spiral notebook and keep it by the phone with a pen to record incoming messages. Put the date, who the message is for, the caller's name and number, and a brief message. Each person is responsible for checking the book, returning calls, and crossing them off when done.
- Purchase an oversized three-ring binder and fill it with plastic pockets for storing appliance and equipment manuals, original receipts, serial and model numbers, and warranties. Have a master locater sheet (like a table of contents) at the beginning to note each one for easy retrieval.
- Use binders and plastic pockets for medical records; kid's artwork; and travel, decorating, and landscaping articles.
- Set up a tickler file for time-sensitive documents. Rather than putting travel and entertainment tickets, meeting memos, and wedding, birthday, or shower invitations on a bulletin board, on the fridge with a magnet, or tucking them into your date book, place them in a special file sorted by month and date.
- Keep a record of those who have borrowed books, tools, or kitchen items, along with the date.
- "Let us strip off anything that slows us down or holds us back" (Hebrews 12:1 TLB).

18

Sanity Secret #14

Boost Your Drooping Body Image

When More Than Your Confidence Is Sagging

Let's face it—it's not easy to maintain a positive body image if you're a woman in today's society. Everywhere we look there are opportunities to compare ourselves with seemingly perfect bodies, even if we suspect they've been computer-enhanced. (If it were possible, some of us would computer-enhance our bodies before dressing in the morning.) Being disgruntled with our bodies robs us of our sanity all day, every day.

I know from experience it's difficult to feel good about our bodies, especially at the beach. There we are, lathering suntan lotion all over those clown-white thighs and upper arm flaps (no, the underarm swing is not a new dance), and we notice the 24-year-old Barbie-shaped woman stretched out nearby. She's blond, tan, and wearing a hot pink, size zero swimsuit as teeny as your credit card (just kidding...I meant to say postage stamp). She's the one you see in restaurants wolfing down an entire double-chocolate cheesecake that has to be transported to her table in a wheelbarrow, yet she never gains an ounce. If you asked, she'd most likely be quick to point out the extra two ounces of flab on her tummy. In the meantime, you've decided to put yourself on the South "Beached Whale" Diet.

In situations like this it's natural to feel insecure and wonder if your husband is secretly wishing you had the body of a 24-year-old. Little does he know you're wishing he had the body of a person who would put his dirty laundry in the hamper, help tidy the house, and manage to get his coffee cup inside the dishwasher. What happened to all those promises that you were going to be equal partners in sharing household duties? Aside from refilling the ice cube trays or brewing the occasional pot of coffee (after all, the Bible does say "Hebrews"!), all the other kitchen duties have been left up to you, including taste-testing the spaghetti sauce, the soup, the gravy, and sometimes as much as half the unbaked cookie dough.

(Hmmm...no wonder I don't look like that bathing beauty. I like to tell myself she obviously works out at the gym 72 hours a day and has probably had so much cosmetic surgery that for easy maintenance and repeat procedures some of her parts are attached with Velcro. Also I'm not totally responsible for my recent weight gain. The "monthly hormonal crazies" compelled me to stop at the donut shop so often they finally gave me my own parking spot.)

Seriously, I knew I was gaining weight and where it was *ending* up (pun intended) because I was "getting taller" when I sat in my car. I had to keep adjusting the rearview mirror. (I'm not making this up.) As my full-bodied hair was being squashed against the roof of the car, my friend suggested I take advantage of my driving time by doing some butt scrunches and muscle-tightening exercises. I think it's working, but as my body rises and falls with each scrunch, I've noticed a few odd looks from drivers in the passing lane.

Over the years I don't think I've met more than half a dozen women who are completely at peace with their bodies. Even my gorgeous and fit friends complain about an imperfect nose, hefty hips, pudgy thighs, flat feet, a plump rump, or a tiny wart behind a left knee. One woman told me she has furniture disease. When I asked her about it, she replied, "It's when your chest falls into your drawers!" She also complained of having "thankles" which happens when gravity pulls your thighs down to your ankles! Another woman confessed she's started going braless because she discovered it pulls all the wrinkles out of her face. She says she used to pack her ample bosom into a push-up bra, but now it's easier to simply tuck it all into her waistband. I noticed her trying to smile while she was telling me, but her face was stretched tight. I guess the braless thing is working. Personally I've given up on wearing plunging necklines since enough of me is plunging on its own.

The majority of us are locked into painfully distorted views of our bodies. It's nearly impossible to be stress-free when we hate the bodies we live in. Most men don't seem to have the same image problem. While many women worry if they can't fit into their tightest pair of jeans, some men don't worry until they can't fit into their cars. Women tend to see themselves as ornaments, while men see their bodies as instruments. A man might think, *Maybe I'm not the most handsome and strapping male specimen, but I can run, jog, play racquet ball, hunt, and fish.* He looks in the mirror and sees a brawny physique with muscles and broad shoulders regardless of the shape he's in. A woman looks at her reflection and sees only flab, flaws, and faults. When women were polled to see if they wanted to change one thing about their personal appearance, 99 percent said most definitely. Twenty-nine percent said forget one thing...they wanted a complete overhaul.

If you look in the mirror and loathe what you see, you won't be motivated to care for it properly.

It's not hard to see why so many women resort to going under the knife in order to feel better about themselves. We are looking to face-lifts, laser surgery, liposuction, and even duct tape to help ward off the aging process. We're caught in a frightening and dangerous trap of comparing society's image of beauty with our own image in the mirror...and we invariably lose. Our culture has set impossible standards that leaves nearly every woman feeling dissatisfied with herself. A great part of our sanity and self-esteem will come from being able to accept our bodies. When we do, we treat them well, and they respond with an abundance of energy, vitality, strength, and longevity.

You won't consistently nourish something you hate. If you look in the mirror and loathe what you see, you won't be motivated to care for it, feed it properly, provide it with adequate water, protect it, take it for a walk, stand tall, or give it proper exercise. And there's another startling possibility. Through self-loathing, we may even bring on disaster and injury.

For as long as I can remember I complained about my legs. I believed they were unattractive and grumbled that I'd inherited my father's knees and my grandmother's ill-defined ankles and shapeless calves. After severely banging my shins countless times over the years, occasionally twisting my ankles, and seriously injuring my knees through various mishaps, I began to see a pattern. By hating my legs, I may have been subconsciously inviting calamity.

Bruises and all, I decided to start appreciating my legs and being thankful for them in spite of what I thought about their appearance. Every day, after my morning shower, I'd lather on rich body lotion and speak lovingly to my legs. I told them how much I valued them. Yes, it may sound a bit crazy and it felt strange, but I kept going. I also said a prayer of gratitude, thanking God for these incredible legs he's given me—legs that can stand up, walk, run, and carry me to places I might never go without them. It wasn't long before I noticed a difference. Nowadays it's rare that I bump or bruise either of these stunningly gorgeous legs. Now I talk to other body parts too.

What am I really saying? It's time to quit beating yourself up—literally and figuratively. With the images the media presents to us, it's easy to get hung up on our bodies, thinking that shapely legs; flat tummies; and taut, unwrinkled faces define true beauty. I like what award-winning writer Cynthia Ozick said about this: "After a certain number of years, our faces become our biographies." And that's comforting to know, especially as time goes on and more than our self-esteem is sagging.

A while ago my granddaughters discovered some photographs of me taken during my modeling days. Yes, this gal who suffered with such a poor self-image and virtually no confidence had a successful career in modeling. This same girl who never felt pretty and was so shy she could hardly look a person in the eye during a conversation was out there in front of an audience and working with the camera. "Golly," I said when I noticed my hubby sorting through the photos, looking at my 20-pound thinner frame, "I bet you wish you knew me then." "No way," he whispered, as he gave me a big hug. "You are much more gorgeous now!" Does he know how to get a big steak dinner and control of the TV remote or what!

Learning to Love the Body You're In

Accepting, nurturing, and enjoying our bodies are fundamental to staying healthy and whole. You might be haunted by voices from the past that convinced you that you were too "chubby" or "lanky" or "skinny" or "pudgy." Here are some healthy practices that can act as a healing balm to soothe your wounded body image.

- Use kinder, gentler terms when referring to yourself. If you are underweight, tell yourself you are slender, slim, petite, willowy, or trim, and get rid of words like skinny or scrawny. Do the same if you carry extra weight. When I put on extra pounds during menopause, I chose to start seeing myself as curvaceous, voluptuous, and shapely. (After all, a heavyset man would be called nonjudgmental things like beefy, brawny, stocky, stout, or even cuddly.)
- Stand naked in front of a full-length mirror and take a deep breath. (Stay calm! I know this is scary, but please give it a try.) Study your body, front and back, and try to not to be critical...just observant. Now focus on a favorite feature of yours and tell God how grateful you are that you were made this way. Next, look at your least favorite part and do the same thing.
- Create a unique fashion look for yourself, an image that expresses something new for you—an air of energy, sparkle, or dynamism or one you could call striking, stunning, elegant, or dazzling. Have fun shopping for your new look.
- Don't buy anything that says "Slim Down" or "Push Up" on the label.
- Quit wearing clothing and undergarments that leave little red marks all over your body. The discomfort is a constant reminder of any perceived physical imperfections. That includes shoes that are too tight. Someone said, "When a woman gets dressed to kill, her feet are usually her first victims." When I polled a mixed audience to find out how many were wearing shoes that pinch or bind, the men looked at me like I was crazy while most

of the women raised their hands. Men just can't imagine why women would do this to themselves.

- Repeat to yourself, "I love my body just the way it is. I am comfortable in it. My body is a gift from God. It is bursting with beauty, vitality, and health." Walk, move, and carry yourself the way you would if you believed those statements. Do this every time you're walking, biking, swimming, dancing, exercising, or doing any kind of movement. Act as if you truly felt this way. Eventually you'll begin to believe it! It's possible to fake it until you make it.

❀ ❀ ❀

There is a way to be happy no matter what:
Take up acting!

The stress-free life includes an appreciation for what is important. While we realize that breasts will sag, hips expand, and chins double, our life experiences along the way make it all worthwhile. Would we really trade the opportunities, relationships, insights, and knowledge we have now for the bodies we had way back when? Maybe our bodies simply have to expand to hold all the wisdom and love we've acquired. That's my philosophy, and I'm sticking with it.

Sanity Savers & Survival Hints

- For fun, visit a cosmetic salon that offers complimentary makeovers. Experiment with a brand-new look. Purchase a lipstick, blush, or eye shadow to complement your new image.
- Treat yourself to a new outfit in a style that flatters your figure.
- Comfortably camouflage a flabby tummy with an empire waist or wrap-style top or dress. Hide a large bottom with tops and jackets that cover that area. Enhance a flat bottom with pants or jeans that have embroidered or bejeweled back pockets.

- Cover flabby, pudgy, or saggy upper arms with loose fitting sleeves or wraps. Avoid sleeveless tops and spaghetti straps.
- To create a long, lean appearance choose a monochromatic look. Your skirt or pants, stockings, and shoes should all match.
- Treat yourself to a spa day with a relaxation massage, scalp treatment, full-body scrub, pedicure, and manicure.
- "You can be pleased with nothing when you are not pleased with yourself" (Lady Wortley Montagu).

19

Sanity Secret #15

Redefine Contentment

Stop Shopping 'til You Drop

Last week I was alone in my hotel room and did something you may be astonished to hear. After reading the notice recommending I avoid drinking city water in favor of the five-dollar bottle that was placed in my room, I did the unthinkable. You guessed it. With reckless abandon I turned on the tap, filled a glass with water, and drank it. (There's this little part of me that enjoys taking a risk now and then.) I'm still around to tell you about it!

I'm sure you've noticed that it's all the rage to carry bottled water everywhere. There are even designer holders to carry our bottles around in. It's such a big craze today that few of us would want to be caught drinking water from a tap—it just wouldn't be seemly. Yet recent studies have revealed that there aren't any standards in place for testing a bottle of water for purity, source, or contents. City water is tested regularly—and for free. Bottled water can come from foreign countries with little or no government bottling regulations. And some bottled water comes from tap water! So why do we feel more protected drinking water from a plastic bottle with a label that tells us it came "from cool mountain springs" or "an artesian well"?

As important as it is to drink water every day for health benefits, and to be especially cautious while visiting certain parts of the world where drinking bottled water is probably the sane choice, here at home bottled water has almost become a status symbol. Aside from our drinking water, multimillion-dollar promotion campaigns have been devised to convince us that there are specific ways to appear "chic" and "trendy," whether it's from the SUV we drive, the protein bar we snack on, the sports shoes we wear, or the designer bags we carry. Through the labels on our apparel, we've become walking billboards.

Shopaholics

❀ ❀ ❀

"The best things in life aren't things."
ART BUCHWALD

After years of being the target of massive advertising and marketing campaigns, many of us now allow the products we use to define who we are. Beyond that, we're inclined to rely on these products to bring us the sanity and inner peace we long for. Or is it the spending *experience* that's become our comforter, keeping us sane? When we shop and spend, we get instant satisfaction and feel emotionally validated, cared for, understood, and nurtured. That's important since we each have a deep inner longing for those.

But what we're truly craving is something only God can provide. In his word he promises to never leave or forsake us. God offers us peace that passes understanding, and that peace is not dependant on anything we can buy in a store. The Bible says, "Seek first his kingdom and his righteousness, and all these things will be given to you" (Matthew 6:33 NIV). Don't seek satisfaction first—seek to know God. Don't seek to be validated, cared for, understood, nurtured, gratified, or anything else through what the world tries to offer. Only God can truly bring those to your life. First seek him, and then everything else will follow.

You may have noticed that these days so much of what we shop for is related to stress relief. Items or practices that promise to provide a tension-free existence are hot. At one time stress was considered a fatal disease until the advertisers caught on to our dilemma and turned it into a marketer's dream come true. Now we have aromatherapy creams and lotions, scented candles and oils, calming herbal teas, special relaxing pillows, soothing massage oils and foot creams, and bean or rice bag neck rolls we can heat in our microwaves. These are designed so that we can come home, put our feet up, and feel the anxieties of the day drift away. Some restaurants feature specific comfort foods to help us unwind by reproducing the same types of meals our moms used to prepare.

What if we came home and made ourselves some macaroni and cheese, a meat loaf with tomato sauce, or mashed potatoes with gravy? Or maybe we could treat ourselves after dinner once in a while to some homemade coconut cream pie, butter tarts, or chocolate chip cookies? Perhaps instead of buying faux stone water fountains for our homes that bring us the gentle sound of water running over rocks, we could actually take time to go out and sit by a brook and hear water running over real stream rocks? Imagine if we spent a few moments in nature listening to the birds sing and the breeze rustling in the treetops rather than buying a tape with those recorded sounds.

Instead we keep shopping for more and more stress-relieving products, from new clothes to convenient appliances, from exercise equipment to filing cabinets where we store more stuff. God says, "Don't be obsessed with getting more material things. Be relaxed with what you have" (Hebrews 13:5).

What is this preoccupation with shopping really all about? For one thing, shopping is fun and buying is satisfying. The problem is we get hooked on the pleasure of acquiring things and spending money. Often the incentive for shopping isn't the valid reason of needing the new item, but for inner satisfaction. Gathering and collecting more possessions stimulates the pleasure center in our brains.

I know a wonderful lady who overspent regularly and charged all her credit cards to the max. Yet she continued to feel the need to go out and shop. "After all," she told me, "there must be money in the bank because I still have checks!" When I attended one of her lawn sales, there were racks and racks of clothing with the original tags still attached. None of the outfits had been worn. Obviously she didn't need those clothes. What she needed was a closer relationship with God, more time with her husband

and kids, more genuine friendships, more exciting interests to pursue, and more self-nurturing so she could be fulfilled and go out to nurture others with her time, talents, and dollars. She is a caring, loving, giving person missing a more valuable outlet for using her gifts.

In generations past, people met their social needs by connecting with others. Among my fondest childhood memories are the times my parents had friends over to the house for the evening to savor good food and enjoyable conversation. Eventually they'd all gather around the piano as Dad belted out lively tunes. My sisters and I would lie in our beds upstairs listening to the sounds of spirited singing and occasional bouts of laughter mingled with the aroma of coffee brewing and sandwiches being prepared. I wonder if they were getting the same sort of pleasure that we try to get today through buying new stuff. Shopping is one of the few pleasures that doesn't have a warning from the surgeon general. Maybe if it did, we'd be more apt to cut back.

Recently I traveled to England to present a series of stress-and-time management workshops. While I was there I spent time meandering through a local shopping district. The marketplace there is very different from our typical cookie-cutter shopping malls. Here we all buy from the same 20 or so stores no matter which city we are in. In England the small shop owners were in the midst of a struggle to keep the big box stores from taking over. The entrepreneurs were in favor of keeping their unique and independently owned stores alive. Shopping in the marketplace meant customers could meet the owners and chat with someone actually involved in producing the products they sold. There was a human element that is missing from so many of our chain stores.

> For many women shopping is a substitute form of nourishment. It makes us feel like we've done something constructive, which makes us feel better about ourselves.

I enjoyed the alluring aroma of fresh breads and pastries in the bakery and the brightly colored flower arrangements next to vivid displays of fruits and vegetables set up on the sidewalks. The ladies' shop was brimming with unique clothing, handmade knitted pieces, pretty hats, and exclusive jewelry. The owner was there in person to help me find a style that would suit me, my figure, and my budget. The stores had personality, like the craft studio with the artist's workbench sitting right out in the open. Shopping wasn't just a corporate experience. It nurtured my soul. But even this kind of shopping needs to be done in moderation.

Please don't get me wrong. Shopping has its place in our lives. And I'm grateful for the large chain retailers—especially the ones that offer my books on their shelves. But let's make shopping a human experience again...where we connect with one another. And let's quit shopping for things just because everyone else is or spending our money simply to fill the need for pleasure or comfort.

I know it is said jokingly when we tell each other we'll "shop 'til we drop." But wandering around the mall for hours until we're exhausted has become a perfectly acceptable pastime. For many women shopping really is a substitute form of nourishment. After all, we've just spent a lot of money to enhance our lives, our homes, and our appearance. It makes us feel like we've done something constructive, which makes us feel better about ourselves. It's an attempt to boost our self-image. Playing on our self-esteem and sense of worth is another way massive advertising and promotional campaigns have altered our thinking and robbed us of our sanity. Let's get some of it back and enjoy less stress and more joy by redefining contentment. While the media continues to tell us we can't possibly be happy without all the frills, let's keep to the truth.

Sanity Savers & Survival Hints

- Take a stand and move away from consumerism and materialism. Use up what you already have and wear what's in the back of your closet.
- Seek out free, or nearly free, events in your area—a café that has board games such as Scrabble, chess, and checkers; discounted theater tickets for stage plays, musical performances, discussions, seminars; and author readings at bookstores.
- "What I'm trying to do here is to get you to relax, to not be so preoccupied with getting, so you can respond to God's giving" (Matthew 6:31).

- Go to an evening church service at your church or visit a new one.
- "God's blessing makes life rich" (Proverbs 10:22).
- Volunteer as a single, couple, or family. Read to schoolchildren or the blind, share special talents in a nursing home (music, making crafts, photography), serve at a shelter or soup kitchen, do indoor/outdoor chores for shut-ins.
- Ride the local ferry, trolley, or bus to the end of the line. Visit a park, do some people watching, and have a picnic before returning.
- For an afternoon of fun, gather your family and friends and go bowling, roller skating, ice skating, or bike riding. Play tennis at a public court or have a round of miniature golf.
- Go outside at night and snuggle inside sleeping bags in the backyard for some stargazing and watching the planets.
- Join outdoor groups that offer hikes, bird-watching expeditions, canoe or kayaking trips, and cross-country ski trips.

20

Sanity Secret #16

Celebrate the Joys of Aging

When You're Having a Mid-Yikes Crisis

In this chapter we're going to deal with…with… Wait…it's on the tip of my tongue. Hmm. Oh, now I remember—aging! Forgetfulness is one of those frustrating stressors that seems to come along with getting older and many times it's no fun.

> Three ladies were discussing their memory problems when one confessed, "I get so annoyed with myself when I go the refrigerator, stare inside, and haven't a clue what I want." The second one said, "That's nothing. I go to the top of the stairs and have to come back down again to remember why I went up there." The third lady was pleased as she boasted to her friends, "Thank the good Lord I'm not as bad as the two of you. Knock on wood." After tapping loudly on the tabletop, she jumped up and announced, "Excuse me while I get the door!"

Maybe you have trouble remembering what you did yesterday or even a minute ago. Do you often forget the words for common things such as "husband" or "vacuum cleaner"? Are younger people starting to call you "ma'am"? Do you look in the mirror and cry, "Who are you and what have you done with my body?" Does the image there reflect your mother's face more than your own? If any of this sounds familiar, welcome to midlife. Don't run away screaming about your "lost" youth or the fear that you're "past your prime." Now is the time when you can have more fun, more meaning, and more passion than you've ever imagined.

If we listen to messages from the outside world, it may be difficult to believe that's true. For instance, a radio commercial I heard the other day started off by saying, "Ladies, quit lying to yourselves. The age spots on your skin *do* make you look older." It went on to introduce a miracle-working product, which costs per tube about the same as a sporty convertible. With the great effort and strides we've allegedly made in regard to accepting ourselves and feeling good regardless of our physical features, I could hardly believe my ears.

✲ ✲ ✲

Did you ever stop to think and
forget to start up again?

When I first noticed a few "freckles" of my own, I went into shock and had to stop at the bakery where I bought a dozen chocolate chip cookies to drown my sorrows. Those were the only brown spots I could handle that day. After that I started playing connect-the-dots on my body and found when they were joined they formed the Big Dipper. At least that made me smile...until I happened to notice I'd developed some laugh lines. And frankly, they just aren't very funny.

Time may be a great healer, but it's a lousy beautician. Fortunately, thanks to the caring, compassionate people who operate the cosmetic industry, I found out that it's possible to keep a youthful appearance by investing no more time or money than it would take to construct a state-of-the-art, 5000-passenger cruise ship. So with my cache of "quality" skin-care products (meaning they cost per ounce about the same as a four-week trip to Fiji) that I keep in my cosmetic warehouse, along with my handy Black & Decker Makeup Applicator and an emergency supply of whiteout for under-eye circles, I feel equipped to battle the aging process until the grave (or at least until the casket is closed!). The only problem is that to be ready for work at nine in the morning, I have to start applying products at suppertime the night before.

When one woman complained that her new photo wasn't nearly as good as the last one she took, the photographer very politely replied, "You must forgive me. The last time I took your picture I was ten years younger."

We strive to hold on to our youth because it's so easy to think that personal worth and value come from being young. Today there are pills, potions, and procedures to smooth, tighten, and lift body parts that are bound and determined to go their own way. Bookstore shelves are full of books on anti-aging and ways to halt the ravages of getting older. I'm thinking that if we don't age, the only alternative is to die. So what do we do—take a daily dose of anti-aging vitamins and minerals? I wonder if worrying about what's in them is what's creating most of our aging. Do we invest in the latest herbal supplements that will increase our libido even though it could make facial hair grow? Sure, we may be in the mood, but before we get started, we'll need to tweeze our chin hairs.

❊ ❊ ❊

"When your friends begin to flatter you on how young you look,
it's a sure sign you're getting old."
MARK TWAIN

There's a big difference between being young and being youthful. The Bible says that "though our outward [woman] is perishing, yet the inward [woman] is being renewed day by day" (2 Corinthians 4:16 NKJV). How would you live if you began to relate to age as a spiritual *ascent* rather than a physical *descent?* Midlife can be a time to really get started and give life all you've got. Instead of aging on autopilot, you can reach beyond the stereotype images you may have about what's possible at this time in your life. Give yourself permission to stretch forward and embrace what can be!

❊ ❊ ❊

"Retirement at 65 is ridiculous.
When I was 65, I still had pimples!"
GEORGE BURNS

No matter what you have been through, it's never too late to be what you might have been. Life really can begin in the middle…middle age, that is. It did for me. That's when I wrote my first book and fulfilled my lifelong dream of becoming a published author. Since then everything's been uphill (except for some body parts) regarding joy and contentment. What we've labeled middle age doesn't need to be seen as the turning point toward the end. It can be viewed as a delightful and enjoyable time of experiencing new opportunities. No matter what did or didn't happen in your past, the present remains an endless wellspring of exhilarating possibilities.

In our youth-obsessed society, we tend to forget the wonderful parts of maturing. Begin to appreciate your age by becoming a sage and sharing your wisdom by being a mentor. Whether through volunteer work within a community organization, a boys' and girls' club, a church group, or informally with your own kids and grandkids, now is the time you can pass on valuable information, skills, and insights you've spent years gathering. And when you mentor young people, you'll be blessed too.

If you're feeling "youthfully challenged" with the stresses of aging, decide to bring some enchantment into your life. Maybe you've lost all your marvels. It's time to recapture your sense of adventure! Let go of the weight of past stressors and embrace the lightheartedness of the free spirit within you. Rewrite the script of your life to include simple pleasures and innocent indulgences. If you're not sure how to go about that, here are 21 helpful hints garnered from my life and my friends.

- Rethink old attitudes. "My hubby and I could never understand people who referred to themselves as Mommy and Daddy when talking to their pets. Now, not only have we become parents to our cat, Daffy, but I am embarrassed to say we talk to our 'widdle kitty' in baby talk and can't imagine what life would be like without her."
- Get some pretty flannel pajamas. Silk is luxurious, but flannel is cozy.
- Dance with abandon. Alone or with your sweetie. Have fun!

- Buy that perfume you've always wanted. You can even wear it to bed.
- Wear lacy lingerie under your jeans, sweats, and everything else.
- Give away clothes that don't flatter your figure.
- Get a fresh look with a complimentary makeover.
- Treat yourself to a spa day. Get a massage, facial, pedicure, and manicure.
- Say no to vitality-draining activities you really don't want to do.
- Eat grilled cheese sandwiches on your good china.
- Drink juice from a stemmed crystal goblet and coffee from your best china mug.
- Leave your comfort zone behind. Try something you've always secretly longed to do—tap dancing, furniture refinishing, skydiving, roller skating. If that's a little too risky, start with something less daring—make a new recipe, order a menu item you've never tried, or wear a sweater in hot pink, lime green, or a color you don't normally wear.
- Rearrange the living room.
- Stop listening to the "shoulds" that keep you stuck in a narrow little box: "You should get a real job." "You should cut your hair at this age." "You should retire." "You should wear sensible shoes." "You should downsize your home."
- Eat chocolate and buy only the best.
- Keep a large supply of sticky notes on hand—they're great memory boosters.
- Resist using your age as an excuse for not doing things.
- Volunteer at a shelter, nursing home, or school.
- Start the day with God.

- Pray and read from Proverbs first thing in the day; pray and read from Psalms before going to bed.
- Remember, God loves you just the way you are.

A friend sent me this great quote she received over the internet: "Old is when your sweetie says, 'Let's go upstairs and make love,' and you reply, 'Honey, it's one or the other!'" She also went on to say that physical intimacy has been one of the most precious and cherished parts of her 44-year marriage. Raised with solid religious values, including the emphasis on virginity until marriage, she and her husband chose to wait for each other. Now she says, "Wow, was it worth it. The intimacy we've enjoyed over the years has become increasingly passionate and intense." That's not to say there haven't been glitches here and there due to stresses at different stages in their marriage. There have also been changes due to aging. But she says over the years, she has learned that timing is everything and quality is better than quantity. "It may take longer to get where we're going," she tells me, "but it's worth the journey. And sometimes the voyage is pleasurable enough even if we don't reach the final destination. It's not that we want to go on the journey less often. It's just that it takes a lot longer to get moving."

* * *

"An archeologist is the best husband a woman can have; the older she gets, the more interested he is in her."
AGATHA CHRISTIE

It seems to me that life is backward. When we're young with voracious, insatiable sex drives, our lives are full with kids, jobs, housework, bills, and so on. We look forward to having the house to ourselves and all the time in the world to make love with no distractions. But when the day comes the sex drive mysteriously vanishes. (Well, it's there somewhere. Just give us a few hours to find it.) We've got the whole night, no kids, no noise, no disruptions—a situation we would have given our right arms for earlier. But then it's good we have all night because that's how long it might take to get the fires burning.

* * *

"If youth but knew, if old age but could."
HENRI ESTIENNE

It's true, we have less energy now, perhaps, but we have far more understanding of what each breath of life is for. And now at last we have a destiny to fulfill—not a destiny of a life that's simply over, but rather a destiny of a life that is finally truly lived. Midlife is not a crisis; it's a time of rebirth. It's a time to accept life and death. It's a time to finally, truly live life as you know deep in your heart God meant it to be lived.

Sanity Savers & Survival Hints

- "A man may grow old in body, but never in mind" (Cicero).
- "My son, do not forget my teaching, but keep my commands in your heart, for they will prolong your life many years" (Proverbs 3:1-2 NIV).
- Women have hormonal ups and downs as they age, but men buy motorcycles.
- "Getting old is not for sissies!" (Bette Davis).
- "Age is something that doesn't matter unless you are a cheese" (Billie Burke).
- "The best mirror is an old friend" (George Herbert).
- "The ways of right-living people glow with light; the longer they live, the brighter they shine" (Proverbs 4:18).
- Midlife is when you want to grab every firm young lovely in a tube top and scream, "Listen, honey, even the Roman Empire fell and those things will too!"
- "Nature gives you the face you have at twenty; it's up to you to merit the face you have at fifty" (Coco Chanel).
- "Live now, believe me, wait not till tomorrow; gather the roses of life today" (Pierre De Ronsard).
- "Be content with what you have" (Hebrews 13:5 NIV).

- They say the mind is the first thing to go…at least, that's what I think they say.

Exercise for Seniors

This great routine by an unknown author is for older people. Younger people try it at their own risk. For those of us getting along in years, here is a little secret for building your arm and shoulder muscles. Three days a week works well.

Begin by standing straight with a 5-pound potato sack in each hand. Extend your arms straight out from your sides and hold them there as long as you can. Try to reach a full minute and then relax.

After a few weeks, move up to 10-pound potato sacks and then 50-pound potato sacks.

Eventually try to get to where you can lift a 100-pound potato sack in each hand and hold your arms horizontally, straight out from your sides, for more than a full minute.

After you've reached a reasonable level of confidence at the 100-pound sack level, start putting a couple of potatoes in each of the sacks, but be careful not to overdo it.

Great Truths About Growing Old

1. Growing old is mandatory; growing up is optional.
2. Forget the health food. I need all the preservatives I can get.
3. When you fall down, you wonder what else you can do while you're down there.
4. You're getting old when you get the same sensation from a rocking chair that you once got from a roller coaster.
5. It's frustrating when you know all the answers, but nobody bothers to ask you the questions.
6. Time may be a great healer, but it's a lousy beautician.
7. Wisdom comes with age, but sometimes age comes alone.

21

Get Your Finances in Shape

When Too Much Month Is Left at the End of the Money

Do you ever...

- get discouraged about your money situation?
- feel uncomfortable spending money on yourself?
- have no idea where your money goes?
- wonder exactly how much your husband earns, what would happen if he died, or what kind of joint savings, investments, or debts you have?
- feel you can't afford things you truly need for yourself and your family?
- have more debt than you believe you can pay back?
- find your financial situation causes marriage and family problems and keeps you awake at night?
- imagine that you may end up homeless and living on the street?

Let's face it—money causes a lot of stress for most of us. When surveyed, many people say money is their number one source of trouble. And women have some additional money stressors. While we can appreciate that there are definite physical, emotional, and psychological differences between men and women (I know—you're shocked, but it's true), we need to recognize that there are also differences when it comes to finances:

- In certain situations, women are still limited when it comes to making financial transactions, such as taking out business loans or getting mortgages because of outdated policies and regulations.
- Girls are still raised to believe they can't understand facts and figures in the same way boys do.
- In most instances women continue to be paid much less than men for the same work. Although we're seeing changes, historically women's pay scales have been lower than men's in positions typically held by men, such as engineers, truck drivers, forklift operators, doctors, lawyers, and construction workers.
- Most North Americans who live below poverty level are women.
- Millions of fathers don't pay child support, leaving the financial burden on single mothers.

These are very real issues, and we can't wish them away. But how *we feel and think* determine how these concerns affect us. The role money plays in our lives is vitally important to feeling peaceful. Both our resistance to stress and our self-esteem are often intricately linked with our income and bank accounts. That's something we can work toward changing.

In order to break free from past limitations, take some steps to improve your financial self-worth.

- Build a good credit history. Apply for a credit card in your own name and always pay it by the due date to avoid interest charges and to get a high credit score. Use discipline and never charge beyond your ability to pay the full amount each month.

- Develop a good relationship with your bank by having both a savings and a checking account. Apply for a small loan and pay it back on schedule or ahead of time.
- Increase your income by asking for a raise, taking a second job, or turning a hobby into a paying venture.
- Recognize your worth and value to the company that employs you. Don't berate yourself—privately or to others. Take inventory of your strong points and all you have to offer your organization. Present these at reviews or when seeking a new position.
- Look into getting a better paying job by going back to school, earning a degree, learning new skills, starting your own business, or going into direct sales or network marketing (where the sky is the limit).
- If you're married, familiarize yourself with all aspects of your joint financial situation. Don't let your mate keep monetary secrets from you. No matter how much you love and trust your husband, relationships and circumstances can change. Be sure you can survive on your own if necessary.

❊ ❊ ❊

Make all you can, save all you can, give all you can.
JOHN WESLEY

Maybe money can't buy happiness, but poverty can buy misery. I like how motivational speaker and author Zig Ziglar put it. He said there have been times when he's had money and times when he hasn't, and he's found out he'd rather have it. What extra money can do is buy you some help with the housework; pay for a babysitter when you need time out; help make your home a comfy, cozy, inviting haven; and provide a vacation or other treat you can look forward to occasionally.

One important sanity secret for financial stress is to find more accurate and reliable ways of measuring your self-worth. You are *not* your finances and your finances are *not* you. If you've fallen behind, whether through your circumstances or your choices, remind yourself that there are more constant and reliable elements to use when determining your value, including loving relationships; friendships; community involvement; contributions you make through work, personal gifts, unique talents, hobbies, and other special interests; and beyond all else—what God thinks of you. Don't fall into the trap of measuring your worth in dollars or debts. God says in his Word that you're made in his image and worth far more to him than diamonds (Proverbs 31:10)! He also says he will never leave you or forsake you (Hebrews 13:5).

You've probably seen the T-shirt that says, "When the going gets tough, the tough go shopping." For many women, it's no joke. Buying nice things has become a major way to cope with pressure and tension. But some women are just the opposite. They feel guilty or uncomfortable about spending money to nurture themselves. If this latter one is you, you're not recognizing your personal worth or value. With a martyr mindset, you'll spend the rest of your life saying, "After I get my raise" or "When I get that new position" or "Once I sell my quota" or "When I'm finally out of debt, the kids are raised, and the mortgage is paid, then I'll do something good for myself." Happiness will elude you often and stress will make your life hard. Start now to regularly treat yourself in small, healthy ways.

If you want to find the money you need for healthy self-care, it's essential to determine your priorities. To identify what they are, keep a journal of your spending habits. You'll soon notice a pattern emerging. If caring for yourself is not part of it, decide to make some healthy changes. The goal is not to use shopping as a way to handle your stress but to pamper and nurture your life back into wellness and balance.

❊ ❊ ❊

By the time you make ends meet, they move the ends!

If you have a problem with overspending or have a lot of debt, you'll want to get your financial papers organized so you can take a hard look at your income and expenses. See what you can eliminate or economize on. Keep records and note where your money comes from and where it goes. You might want to carry a pocket notebook and keep an account of every purchase and expenditure for a few weeks. If necessary, change your shopping habits and cut back to bare necessities for a time to clear up any debts. Set realistic goals, make a budget, and save for things before you buy them. Also work toward establishing a financial cushion for emergencies. Once you get debt under control, think about opening a savings account and making investments toward your future. You may want to meet with a financial planner who can make recommendations for your unique situation.

Situations will always arise that are beyond your control. When that happens, a wonderful coping mechanism is to count your blessings. Be grateful for what you have. This may sound simplistic and naïve, but it isn't. Free yourself from money's merciless grip by taking stock of all that is good in your life right now. Don't focus on what is lacking. And don't limit yourself to material things or bank balances. There was a time when I lived in fear if my bank balance was less than what I felt I needed or if my calendar wasn't full of speaking engagements. The best remedy I found was to list all the blessings in my life and everything I could be grateful for: a roof over my head, my health, family and friends who love me, a cozy bed to sleep in at night, food on the table, clothes to wear, eyes that see and ears that hear.

❊ ❊ ❊

I owe, I owe, so off to work I go!

AUTHOR UNKNOWN

Many of us feel stressed because we're broke before the month is up, but we often have places where we could cut back on our spending. Research shows that by trying to maintain a lifestyle we can't afford, we're more likely to suffer stress-related health problems. Invest some time in examining where your money goes and determine where you spend on things that aren't top priority. You may be able to save by cutting back on entertainment, specialty coffee, take-out food, cable television, excess car trips, and trendy clothing. Take a sack lunch to work, put coffee in a thermos, and use coupons when shopping.

Pay off your loans by tackling the smallest ones first and doubling up on payments. When one is paid off, take that amount and add it to the next smallest loan, and so on. Once when I had paid off a business loan this way, I continued to make that monthly payment except I deposited it in a savings account toward a vacation in Hawaii. It took two years, but the trip was worth the discipline.

At one time in history, money was a simple medium of exchange. Today it's taken on a powerful life of its own. But it's not actually money that causes our stress. Our *state of mind and attitude* toward money is more important than how much we earn, how much we spend, and how much we save. The Bible says the *love* of money is the root of evil not money itself (1 Timothy 6:10 NIV). We've given this neutral commodity too much power and allowed it to run our lives.

In years gone by, bartering was a common method of exchange. To help you get a new perspective on cash, consider bartering for something you want. This will also help when you're having a cash flow problem. You might think you have no services to barter, but think again. Everyone has something to offer. What about your unique gifts and particular talents? If you love babies and small children, you might trade babysitting time with a parent who can supply something you need. One massage therapist I know is a mom with young children who is more than willing to trade her services for the opportunity to have a couple of free nights for dates with her husband. Do you have a talent with photography, calligraphy, decorating, or stenciling? Maybe you own a piece of equipment that someone else needs to use. Would you like to walk dogs? Are you good at caring for horses? How about woodworking, furniture refinishing, quilting, or sewing? Find someone who has what you need and is interested in what you have to offer.

Whether you choose to barter, compose a detailed plan to get back on track, pay off a debt, or save successfully for a special purchase or trip, remember to reward yourself. Decide ahead of time what type of reward will encourage you to keep your commitment to yourself. Rewards don't have to cost a lot, and you don't want to go into debt, but having something to look forward to can be a powerful motivator. The biggest reward will be the financial freedom you experience.

Give me enough food to live on, neither too much nor too little.
If I'm too full, I might get independent, saying,
"God? Who needs him?"

If I'm poor, I might steal and dishonor
the name of my God.

Proverbs 30:8-9

Don't hoard treasure down here where it gets
eaten by moths and corroded by rust or—worse!—
stolen by burglars. Stockpile treasure in heaven, where
it's safe from moth and rust and burglars.
It's obvious, isn't it? The place where your treasure is,
is the place you will most want to be, and end up being.

Matthew 6:19

Don't be obsessed with getting more material things.
Be relaxed with what you have.
Since God assured us, "I'll never let you down,
never walk off and leave you," we can boldly quote,
God is there, ready to help; I'm fearless no matter what.
Who or what can get to me?

Hebrews 13:5-6

Sanity Savers & Survival Hints

- Be sure your income exceeds your expenses.
- Escape the credit card trap. Never buy nonessential items on your credit card or charge more than you can pay when the bill is due.
- Save for things before you buy them.
- Make shopping lists and stick to them.
- Shop for food when you *aren't* hungry and clothing only when you need to.
- Don't shop when you're depressed or upset.
- Always stay within your budget.

- Do regular preventative maintenance on your home and vehicles to avoid costly repairs.
- Talk with a trusted friend or family member before making major purchases.
- Ask for help in organizing your bills and paying them.
- "My God will supply all your needs according to His riches in glory in Christ Jesus" (Philippians 4:19 NASB).
- Review all insurance policies—home, car, life—to see if premiums can be reduced.
- Familiarize yourself with your benefit plan at work to see if it covers therapeutic massages, chiropractic treatments, dental work, and eye care.
- Stay away from get-rich-quick schemes. If it sounds too good to be true, it probably is.
- Resist doing business with phone solicitors. If what they're offering sounds legitimate, ask for details in writing before committing to anything.
- "Honor God with everything you own; give him the first and the best. Your barns will burst, your wine vats will brim over" (Proverbs 3:9-10).
- Be content at your present income level.
- "Bring your full tithe to the Temple treasury so there will be ample provisions in my Temple. Test me in this and see if I don't open up heaven itself to you and pour out blessings beyond your wildest dreams" (Malachi 3:10).
- Recognize that everything belongs to God, and you are stewards of his property.
- In spite of the cost of living, it's still popular!

The First Resort

Although there are so many things we can't control, there are no accidents or senseless events. Nothing happens to you that surprises God. You will never hear him say, "Oops! Things are so bad there's no hope." God controls the blessings and the difficulties you encounter in this life. He is sovereign over your life. He's the supreme ruler over your health, your marriage, your children's lives, your extended family, your job, your bank account, your debt, and your investments. He is sovereign over the doctor's report you just received, the car accident that just happened, the important papers that went missing, and the flight you missed. He rules over your choices and decisions, whether good or bad.

When you come to him as a *first resort* and live in the light of his supreme authority in each aspect of your life, everything changes. Suddenly you have a new perspective. If God truly is sovereign, why would you try to take control? Why would you stay up all night worrying and fretting? Why would you push yourself to work around the clock? If he is sovereign, *everything* rests on *his* shoulders, not on yours.

Jesus says, "Come to me, all you who are weary and burdened, and I will give you rest" (Matthew11:28 NIV). Have you come to him? Is he the sovereign one in your life? If yes, then it's time to lay down your burden, lean on his strong arms, and thank him for being in control. If not, why not take the time right now to invite him into your life as your Savior and Lord? Although it's a big commitment, the process is simple and the rewards everlasting. You can pray this prayer or one similar...

> Lord Jesus, I want the peace and contentment and joy you offer. Today I give my life to you and embrace the love and relationship with you made available through your death and resurrection. Forgive me for all the wrongs I've committed against you and the people I've encountered. I'm so excited to be part of your kingdom! Thank you! In your name I pray. Amen.

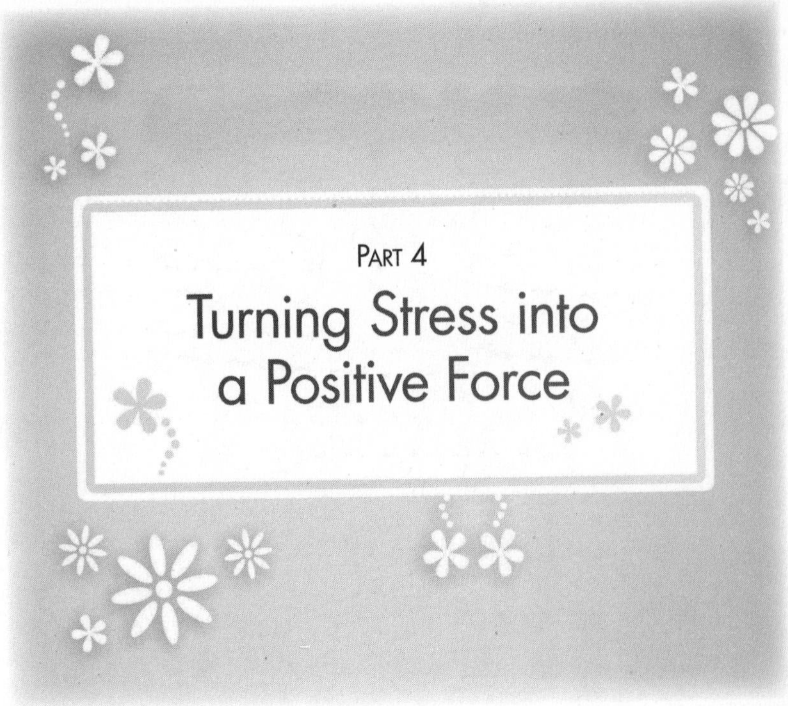

Part 4

Turning Stress into a Positive Force

22

Discover the Stress Cycle

I'm not certain, but I think I lost my sanity somewhere between the rinse cycle and the menstrual cycle. In any case, I started to regain it once I discovered the "stress cycle." (Don't bother talking about this cycle around your kids—they'll just start fighting over who gets to ride it first.)

When stress hits us hard, we usually end up functioning on autopilot. We tend to have a predetermined reaction to high-pressure situations based on past programming. A "spontaneous" cycle of mind–body–spirit effects is set into motion. Often our responses aren't all that healthy. Typically we don't even realize it's happening or that we can consider optional action. We simply react. Once we understand our stress cycle we can find ways to interrupt the sequence *before* the pressure and tension take over.

Stress generates energy. This energy propels us from the initial stress of a situation right on through the various phases of the cycle. Here's how it all evolves.

An event occurs, and your brain automatically searches for similar events in your past and how you handled it. You immediately form a perception of whether you can control the situation or not. If the assessment is, "No, I can't control the outcome the way I want to," the stress cycle kicks in. Your thoughts take over, causing you to talk to yourself in stressful ways. Before you know it, strong emotions kick in, which helps trigger the *fight-or-flight* mechanism. This physical response gives you the energy you need to protect yourself by going into battle or fleeing the situation. With the threat of danger, you also may go into defensive mode, which triggers even more emotions, and the cycle continues with each element feeding the next. As mentioned, most of the time we get caught up in this pattern before we realize it.

To control stress before it controls us, we have to intercept the cycle, choose our responses, and make stress work *for* us instead of against us. Figure 3 shows what the stress cycle looks like.

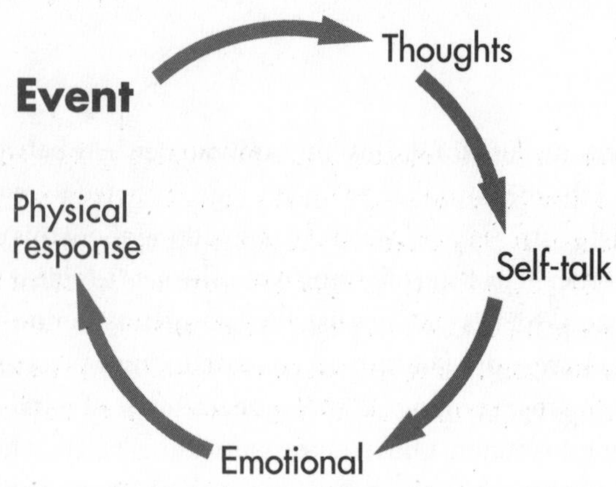

Figure 3: Stress Cycle

Your overall health, wellness, and ability to handle difficult situations are dependant on your balance of mental, emotional, spiritual, and physical well-being. In the next chapter we'll take a closer look at each stress cycle component.

23

Sanity Secret #18

Take Charge of Your Perceptions

Much of our stress, tension, and emotional anguish begins with the way we perceive events around us. In fact, most stress experts agree that approximately 90 percent of the stress we experience comes not so much from the circumstance or situation we're facing but from our *assessment* and *viewpoint* of it. When an event happens, we perceive it as positive or negative and something we can or can't control. When we interpret it as upsetting, frightening, shocking, disturbing, or unpleasant, stress takes over.

I am a master at this. I can drive myself nutty in a couple of minutes. I'm pulling onto the highway, in a hurry to get where I'm going, only to find traffic barely moving. Ah—it's a plot. Drivers purposely got up early and drove out here before I did to block the flow and make me late. Besides, why aren't they already at work? Doesn't anybody have a job? Why are they all driving on the highway at this time of day!

Let's say you and the kids are in line to drive into the parking area of an amusement park. There are several lanes to choose from, and you pick the fastest moving one. Yippee! You're going to get into the park ahead of everybody else. All of a sudden the other lanes around you move forward, but yours has come to a halt. You think, *Oh no! Not again. Why me? Why do I always get in the wrong lane? This always happens to me. Now my whole day is ruined!* You grumble out loud a bit. What happened? You took a simple event and, by distorting it, perceived it as a horrible thing. Now you've put a negative spin on the day for yourself and those with you. The idea that it's not the worst thing to ever happen to you or that you could accept that you're going to get in eventually, thereby solving the problem, doesn't occur to you at that minute.

So what can you do? Stop believing some people have been assigned the special task of ruining your day. Believe me, there is no one that has been given the sole job of annoying you. I know it may seem that way, but sometimes stuff simply happens.

Even though I speak, write, and read everything on the topic of relieving stress I can get my hands on, I still fall into the trap of distorting my perceptions. This usually happens when I'm in a rush and haven't prepared adequately. Recently I was scheduled to give a morning presentation and was asked to arrive at eight o'clock. Now I'm not a morning person. I can manage if I have to with considerable effort, but it doesn't come naturally. I had time the night before to set out my clothing...but no, for some strange reason, I decided to get up early and do it. Well, I overslept and was running behind when I realized I couldn't find the earrings I wanted to wear. They matched my suit perfectly. You know how that is. I made the decision to wear them, and I wasn't about to change my mind.

I began my search calmly, but my jewelry drawer was quickly turning into a disaster area. With each passing moment, I exhibited more and more signs that Mount Sue was about to erupt. Earrings and bracelets and necklaces started flying everywhere as I desperately searched for the right pair. Eventually I discovered one, but the other was nowhere to be found. "I knew something like this would happen!" I shouted. "Where did it go?" Naturally I had to add, "All right, *who took* my other earring?" Have you noticed that as soon as you assign blame, the missing piece mysteriously reappears? (Buying a replacement for the lost item also works quite well in causing the original to reappear.) In the meantime, the minutes were swiftly passing by and I needed to leave the house. But I was on a mission similar to finding the Ark of the Covenant. I was determined to find that earring. Nothing else mattered—except discovering who took it. Well, the only ones living in our house are my husband and me and our cat, Daffy. So guess what? It wasn't me, and the cat had let us know a long time ago she had no interest in earrings. (That's another story.) So it had to be Cliff. It never occurred to me, in my fury, that a burly, bearded, six-foot-three man of 260 pounds would not want one pearl earring, especially since it didn't match any of his outfits.

I was finally able to laugh at the whole situation when I got a vision of my husband in coveralls, working in his garage, wearing one pearl drop earring. Honestly, sometimes I'm convinced we don't need television because we star in our own sitcoms.

> We get to decide whether an event is going to be positive or negative. We can control and shift our perspective.

When I share this story with audiences, it's incredible how many women relate. So many of us fall into this trap and upset ourselves with our view of a situation. Perceptions are usually knee-jerk reactions that seem to appear out of nowhere. They most likely come from programming we've picked up over the years.

When events, situations, and circumstances come into our lives, they are basically neutral. Most of them aren't good or bad until we assign our perception to them. Yes, we get to decide whether an event is going to be positive or negative. We can control and shift our perspective on situations that upset us by looking at the flip side. We can choose to become calmer and more resilient people.

Does this sound unreal? You might think so, but I know this is true because when two people in identical situations have opposite perceptions, they have different outcomes. One person has a little fender-bender on the way to work and cries the blues because of a dent in the car door. Another person rolls the car in the ditch several times, manages to walk away, and thanks God she's alive. It's not what happens to us so much as how we view it. Shifting our point of view allows us to see our world through a different lens.

While I was giving a keynote address at a large conference, two individuals came to talk with me at different times about what was happening at work. One woman told me she'd been let go from her position as a result of downsizing within the company. She was horror-struck and had little hope for a positive future. Later I talked with a second woman who let me know the same thing had happened to her. But she had a different view. She'd always wondered what it would be like to turn her hobby into a small business. "Now," she said with hope, "it looks like I'm going to have the chance."

Similarly, when I ran into two sisters on separate occasions, they both shared with me that their mom had suffered a stroke. The first one told me how distressed and sad she was that something so dreadful could happen. When I saw her sister, she said that the stroke had affected her mother's memory so she could no longer remember a very difficult portion of her life. As a result she seemed to be a happier person and had developed a delightful sense of humor—a trait she'd never had before. Now this sister was enjoying time with her mother more than ever. The same situation with two different views resulted in entirely different outcomes.

To remember the power of perceptions, I've come up with a little formula that helps me...and will help you...implement this principle. I call it "Sue's CPR Sanity Secret":

C + P = R
Circumstance + **P**erception = **R**esult

Why not write this on an index card and post it in plain view for 21 days? That's how long it takes to develop a habit. Many of our perceptions are habitual. While the actual circumstances of life can be upsetting, exasperating, annoying, or frightening, in reality they play only a small role in the stress we experience. It's when we combine those events with our chosen perception that our stress level is determined. While we may not be able to control many of life's circumstances and events, we can always control our perceptions. How we see a situation accounts for a large portion of our stress load.

On one business trip I was driving a rental car and noticed a document on the passenger seat I'd forgotten to fax to my next client. I happened upon a convenience store with a sign saying a fax machine was available. With only a few moments to spare, I ran in to find one store employee on duty. She was facing away from me and talking on the phone. It was obviously a personal call. I tried everything I could think of to let her know I was in a hurry and needed to be helped. As a customer I felt I deserved priority over a personal phone call. My stress level began to rise. To get her attention, I paced the floor loudly, tapped on my watch, drummed my fingertips on the countertop, and jingled the keys in my pocket.

After some time, she did put the phone down. When she turned around there were tears streaming down her face. She explained that she'd been talking to her mom who was at the hospital emergency room with her dad, who had just suffered his second heart attack. They didn't expect him to live, and she wasn't sure whether she'd make it there in time to say goodbye. In a shaky voice, she told me she'd been trying to calm her mother down.

Did my perception change after hearing her explanation? Absolutely. Suddenly I had new goals. I could stay and look after the store while she went to be with her dad and family, or we could lock up the store so I could drive her to the hospital. Everything had changed…yet nothing had changed. The circumstances of that event were the same. She was talking on the phone rather than waiting on me. I was in a hurry to get the document faxed. Only my perception was different now. I could see the situation from another's perspective and my stress was gone.

I use this technique when I'm facing a potentially stressful situation. I've discovered that I can tell myself anything I want, so I might as well say something that *defuses* my stress rather than intensifies it. This sounds like common sense, doesn't it? Yet how many of us really understand this principle? Our perceptions determine what we think about, those thoughts result in self-talk, which results in our feelings, which result in a physical biological response, which is followed by our behavior.

While some people drive through their days saying, "Thank God I'm getting to my destination safely!" others spend their driving time with jaws clenched and fingers clutching the wheel, asking, "Did these idiots get their licenses from a popcorn box?" We can blow things so out of proportion that we get as stressed-out and tense over someone leaving wet towels on the bathroom floor as we would if we were being held hostage by a carjacker. We think we're burned out from external pressures and situations. But most of our stress comes from how we label and judge what's happening. If we look at it right, stress can even be a source of fun. Remember, *stressed* spelled backward is *desserts!*

Sanity Savers & Survival Hints

- Challenge your automatic perceptions.
- Search for the opportunity or positive lesson in every problem.
- Step back and see the big picture...in the current situation and in reference to its impact to life in general. Ask, "Will this matter in one year? In five years? In eternity?"
- Detach temporarily and reframe the situation by taking a mental vacation.
- Examine deep-rooted beliefs you've held for a long time. Are they accurate? Are they positive? Do they need to be updated or changed?
- Name the most persistent obstacle in your life, and practice reframing or redefining it.
- Get outside the box by doing routine things differently—reverse the route of your daily walk or drive to work, put the toilet paper roll on the other way, fold the towels in half instead of thirds, wear your watch on the opposite wrist for a day.
- Learn something new. Start a hobby, sign up for a class, or join a sports team.
- Get out of your rut. If you've always enjoyed jazz or country music, try classical. If you always read business and professional books, choose a good novel.
- Go somewhere new. Attend the ballet or opera, go to an amusement park, or spend an afternoon at the library.
- Miracles have a habit of happening to those who expect and believe in them.
- Go to God first to unleash your fears and frustrations when stress is piling up. He will help you gain a fresh perspective.
- Through prayer you'll gain the clarity to think things through.

Take Charge of Your Thoughts

The stress cycle continues. You now know your perceptions determine how you think. What you dwell on and mull over is a direct result of the judgments you make and the impressions you form in your mind. If you don't monitor and direct them, your thoughts can make you crazy. Almost every day we blow something out of proportion and put a negative spin on an event. Our faulty reasoning can lead to what motivational speaker Zig Ziglar calls *stinkin' thinkin'*. Zig adds that what most of us need is a "check up from the neck up."

Habitual thinking is a major hidden source of stress. Incessant thought patterns are such an integral part of what goes on in our heads that we tend not to even realize we're having them. That's why it's important to "tap the phone lines" of our minds every now and then. Listening in on what we tell ourselves may surprise us. According to studies, when our thoughts are monitored on an average day, over 80 percent of what we think about is negative. Remember, that's on an average day. Can you imagine how that percentage escalates on a *bad* day?

Where does all this negativity come from? Much of it comes through the media, especially the news programs. In our home we don't read the newspaper or watch or listen to the news just before going to bed. Since our subconscious minds play over and over what we program into it before falling asleep, we try to keep our thoughts positive. Cliff and I also agree that first thing in the morning isn't a great time for negativity either. It's a nasty way to start the day. And the middle of the day isn't such a good idea either! I'm not sure when or if there's a best time to become current on the world situation. I do believe in keeping up with what's going on in the world, but we need to be selective as to when and how much information we put into our minds. Since we can't do a lot to change what we hear, how much and how often do we really need to know what's going on? What we hear on the television morning news will be replayed at noon, at six, and at eleven. Much of it will be repeated in the newspaper and on the radio. One friend of mine says if it's really important, someone will tell us. I guess that's true. However, I still watch and listen to enough news to stay in touch with what's happening in general.

❋ ❋ ❋

A strong positive mental attitude will create
more miracles than any wonder drug.
PATRICIA NEAL

To improve your ability to deal with stress through your thought life, put yourself on a "21-Day Positive Mental Attitude" diet. Decide you will *not* entertain any negative thoughts about yourself, anyone else, or anything for three weeks. Once you've accomplished this, it will be a habit, and you may find your life outlook transformed. The Bible says to "be transformed by the renewing of your mind" (Romans 12:2 NIV). You may have to cancel the newspaper and shut off the TV and radio at the beginning, but it will be worth the effort. You may also want to limit the time you spend with any "Negative Neds and Nellies" out there. You know, those anti-happy people who never seem to get ulcers...just give them. They're the ones who brighten a room each time they leave. Oscar Wilde said, "Some cause happiness *wherever* they go; others, *whenever* they go." These poor souls not only see the glass as half empty rather than half full, but they'll be quick to tell you it's chipped, they just cut their lip on it, and now they're bleeding. You love them regardless of their negativity, and you can aim to be a positive role model, set a good example, and keep them in your prayers. But be careful their negativity doesn't rub off on you or add to your stress.

Make the choice to be an optimist. That's what I've done. And not because it comes naturally to me, but because I've found out that optimists have less stress. It's also been shown that people who choose to see life through rose-colored glasses are happier, healthier, have better relationships and more friends, live longer, enjoy life to the fullest, and even earn more money. In one interesting experiment, when autopsies were performed on seniors who apparently died of old age, it was discovered that many of them had physical ailments, tumors, growths, and other diseases that should have taken their lives years earlier. When family members were asked what these people were like, they all reported that their relatives were positive, fun loving, forgiving, and always saw the good in others. They chose to notice the bright side of life. I say, "Get me some rose-colored glasses!"

Have you noticed some people just can't stand being around others who are perpetually happy? They refer to optimists as the Pollyannas of the world. They want those unrealistic thinkers to get back down to earth and realize that life is tough. While it's true that pessimists are often more realistic, optimists are usually having more fun.

❊ ❊ ❊

It's easier to go down a hill than up it,
but the view is much better at the top.
ARNOLD BENNETT

As the saying goes, "A positive attitude may not solve all your problems, but it will sure annoy enough people to make the effort worthwhile."

What Were You Thinking?

Take a few minutes to become aware of the habitual thinking you engage in that may be causing you to feel stressed. Do any of these common faulty thought patterns pop up?

- Self-criticizing—"I can't do anything right" and "I'm a terrible person."

- Obsessing—"I still can't believe I made that remark at the party last month."
- Fearing—"My boss probably asked to see me because he hated my report."
- Controlling—"Why can't everyone do things the way I do?"
- Pity party—"Poor me. I'll never be successful. Why should I even try?"
- Hysterical—"If things get any worse, I'll probably lose everything and have to live on the street with all my belongings in a garbage bag."
- Catastrophizing—"My hubby's late. He's probably injured or dead in a ditch somewhere."
- Over-analyzing—"My friend walked right past me at the meeting. She probably doesn't like me anymore."
- Over-generalizing—"Nobody cares about me." "Nothing I do ever turns out right." "I always mess up." "Things are never going to change."

I don't know about you, but I can drive myself crazy playing and replaying some of these conversations in my head. My inner critic loves to sabotage my efforts to be stress-free by causing even more pressure. I spend valuable minutes going back and forth like a tennis ball in a tennis match, mulling over who said what and how upsetting it was. It becomes an obsession, like a tune I can't get out of my head no matter how hard I try. Can you relate?

> Wherever your thoughts are going, that's where you're going.

The most important sanity secret in dealing with stressful perceptions is to challenge your habitual thinking patterns. Sometimes you have to interrupt the pattern by using "thought stoppage." Imagine quieting a child who is out of control. You might hold her firmly by the shoulders while saying, "Calm down now." When you find yourself "awfulizing" or "catastrophizing," tell yourself the same thing. Or you may simply say "Stop it!" or "That's enough!" You could also try "Cancel," like you would when pushing a button on a machine or "Delete" like hitting a key on a computer keyboard. Be firm and compelling, but also pay attention to your surroundings when you do this. When I was having a frustrating inner dialog one day while gardening in my backyard, I decided to take some vigorous action. I shouted out loud to my internal critic, "Just quit it! I've had enough of you!" I hadn't noticed the meter reader who'd entered my yard. After hearing me holler at the top of my lungs, he got scared and ran off.

Thoughts are powerful. View your thoughts as entities, as things. They *are* real. And wherever your thoughts are going, that's where you're going. Everything that happens *to* you first happens *within* you. The Bible says, "As [a woman] thinks in [her] heart, so is [she]" (Proverbs 23:7 NKJV). As within, so without. Change your thoughts; change your life.

Sanity Savers & Survival Hints

- Change from being a pessimist to an optimist by deciding not to turn a molehill into a mountain.
- Anticipate that something good can happen that will change negative things. Chances are you may not always be trapped in a particular situation, job, or lifestyle.
- Accept some things as they are—if you're short, you won't get taller; if you have to drive one hour to work, your only other option is to change jobs; if your in-laws drive you nuts when they visit or your spouse is grouchy in the morning, think of ways to cope.
- If you keep on saying things are going to be bad, this may become a self-fulfilling prophecy.
- Think about an incident when you were in the right place at the right time and what you were thinking about that made a difference.
- Contemplate all you have to be thankful for and develop an attitude of gratitude.
- Listen between the lines regarding what you're thinking about your

health, energy, relationships, finances, abilities, talents, gifts, and skills.

- "Summing it all up, friends, I'd say you'll do best by filling your minds and meditating on things true, noble, reputable, authentic, compelling, gracious—the best, not the worst; the beautiful, not the ugly; things to praise, not to curse" (Philippians 4:8).

25

Take Charge of Your Self-Talk

Whether you realize it or not, you talk to yourself all day every day, and your words are the result of what you're thinking about. So look at your words as seeds. One of God's fundamental laws says that whatever you plant, you will also reap. And you get to decide what seeds you will sow and grow. What you say to yourself about your stressful situation is always your choice. From the time you wake up in the morning, before you even get out of bed, you can say, "Good morning, Lord" or "Good Lord, it's morning." Depending on your choice, you'll experience a positive or negative outcome. Your day will then tend to get better or worse, depending on your attitude. Through your words, you can alter the course of your day and your life.

Close your eyes for a moment and think about one of your current stressors. What do you typically think about it? What are the words that come? When we're stressed we tend to use a lot of generalizations and absolutes. Do you recognize these negative automatic stress responses?

- "I can't believe this is happening to me again."
- "The cards are stacked against me.
- "I always get in the slow lane."

- "Everyone gets waited on before I do."
- "I'll never lose weight."
- "Here we go again."
- "Of course the weather is bad—it's my day off."
- "The whole world is out to get me.
- "She makes me so frustrated."
- "Why does he always act that way?"
- "I'm not surprised I've misplaced those important papers."
- "This situation is terrible, and it's only going to get worse."
- "I guess I'm just not meant to be happy."
- "I'll show them."
- "It's going to be one of those days."
- "I think I'm getting a headache."
- "I'll never get out of debt."
- "I don't get paid enough to take this nonsense."

With comments like these, you could be creating even more stress for yourself. First you "globalize" and make an event all-inclusive. Then, in your mind, it becomes permanent and everlasting. Without realizing it you can even start suffering in advance: "I'm going to the store, and the lines at the checkout aisles are probably going to be horrendous. I just know they won't have enough registers open or enough staff to serve everyone." When you arrive, your prediction comes true. You've done your advance preparation, and now you get to suffer for real. On the way home you review what happened so you can suffer all over again. You get three times the suffering for one event.

By simply changing the way you talk to yourself, it's possible to minimize the stress you experience. Before you get to the store decide that if there's a long line you'll enjoy people watching or possibly chatting with other shoppers. Then, when you arrive at the store, implement your plan. Or consider shopping at a different time of day when it's less crowded. One of the best things to remind yourself of is that if others didn't shop here, the store would be out of business and you'd have to go someplace else.

When you catch your automatic responses and counter them with rational replies, you'll be able to:

- pull yourself out of a bad mood in minutes
- become more optimistic even if you feel trapped in a situation
- react to emergencies, failures, and crises with less anxiety

Normally we think we have to fix a problem to minimize stress. Coming up with a viable solution will eventually solve the problem, but you can get *immediate* results just by changing the way you talk to yourself. Here are some steps to take.

1. Listen to the words you speak. Really pay attention, and you may be surprised. Catch yourself or ask someone you trust to listen in and provide feedback. Be open to what you hear.
2. Change unproductive words to new ones that lead you toward your desired goals. Avoid a rigid vocabulary that includes *should, have to,* and *must.* Replace these with *I choose* or *I prefer.*
3. Answer negative statements with rational responses. Rather than saying "This is terrible," ask, "Why is this upsetting?" or "What's the worst that could happen?" Instead of "I should quit my job" or "I guess I have to call my friend," ask, "What are my options?" Replace "I shouldn't spend that money on a massage" or "I can't take time to meet a friend for a coffee" with "Why not?" Rather than "I have to visit my grandmother" say "I choose to visit because I know Grandma gets lonely" or "I choose not to visit this week because of the time pressure I'm facing right now."
4. Develop the habit of regularly sowing positive "word seeds." Eventually your mind won't know the difference,

your brain accepts it as truth, and you will grow more of what you've planted.

- "I stay calm and composed in stressful situations."
- "There is no stressful situation I cannot overcome."
- "I will sail right through my hectic day."
- "I'm always at the right place at the right time."
- "My body, mind, and spirit are happy, healthy, and energetic."
- "I enjoy my life, my job, and my relationships."
- "Every day in every way life is becoming more stress free."
- "I discover new stress relievers every day."
- "For every obstacle, there is a solution or alternative."

For all the negative things we say about ourselves and our situations, God has a positive answer. Look over this list a friend sent to me:

- You say, "It's impossible." God says, "All things are possible" (Luke 18:27).
- You say, "I'm too tired." God says, "I will give you rest" (Matthew 11:28-30).
- You say, "Nobody really loves me." God says, "I love you" (John 3:16).
- You say, "I can't go on." God says, "My grace is sufficient" (2 Corinthians 12:9).
- You say, "I can't figure things out." God says, "I will direct your steps" (Proverbs 3:5-6).
- You say, "I can't do it." God says, "You can do all things" (Philippians 4:13).
- You say, "I am not able." God says, "I am able" (2 Corinthians 9:8).

- You say, "It's not worth it." God says, "It will be worth it" (Romans 8:28).
- You say, "I can't forgive myself." God says, "I forgive you" (1 John 1:9).
- You say, "I can't manage." God says, "I will supply all your needs" (Philippians 4:19).
- You say, "I'm afraid." God says, "I have not given you a spirit of fear" (2 Timothy 1:7).
- You say, "I'm always worried." God says, "Cast all your cares on me" (1 Peter 5:7).
- You say, "I feel so alone." God says, "I will never leave you or forsake you" (Hebrews 13:5).

Sanity Savers & Survival Hints

- You *always* have a choice when it comes to what you tell yourself.
- To change the way you talk to yourself, say positive, affirming statements daily.
- Negative words keep the body in a state of tension, constricting muscles and blood vessels, creating an atmosphere of disharmony and frayed nerves. Positive words create an atmosphere of peace. They calm our nerves.
- Alter your stressful vocabulary by moving beyond your habitual favorites. Instead of saying, "I feel awful," try identifying your experience specifically by stating "I'm overwhelmed...insecure...frightened... embarrassed."
- Eliminate the word *hate* from your vocabulary. This word allows your mind, body, and soul to be filled with disgust, loathing, and repulsion—not good seeds to plant.
- "Death and life are in the power of the tongue" (Proverbs 18:21 NASB).

- It takes just as much energy to say a positive word as it does a negative one.
- Research has shown that when we speak positive words, even in difficult circumstances, we become more relaxed. As we loosen up, the flow of blood to the brain increases, and we can think more creatively, make wise decisions, find innovative solutions, and generate insightful answers.
- Instead of telling yourself you can't cope, remember Joel 3:10: "Let the weak say 'I am strong'" (NKJV).

26

Sanity Secret #21

Take Charge of Your Emotions

After our perception is formed, what we think and tell ourselves about a stressful situation produces an emotional response. Regardless of the circumstance, healthy thoughts produce healthy emotions, which result in peace, joy, and an abundance of energy. When we hold unhealthy emotions inside, they will eventually squeeze the energy and happiness right out of us. Aside from that, our emotions will eventually determine our actions and behaviors. To use stress as an ally, not an enemy, it is imperative that we get a grip on our emotions.

It's easy to fall into the trap of believing our feelings have control over us rather than the other way around. I will never forget the day I had the divine revelation that I do not have to be ruled by my emotions. Instead, I can *choose* how I will respond when certain emotions rise up and threaten to take over. In the same way we can change the channel if we're watching a horror movie, we hold the remote control for our emotions. We can reroute the moods and feelings we're having by altering what we think about our situation.

When we feel overwhelmed by life's stressors and are tempted to lie around the house wearing our "Help me, Lord—I've messed up my whole life" tattered sweat suits, we need to remind ourselves that we have the ability to switch to a different station. Unless the emotions we're experiencing are caused by chronic conditions, such as clinical depression or a chemical imbalance, we can *always* take charge and decide what we will dwell on. No one else can determine our focus. What we mull over and concentrate on will determine the direction of our emotions.

At times, life is filled with sadness, frustrations, hassles, disappointments, and losses—big and small. These are inevitable. Upsetting moments invade our lives regularly: dealing with a family conflict, having a disagreement with a friend, gaining weight, paying taxes, never having enough time. Our emotional reactions to stressful events are normal human responses. It's when we give in to negative feelings or ignore them that we create extra stress. Trying to conceal our emotions can also lead to misery and despair. Dealing with our frustrations, irritations, and pain as they arise promotes health, increases energy, and frees us to live fully in the moment.

In our culture, letting our unpleasant emotions out is not always encouraged. We've all been told at some point in our lives to "just calm down" or "stop crying." Have you come to believe that it's best to curb your anger and hold back unpleasant feelings? Rather than turning harmful emotions inward, use creative, healthy ways to handle them and keep them from taking over. Here are some sanity tips to get emotions caused by stress under control.

1. *Journal your feelings.* Put pen to paper and jot down what you're experiencing. Whether you're angry with a friend, having marital problems, frustrated with a child's behavior, enduring the search for a job, or suffering some other traumatic experience, expressing your feelings relieves some of the stress and helps you cope. Observe your mood, disposition, and frame of mind calmly and objectively. Identify the specific dominant emotion: fear, anxiety, worry, dread, exasperation, bitterness, frustration, jealousy, or envy. Often we know we're upset but aren't sure exactly why until we attempt to get it in writing.

2. *Decide to stop being a worrywart.* Some of us have PhDs in worrying. Others wear worry as a badge of honor. Have you said, "If I don't worry for my family, who will?" Are you the "designated worrier" for your loved ones. Maybe you've inherited the worry gene from your mom or dad,

grandma or grandpa, and now it's become one of your jobs. The problem is that worry is like trying to travel in a rocking chair—you expend a lot of energy but you don't go anywhere. It's also like reviewing a bad movie over and over. So what can you do?

Instead of dwelling on the negative aspects of a stressful situation, make a "worry appointment" with yourself. One woman I know marks it on her calendar. She schedules 30 minutes each week so she can do all her worrying at once. That way she's not using valuable time during the week. Besides that, once the day comes, she's often not "in the mood" to worry so she puts it off another week. This is called "positive procrastination."

3. *Talk it out.* Turn your worry energy into prayer power. That's what prayer is—talking things over with God. When you do, he will give you supernatural peace that passes all understanding and inspire you with answers and valuable insights for handling your emotions. You can also share your worries with a trusted friend or trained professional. It's amazing what happens when we open up and share what's bothering us. Chances are, as you talk, you'll see your situation more clearly and come up with some viable solutions.

4. *Change your interpretations of stress-causing events.* Logically you know that fretting doesn't make anything better, but in an emotional state, you can interpret everything as the end of the earth, creating more stress, tension, and fear. Your son is a few minutes late coming home, and you become convinced he's had a terrible accident. A friend doesn't return a phone call so you're sure you've offended her. You're late paying some bills and now you see repossessors around every corner. When panic strikes, ask yourself what actions, if any, you can or should take. If the situation is something that won't matter in a year, five years, or in light of eternity, is it worth losing sleep, making yourself ill, or ruining a relationship?

5. *Get rid of "peace of mind" thieves and sanity robbers.* In today's world there are a lot of reasons to worry, but God says, "Be anxious for nothing, but in everything by prayer and supplication with thanksgiving let your

requests be made known to God" (Philippians 4:6 NASB). Much of the information we get from newspapers and TV is dreadful—murders, wars, drugs, political misconduct, car crashes, shootings. We hear staggering reports about incest, physical abuse, and sexual infidelities. It sometimes seems like everyone is a criminal and nothing good ever happens in this world. We start to believe that life will only get worse.

Horrendous things have been happening since the beginning of time and have been recorded throughout history. Remember Cain and Abel? Noah and the flood? Jonah and the whale? One big difference is in days gone by, people didn't have the added stress of knowing about everything that was happening at the moment around the globe. Today we view images of bad news the second it happens. Even the weather reports can rob us of our peace with the seemingly constant hurricanes, storms that cause flooding, and lightning-caused fires. And what about the documentaries on mad cow disease, E. coli, bacteria, dust mites, mosquito bites, and bed bugs? You may want to temporarily cancel your newspaper or turn off the TV to gain a little inner peace and sanity.

6. *Decide how long you will experience an emotion.* Whatever feelings you're experiencing, you can choose how long you will stay upset. You can say, "Yes, I am frustrated over this situation, and I will stay annoyed for two hours. Then I will get on with what has to be done to improve things." When you're outraged, you can tell yourself, "It's no wonder I feel angry after what's happened. I think I will continue to be infuriated until tomorrow at noon. Then I will let it go." If you've made a mistake, you can continue to feel bad about yourself or you can go to God, ask for and accept his forgiveness, forgive yourself, and then close the door on the past. You might have to remind yourself you're forgiven and free to move on, but chances are with a more balanced perspective you'll center on the more productive and promising aspects of your life.

7. *Give yourself permission to cry.* Tears are a natural form of emotional release. Yet in our society crying is often seen as a sign of weakness. When a stressful event makes you sad, irritated, or depressed, let the tears flow. Allow yourself the comfort of this God-given source of emotional release. From scientific research, we know there's a difference between biological

tears—the type shed when we poke ourselves in the eye with a mascara wand—and emotional tears that come when we're stressed to the limit. Emotional tears carry toxic poisons out of our bodies. Crying cleanses and purifies our bodies, keeps us free from illness, and helps restore life balance.

When you cry, allow yourself to moan and wail too. These instinctive groans can actually be a form of prayer and provide remarkable relief from emotional pain. If you recognize the need to have a good cry but find the tears won't come, use some "tear triggers"—watch a sad movie, listen to some stirring music, read a touching poem—that get your feelings and tears flowing.

8. *Plan to have more fun.* Many people tell me I look like I'm having a lot of fun on stage when I'm giving a presentation. It's true—I love to entertain audiences and get them laughing while offering powerful principles that can better their lives. To enhance personal growth and deal positively with stress, we need to tap the healing power of humor. Laughter can be a healing balm to frazzled emotions. It has mood-altering qualities and can act as a tranquilizer without the negative side effects. Rather than getting caught up in "being funny," choose to see the silly things in everyday life. It's more important to *have* fun than to be a comical person. Laugh at yourself; laugh at your situation. See the hilarious side of what's happening.

One time I thought Cliff was being too controlling. Out of exasperation I called him a "control freak." Later on he felt I was trying to take control of a situation and decided he'd return the comment. Instead, he misspoke and called me a "controlling freak"! Now I don't know about you, but I think there's a big difference between being a control freak and being a "controlling freak." When I pointed out the difference, we laughed so hard we almost fell over. Now anytime we want to break a tense mood, one of us shouts out "controlling freak" and we collapse into each other's arms with laughter.

While negative emotions aren't wrong in and of themselves, and may be quite understandable given the particular circumstance, they negatively affect our health, peace of mind, and relationships when not handled properly. When our feelings govern our actions, we run the risk of having unresolved emotions surface when we least expect them. This can result in sarcasm, cynicism, and accusatory comments to family or friends. Whether it's jealousy; guilt; shame; or the hormonal crazies that come with PMS, pregnancy, or menopause, we may not always be able to fully control our emotions the way we'd like. But God created us this way, intense emotions and all, and he wants to use our deepest passions and authentic feelings in ways that bring him glory. Trust your Creator, for he "has not given us a spirit of fear, but of power and of love and of a sound mind" (2 Timothy 1:7 NKJV).

Sanity Savers & Survival Hints

I only have two emotional flare-ups each year.
The only problem is they each last six months!
AUTHOR UNKNOWN

- Look for the positive lessons. Ask, "What did I learn? What will I do differently next time?" Then close the door to the past and don't look back.
- See the big picture to regain your perspective. Too often we get tunnel vision and see only the problem facing us. Step back, notice all the blessings that surround you, and practice being grateful.
- "Don't fret or worry. Instead of worrying, pray" (Philippians 4:6).
- For fun, blow a stressful situation ridiculously out of proportion in your mind. Imagine the worst scenario possible, have a laugh, and then bring it back into proper perspective.
- Resist the urge to assign blame. Accept 100 percent of the responsibility for what you are experiencing. Blaming others robs you of the power to make changes for your well-being.
- Remember the ten most powerful two-letter words strung together: "If it is to be, it is up to me."

- "People are always blaming circumstances. I don't believe in circumstances. The people who get on in this life go out and find the circumstances they want, and if they can't find them, they make them" (George Bernard Shaw).
- Consider the price you're paying when harmful emotions take their toll—sleeplessness, being prone to illness, ruined relationships, and wrinkles.
- "Do not let the sun go down while you are still angry" (Ephesians 4:26 NIV).

27 Sanity Secret #22

Get Moving!

When the stress alarm sounds our adrenalin rises, the stomach "sinks," muscles tense, the heartbeat races, and the entire body, including emotions, primes itself to be alert and ready to act. This reaction to stress is known as the *fight-or-flight* response mechanism, which our bodies use to respond to impending danger. A series of biochemical changes prepares us to deal with ominous hazards. In days gone by, when people were threatened they either went into battle with the enemy or headed toward safety. In either case, energy would increase and built-up tension would be released to facilitate the appropriate action.

This was a great idea about a million years ago. People had to defend themselves against a herd of woolly mammoths or an enemy tribe attacking their camp. The fight-or-flight response was essential—people couldn't survive without it. They needed that burst of energy to get moving.

Let's say you are in your car on a freeway. You're irritated so you're honking your horn and flashing your lights at the "enemy," an 81-year-old man who is driving too slowly in the passing lane when you're running late for an appointment. Or maybe you're at the supermarket fuming at a customer with 11 items in the 8-item register line or you're angry with management for having only 3 of 12 checkout lanes open at the busiest time of day.

Your heart rate and blood pressure go up. Your hearing becomes more acute and your eyes narrow to see into the distance more clearly. Your hands and feet get cold as blood is directed away from your extremities into the larger muscles that will help you charge into battle or flee from danger. Since your body doesn't know whether you're in the jungle, on the highway, or at the supermarket, it responds to what it thinks is life-threatening danger.

During these moments common sense, rational thoughts, and self-control can give way to exasperation, reckless anger, and impulsive behavior. Often unwarranted haste in these situations can cause great harm. The subsequent build-up of tension and pressure—physical, mental, and emotional—may feel unbearable if action doesn't follow. Biological changes that take place when the body is preparing to fight a dangerous enemy or flee from a perilous situation can cause prolonged effects, robbing us of peace and physical vitality. Let's explore how exercise helps boost and harness our energy.

Exercise Your Stress Away

Even a little exercise goes a long way. It doesn't take much to release pent-up tension and recharge our battery. Whether we get away from a stressful situation to do some running or sneak in a few jumping jacks, we'll feel the stress draining from our bodies. The problem is that some of us are like my friend who says every time she gets the urge to exercise, she lies down until the feeling goes away. She says whenever she uses the word *exercise* she has to wash her mouth out with chocolate. Maybe you can relate.

Studies reveal that only a small percentage of us are getting enough exercise to achieve cardiac fitness, build strong muscles, and maintain healthy body weight. Yet we all know how our lives would suffer if our bodies suddenly failed to do what they were created to do.

Our levels of health, energy, and overall well-being directly influence our mood, memory, ambition, thinking capacity, and ability to perform everyday functions. No one has to tell us how important exercise is to keeping our minds fit and our bodies strong and vibrant. Ever since we were kids at the playground, we've known intrinsically that exercise is good for us. Aside from keeping us physically fit, it removes stress from our bodies. Today the impact of exercise is all over the news, and store shelves are full of books and magazines heralding the benefits. We know that even if we've never exercised, we can improve our health immediately by starting now. Here's some good news—the more out of shape you are, the quicker you'll see results.

Despite all this talk of exercise, there's one thing we desire more than anything that's robbing us of the opportunity to exercise naturally: comfort. For the sake of ease, we have drive-through windows at coffee shops, restaurants, banks, and dry cleaners. For our convenience, there's valet parking at hotels and moving sidewalks at airports. With very little effort, we can pick up the phone, order any variety of food we want, and our meals are delivered right to our doorsteps. All we have to do is haul ourselves off the sofa and drag our stressed-out bodies to the door to enjoy what we crave, and what we crave is likely brimming with fat and filled with calories. (I don't know about you, but when I'm stressed, I rarely crave a raw veggie platter.)

With our desire for ease, comfort, and convenience, not only is exercise very unappealing, but we've made it complex and involved when it doesn't need to be. All we really have to do to improve our health is get moving. Let's face it—we don't have to analyze this too much to know that moving is better than not moving and sweating is better than not sweating. It's really a simple process: Move. Breathe. Keep moving and breathing. Break a sweat. Get our heart rates up. Do it some more. That's it.

If all the fuss around exercising stresses you out—finding exactly the right facility, choosing a personal trainer, comparing yourself to "perfect specimens" with chiseled bodies in form-fitting workout gear, feeling life is unfair, counting the seconds until exercise time is over—then get back to basics. If you don't happen to exercise and get fit the way exercise gurus and people who want to sell their fitness products do, it's not the end of the world.

I finally made the decision to join a local gym. I paid my money and bought some nice workout clothes and suitable shoes. Then somebody told me I actually had to *go there* for the process to work. Since then there's one thing I've learned about exercise: Keep it simple. These days I love working out at the gym, but the routine I've worked out for myself is very basic and suits my needs. If you're spending more time and money picking out the right fitness outfit and workout shoes than you are in getting fit, you might want to take a step back and remind yourself why you're doing this in the first place.

The gym may work for you, but whether it does or not, why not get outside with a broom and clean the front walkway or grab a shovel or hoe and do some yard work? Whether you're raking leaves, weeding, planting, or sweeping, you'll be using muscles you don't normally use. Give your heart a workout by purposely making extra trips up and down stairs to get organized and put things where they belong. Park further away at work, church, and the shopping mall. Once inside, take the stairs instead of the escalator or elevator. At home you can jump rope or bounce on a trampoline. Put on some music in the living room, close the drapes, get undressed, and dance to your heart's content. (When I do this, you don't want to be standing too close. There are body parts flapping all over the place. It's not a pretty sight. But oh, what a feeling of total abandon!)

Make a point of getting out into nature (once you're dressed!), where you'll find God has provided ready-made opportunities to exercise. Rather than spending 45 minutes on a treadmill at level 23, how about an afternoon of hiking on a wooded trail or a brisk walk around a park? Instead of a one-hour session on a rowing machine, why not go canoeing or kayaking with a friend on a tranquil lake? What's better for your body, mind, and soul—packing your body into spandex and Lycra workout stretch wear for an aerobics class and a trip around an air-conditioned circuit at a gym or putting on some comfy shorts and a T-shirt to play a game of badminton with some friends in the backyard? (The latter is my first choice, and since my friends and I are such dreadful players, one badminton game gives us more of a workout than we could get in two weeks at the gym.)

> Fitness is caring for your one-and-only body in a way that promotes health, energy, and longevity.

Whatever you do—join a gym, commit to an exercise class, invest in a video to work out with at home, mall walk, or skip rope on the patio—give yourself credit if you're doing more than you used to do. Maybe you're doing just the right amount for *you*. Your body requires movement, and you'll intrinsically know how much is right for the condition you're in. Moving even a little is better than not moving at all.

Making fitness a priority isn't all about looking great, although that's a nice fringe benefit. Fitness is caring for your one-and-only body in a way that promotes health, energy, and longevity. Fitness also builds stamina and endurance. When you're fit, your body bounces back more readily from minor or major illnesses and injuries, you can handle getting less sleep for short periods, you're more able to cope with the inevitable setbacks and stumbling blocks of life, and you'll feel better about yourself.

✻ ✻ ✻

Glorify God in your body.
1 CORINTHIANS 6:20 NASB

Here are more exercise benefits.

39 Good Reasons to Get Fit

Exercising regularly...

- gives you more energy and builds resilience.
- increases your metabolic rate.
- burns up extra calories.
- triggers a desire for healthy food.
- improves your body shape and provides muscle definition.
- increases enzymes in the body that burn fat.
- helps you reach and maintain your ideal body weight.
- relieves depression.
- lifts your spirits.
- improves the quality of your sleep.
- promotes clarity of mind.
- strengthens your heart and lungs.
- improves circulation.
- bolsters your immune system.
- improves your self-image, self-esteem, and self-confidence.

- helps alleviate varicose veins.
- increases flexibility, making you more limber and agile.
- increases strong muscle tissue.
- builds strong bones.
- improves posture.
- eases menstrual cramps.
- reduces risk of developing chronic diseases (osteoporosis, high blood pressure, heart disease).
- promotes endurance.
- tones and firms muscles.
- eases back problems.
- develops coordination and balance.
- reduces symptoms of PMS and menopause.
- slows the aging process.
- improves quality of life.
- improves productivity.
- releases stress and tension.
- stimulates the release of hormones that alleviate pain.
- improves athletic performance.
- enhances sexual enjoyment.
- increases your feeling of well-being.
- offers opportunities to socialize and make new friends.
- encourages the acceptance of responsibility for health and wellness.
- makes you feel better about life.
- helps you live longer.

Now go back over the list and put a check mark beside those reasons that will help motivate you to start or continue exercising. Remember, your exercise routine doesn't have to be costly or elaborate. You don't need a pricey, fashionable wardrobe, membership at a club, or state-of-the-art equipment. It's possible to get moving anywhere, anytime.

12 Creative Ways to Fit Exercise into Your Life

- Rather than going out for coffee or lunch to chat with a friend, go for a brisk walk as you visit.
- While driving, tighten and release your buttocks, thighs, and tummy muscles.
- Do leg lifts or crunches while dinner is cooking or when you're watching TV.
- If you visit a playground with your children or grandkids, take advantage of the equipment to get fit. Spinning a child on the merry-go-round firms up your arms, strengthens your legs, and revs up your heart. Tone your arms by pushing a child on a swing.
- Choose far-off parking spots and walk to the mall or office.
- Take stairs instead of an elevator.
- Work your biceps with a 3- or 5-pound weight while you chat on the phone or watch TV.
- Wash your car at home.
- Walk around the waiting room or in the hall while waiting for appointments.
- Go roller skating, ice skating, or sledding with your kids. Play a game of tag.
- Do housework at a more vigorous pace and wear ankle weights.
- Schedule active fun for the weekend: swimming, dancing, skating, bowling, tennis, hiking.
- Join a swimming or water aerobics program for all the benefits without damaging your joints. (In chest-high water, you weigh a third of what you weigh on land.)

- Go to the mall and walk around the entire interior before or after you do your shopping. Sign up for a mall walking program.
- Work out on a stationary bike or treadmill and enjoy reading, leafing through a magazine, watching a movie, or listening to your favorite music.

12 Exercise Procrastination Beaters

Here are some tips for getting unstuck, overcoming procrastination, and sticking with exercise goals.

- Exercise at home—you'll save travel time and avoid using transportation or bad weather as "I can't get to the gym" excuses.
- If you work out at a gym, quit berating yourself for missing a day and just get back to exercising as soon as you can.
- If you work out alone, put on lively music.
- Vary your exercise routine to avoid boredom: walking, water aerobics program, strength training. Make at least minor changes every few weeks.
- Keep a journal to record the days you exercised, what you did, and how you felt.
- Whether you exercise at home or belong to a gym, think of your fitness program as a system for becoming healthy, improving the quality of your life, and increasing longevity. Don't focus on appearance or weight loss.
- Put your bathroom scale away and rate your fitness level by how you feel and how your clothes fit.
- Work into an exercise program gradually rather than jumping into a strenuous routine. Overdoing it in the beginning causes injuries such as stiff, sore, or pulled muscles that may cause you to get discouraged and quit.

- Develop the habit of confident expectation. Positive thinking does wonders.
- Be an encourager to yourself and others. Say, "Good job today!" or "You can do this!"
- Give yourself credit for starting the process of becoming healthy. Come up with innovative ways to reward yourself for each exercise period you keep (choose something other than food).
- Remember, the more out of shape you are, the quicker you'll see results.

Exercises to Avoid

Some exercises aren't that great for you. Avoid these if at all possible.

- wade through paperwork
- run around in circles
- add fuel to the fire
- climb the walls
- drag your heels
- jump to conclusions
- grasp at straws
- throw your weight around

Sanity Savers & Survival Hints

Train yourself to be godly.
For physical training is of some value,
but godliness has value for all things,
holding promise for both the present life and the life to come.
1 Timothy 4:7-8 NIV

- Have a physical check-up. If you've been inactive for a long time, are overweight, or have chronic health problems, see your doctor for a medical exam before exercising.
- Choose activities that are fun, not exhausting. You don't want exercise to be boring or routine. Develop a variety of activities that you can enjoy and choose from.
- Wear comfortable, properly fitted footwear and comfortable, loose-fitting clothing appropriate for the weather and the activity.
- Pick a convenient time and place.
- Make exercise a habit, but be flexible. If you miss an exercise opportunity, work activity into your day another way.
- Discover your driving force. Use motivational tapes, audiobooks, music, or the buddy system to keep you inspired and enthusiastic.
- Surround yourself with supportive people. Decide what kind of support you need. Would you appreciate someone who will remind you to exercise? Ask about your progress? Participate with you? Allow you time to exercise by yourself? Go with you to a special event, such as a 10k walk or run? Be understanding when you get up early? Spend time with the children while you exercise?
- Share your activity time with others. Make a fitness date with a family member, friend, or coworker. You can be positive role models for each other.
- Don't overdo it. Do low- to moderate-level activities, especially at first. Slowly increase the duration and intensity of your activities as you become more fit. Over time, work up to exercising on most days of the week for 30 to 60 minutes.
- Keep a record of your activities and progress. Reward yourself at special milestones. Nothing motivates like success!

Eat Your Stress Away

At a time when I was overstressed and close to burnout from a hectic work schedule, I literally wanted to eat my stress away. I thought a balanced diet was a cookie in each hand. When I realized my health—mentally, emotionally, physically, and spiritually—was suffering, I prayed and asked for guidance. Almost immediately God began showing me some things about my eating habits that may seem insignificant but made a huge difference when dealing with tension and pressure.

The first thing I learned was that the human body is an energy system that functions with efficient food fuel. That means we'll only be as healthy and stress free as the food we eat. So now when I attend a business luncheon or eat in restaurants or hotels, I forgo the cream soups, heavy sauces, gravies, rolls with butter, fried foods, and desserts in favor of broiled fish or chicken, steamed vegetables, and a salad dressed with olive oil and freshly squeezed lemon juice. For breakfast I enjoy half a grapefruit and a bowl of whole-grain cereal with skim milk or a boiled egg with a slice of multigrain toast with unsweetened fruit spread or almond butter and a cup of herbal tea in place of fried eggs, bacon, and coffee.

There are always those days when work is grueling or life seems unbearable so I treat myself to a big platter of pasta with sauce, or a veggie and cheese pizza, or maybe even a big piece of apple pie with ice cream. But these days that is the exception, not the rule.

What we put into our bodies affects our emotions, moods, memory, ability to think clearly, energy levels, stamina, endurance, general health, and longevity. According to current medical information, many of the degenerative diseases that plague modern societies—high blood pressure, heart problems, stroke, and certain cancers—are predominantly the result of inadequate diet. The message is simple: To be well, eat well. An ancient proverb states that "a fool lives to eat" whereas a "wise man eats to live."

The best way to take care of our bodies and make them stress-resistant is also the simplest: *Eat food as close to its natural state as possible.* Eat food the way it is grown, with nothing added and nothing removed. Doesn't that make perfect sense? Sugar-coated cereals with pink and purple marshmallows don't grow in gardens. Drinks corrupted by artificial sweeteners, chemicals, and syrups don't flow in streams. The fields are not full of instant rice or fast-cooking oats. This should tell us something about the way we're fueling our bodies. I'm saddened when I see what goes into some people's shopping carts. It's alarming that so many of us have accepted the modern marketing concept that it's better to bury our broccoli in cheese sauce from a packaged mix.

We've accepted this way of eating to such an extent that many of us no longer appreciate the taste of *real* food. We've become accustomed to concoctions that have been artificially enhanced with color and flavor—as though the real things don't have enough of those properties on their own. If you want to see the difference between real and artificial food ingredients, watch children. They are good gauges of this current eating pattern. When kids have been raised on processed food, it's nearly impossible to get them to accept the real thing.

❋ ❋ ❋

Unless we are incarcerated in a prison or hospital,
where we are forced to take what we can get,
we can choose our nourishment.
We can eat simple fresh food, or
we can eat store-bought fabrications.

Helen Nearing
Simple Food for the Good Life

Some of the foods we need to increase in our daily diet are whole grains, nuts, seeds, and legumes. We also need to boost our intake of high-water-content foods. There are only two groups of foods that fall into this category: fruits and vegetables. (A man in one of my stress seminars guessed soup and beer. Wishful thinking, I imagine.) Since our bodies are predominantly made up of water, and we lose so much of it during the day, we need to replenish it regularly. Eating fruits and vegetables, preferably fresh and raw, is one excellent way to get more water into our systems. The water from the food helps transport nutrients to various parts of the body as well as flush out toxins.

Stock your refrigerator with blueberries, strawberries, raspberries, melons, apples, pears, and oranges. Keep ziplock bags full of washed and cut-up broccoli, cauliflower, bell peppers, carrots, celery, and cucumbers. Enjoy them with low-fat dip if you like. Doing this lets you always have an array of sensual delights waiting when you have a craving or want to nibble. Enjoy fresh fruit or a fruit smoothie for breakfast and snacks, a big salad for lunch, and another for supper, along with steamed vegetables on the side, and you'll get your proper intake of nutrients and water. Sprinkle your asparagus, carrots, brussels sprouts, and other vegetables with a few basic herbs or garlic powder and a drizzle of olive oil instead of adding butter and salt. If your family won't go near vegetables, or if you're not fond of them yourself, you can sneak a few in here and there:

- Grate carrots and add to tuna or chicken salad before stuffing in a pita pocket.
- Add a medley of mixed chopped vegetables to your favorite meatball or meatloaf recipes.
- Blend chopped, cooked vegetables into your marinara sauce and serve over pasta.
- Make homemade pizza and toss on chopped broccoli, green beans, or mushrooms before spreading on the cheese.
- Make vegetable lasagna with spinach in the sauce or add chopped and cooked zucchini, broccoli, or cauliflower between the layers.

- Bake your own low-fat muffins and add grated zucchini or carrots.
- Puree cooked carrots and squash and add small amounts to ground beef, chicken, or turkey before shaping into burgers to cook on the grill.
- Serve "make your own" tacos and have different stations for adding diced tomatoes, shredded lettuce, grated carrots, chopped green onions, and cheese.
- Make chicken–vegetable kabobs by alternating chunks of grilled chicken, mushrooms, peppers, tomatoes, onions, and zucchini on skewers. Have a variety of sauces available for dipping, such as sweet-and-sour sauce or low-fat dressings.
- Top a baked potato with chopped broccoli and melted low-fat cheese.
- Get out your wok and have your kids assist with washing and cutting up the vegetables for a stir-fry. Add chicken, beef, or seafood, and pour it over rice or linguini. Serve with chopsticks of course.
- Blend pureed spinach with low-fat plain yogurt or sour cream to make a dip for raw veggies and whole grain crackers.

Even if eating vegetables hasn't been the first choice for you and your family, it's possible to reprogram your taste buds to prefer these simple, basic, nutrition-laden foods.

❊ ❊ ❊

Until I was twelve, I thought spaghetti came from a can,
and that vegetables grew in the freezer.
When I discovered that green beans grew
in the ground, I thought it was a miracle.

Mollie Katzen
Moosewood Cookbook

Aside from eating fruits and vegetables for the water content, we need to drink more water. Once I learned to appreciate basic, simple foods, my tastes also changed regarding drinks. In order to get eight glasses of water per day, I carry around a big bottle of water to quench my thirst. I don't even crave soda pop anymore. Why would I want to fill my body with caramel coloring, sugar or artificial sweeteners, and chemicals when water is fresh, free, and tastes much better? To keep track of my water intake, I place a stack of eight pennies on my desk or countertop and move them over one at a time to another pile each time I drink eight ounces. It becomes a challenge to see how soon I can transfer the whole stack. Eventually the amount of water you need will be dictated by your thirst. When you begin to replace regular tea, coffee, and soft drinks with water and herbal teas, your natural thirst will return. If you still crave the feeling of bubbly carbonation when you're thirsty, switch to a mixture of fruit juice and club soda or sparkling mineral water with a wedge of lemon or lime. It won't be long before you'll be wondering how you ever handled the sugary sweetness and chemical flavors of sodas.

Pulling Your Sweet Tooth

Sugar in any form can make you crazy. It's also highly addictive and one of the main culprits of low energy, exhaustion, and the inability to deal with stress. When you eat sugar, you have an instantaneous surge of energy throughout your body, but too much overworks the adrenal glands, leaving you feeling irritable and exhausted. Sugar robs your body of the important nutrients you need to handle stressful events. When this happens, you don't cope well under pressure. You can experience violent moods swings, feel nervous and cranky, and sleep poorly. You may also become prone to headaches, illnesses, and feel lethargic. For a quick pick-me-up, you'll usually opt for more sugar-laden goodies, which send your sugar levels sky high. Because the pancreas responds to a sugar surge by secreting insulin, which processes sugar, your blood-sugar level then plummets far below where it was initially. The result is that you come crashing down and can suffer extreme fatigue, moodiness, and varying degrees of depression. Then what do you crave to pick you up? More sugar! And the intense cycle of violent ups and downs continues.

To break the cycle, keep your sugar levels on an even keel. Snack on good foods between meals, those that are high in B vitamins—complex carbohydrates such as whole grains and fresh vegetables. Fruit is good since it has natural sugar that satisfies your cravings, especially if you combine it with solid proteins and starch foods such as cheese, nuts, peanut butter on crackers or bread, and hard-boiled eggs. Exercise also acts as a sugar stabilizer and controls the chemical crazies produced by blood-sugar swings.

Stock your shelves with nourishing snacks such as popcorn, yogurt, graham cracker wafers, multigrain crackers, salt-free pretzels, nuts, seeds, and fresh fruits and vegetables.

You may want to clean your house of all sugary snacks. Cut back on your use of white and brown sugars, corn syrup, maple syrup, molasses, and even the natural sugar of honey. Read food labels. Sugar is one of the most common additives and can be found in the most unlikely places—soup, ketchup, mayonnaise, relish, salad dressings, boxed cereals, canned food, pickles, and even toothpaste.

Stock your shelves with nourishing snacks such as popcorn, yogurt, graham cracker wafers, multigrain crackers, salt-free pretzels, nuts, seeds, fresh fruits, and vegetables. I've found that depriving myself totally of sugar is too extreme, so I have dessert once a week and an occasional taste of quality chocolate. Unless you're diabetic or hypoglycemic, a little sugar won't be life threatening and makes life more enjoyable.

If your diet consists mainly of sweets; fast foods; and packaged, frozen, or other processed meals, your body will still crave real food. If your stomach is filled with a mumbo jumbo of chemicals, preservatives, and artificial coloring and flavorings, you'll walk away unsatisfied. You may even feel as though you're starving…and you might be. When this happens, it isn't food you're craving—it's nutrition. As long as you starve your body of the nutrients it requires to function properly, you will continue to feel hungry. Once you decide to switch to natural, nutrient-filled foods, the cravings and hunger pangs will stop. It may take some time to adjust to the flavors of real foods since your taste buds have become accustomed to sugar, chemicals, and additives.

Nutrients that Make a Difference

Ideally we would get nutrients we need in their original form—food. These days it isn't always possible to eat a well-balanced diet for a number of reasons, so supplements provide energy and stress supports. Not only are we on the run with little time to plan and prepare healthy meals, but nearly everything we eat has been altered from its original state by the time we eat it. Either it's been processed before it gets to the store or we adjust it ourselves by our cooking methods. In some cases the earth where food is grown is depleted of its nutritional value. Other times fruits and vegetables are picked green and left to ripen in a truck. Air and water pollution, drugs and alcohol consumption, radiation emitted by modern-day conveniences, and emotional stress and illness deplete our bodies of nutrients. I recommend you do some research about which nutrients you would like to add to your diet. Here is a partial list of supplements.

Vitamin C: It assists every process in the body including the immune system, the healing of wounds and burns, and relief of cold symptoms. Best of all, it's responsible for producing collagen, which is the glue that holds us together. It helps us look better. Food sources include fresh citrus fruits and dark green vegetables.

B complex: This is most critical to the nervous system and our ability to fight the effects of stress. In our house we call our B vitamins "happy pills." Food sources include fish—especially tuna and salmon—dark green vegetables, root vegetables, oats, whole grains, and wheat products.

Vitamin E: This keeps us youthful and provides the best protection against heart disease. I say the "E" stands for energy and endurance, which has been proven with athletes and animals. Food sources include brown rice, wheat germ, vegetable oils, eggs, nuts, and organ meats.

Calcium: This nutrient is essential for ache-free joints and healthy bones, nerves, and muscles. In fact, our bodies will eat their own bones to survive if there isn't enough calcium supplied in our diet. It's also been referred to as "nature's tranquilizer" because it calms the nerves. Food sources include yogurt and other dairy products, apples, cabbage, soy products, and seafood.

Lecithin: This nutrient contains choline, which makes us more physically and mentally alert and is used in the treatment of diseases affecting memory. It's also an important component of the myelin sheath, a covering that shelters our nerves and plays a role in our ability to deal with stress. Food sources include soybeans, corn, and egg yolk.

Garlic: Nature's antibiotic, garlic inhibits the bacteria responsible for staph and strep infections and disease-related yeast.

Alfalfa: Alfalfa sprouts provide protein in its most complete and digestible form and promote strength and endurance.

Zinc: Used by more body parts than any other nutrient, zinc plays a role in healthy hair, strong nails, a clear complexion, disease resistance, emotional control, and vitality. Food sources include liver, seafood, spinach, gingerroot, mushrooms, and some varieties of nuts.

Aside from these nutrients, herbal remedies are another way to calm your nerves and achieve abundant vitality. Herbs have been used for centuries and are often referred to in the Bible: "I have given you all things, even as the green herbs" (Genesis 9:3 NKJV). Some herbs you may want to consider and investigate are:

Ginseng, which helps to handle mental stress and has been called the harmony herb

Chamomile, which acts as a muscle relaxant and nerve soother, making it an ideal bedtime drink

Lavender, which relieves physical fatigue and emotional stress

Peppermint, which is a wonderful tonic that alleviates an upset stomach or indigestion after a meal

I encourage you to do your own studying to find out which herbs and nutritional supplements you'd like to add to your diet. Since we're all different, you need to decide what is best for you.

Your body has been miraculously created to be self-cleansing, self-healing, and self-renewing. With some simple changes in the way you fuel and look after your body, you can enhance or restore its abilities to energize and repair itself. On the whole, with a few basic alterations in your eating patterns, you should notice results almost immediately.

Quick Tips for Eating Healthy

- Check with your doctor before beginning any vitamin, mineral, or herbal therapy.
- What you eat can promote or relieve stress and help or hinder your body in how it handles the physical stress response.
- For a quick, calming effect, eat foods low in fats and high in complex carbohydrates. Choose from cooked whole grains (wheat, oatmeal, buckwheat, barley); low-fat pasta salad with vegetables; or high-grain, low-fat breads such as bagels or pitas.
- To stay stress resistant, cut back on the three white killers: salt, sugar, and white flour.
- Caffeine is highly addictive and is known to destroy vitamin B, which is necessary in coping with stress. Replace coffee, regular tea, cocoa, and cola drinks with water, juice, and herbal teas, such as peppermint, chamomile, and fruit varieties. Try valerian root, which acts as a natural sedative with no groggy side effects.
- If you opt for decaffeinated coffee, choose a water-processed brand to avoid the chemicals used in other methods of removing caffeine.
- Read labels and be alert for artificial additives.
- Avoid fats found in pastries, sauces, gravies, and cream soups. They clog your arteries, steal your energy, and make you sluggish.
- Stress makes the digestive system work erratically and overtime, increasing churning in the stomach, so you may want to avoid highly spiced or greasy foods.
- Replace the nutrients that stress depletes, especially vitamins B and C.

Get a Good Night's Rest

When we're stressed-out, it's inevitable: Sleep becomes difficult and the customary, time-honored tactics to bring about slumber fail. The problem is that the harder we try to fall asleep, the more our brains seem to come alive (although they do a good job of remaining inactive whenever we need to remember the name of our child's teacher or where we put our passports!).

For a while I was having a difficult time sleeping. Between counting sheep, I would lie awake fretting about the harmful effects of long-term insomnia. Research backed up my concern. Scientists have discovered that laboratory rodents, when robbed of sleep for extended periods of time, have difficulty performing tasks such as finding their way through a labyrinth, running on a wheel, or operating equipment. Studies also show that being sleep deprived can contribute to weight gain, especially if you're indulging in midnight snacks such as caramel crunch cheesecake, butter pecan ice cream, chocolate chip cookie dough, or double-decker sandwiches.

While we're lying in bed waiting for sleep to come, we often end up having an internal discussion something like this: *I wonder if I'm going to get back to sleep. I'll be so tired if I don't. If I fall asleep right now, this very minute, I will still get three-and-a-half hours of rest.* If our bodies won't be lulled into sleep, we start commanding. "Okay! Lights are out. It's time to sleep." Minutes later an inner voice tells us that now would be a good time to worry about our finances, and other things we can't do anything about in the middle of the night. By now we've noticed that our bodies are tense and our necks and shoulders are tight. Knotted muscles and stored stress become second nature with this sleepless trend.

* * *

The hand that rocks the cradle is usually attached to someone who isn't getting enough sleep.

Insomnia is a *symptom*. It's not a disease or an illness. It almost always points to something else. There are a number of reasons we can't sleep. I'm going to leave formal diagnoses to the medical profession, but one source of sleeplessness is the disruption of our natural body rhythm.

Our "circadian rhythms" are patterns in our bodies that affect hormone production, blood pressure, sleep cycles, and other functions every 24 hours. When we interfere with our circadian rhythms by cheating ourselves of adequate breaks, relaxation retreats, natural sunshine, social gatherings, and proper nutrition through healthy meals, insomnia may result. Furthermore, due to the invention of artificial lighting, our inner body clocks are often confused and don't function properly.

Although we still might not know the root cause, we do know that sleep disorders are on the rise. There are so many of them we could count them instead of sheep. Their symptoms run the gamut from inconvenience to bizarre occurrences, from mildly disturbing to unbearable. Check out this list of allegedly real-life sleep experiences I received via email.

- A woman who drew a map of United States on her bedroom wall and filled in the capitals—all while she slept.
- A man in the back of a moving trailer who sleepwalked out the door and was killed on the highway.
- A sleeping woman who drove to the airport, bought a plane ticket, and flew halfway to California before waking up.

- An air traffic controller whose only way to keep from falling asleep while working was to stand up on the job.
- A sleeping woman who awoke to find herself in a grocery store aisle pushing a cart filled with 50 boxes of cereal.
- A woman who gained 40 pounds eating chocolates while she slept.

While some of these appear humorous (I'm seriously considering trying to get away with the last innovative weight-gain explanation), others are horrendous. People with sleep disorders really do suffer...as well as some of those around them. Imagine being a passenger in a jet plane while a sleepy pilot drifts off just before landing. Or being in a car on the highway when another driver falls asleep at the wheel. One husband reported being in bed with his sleeping wife while she kicked, punched, screamed, and thrashed hundreds of times a night.

While sleeping disorders are serious and have potentially severe consequences, the most common of all sleep ailments is insomnia. Sleeplessness is no fun. Whenever I find myself lying there, suddenly wide awake in the middle of the night, I usually make a terrible mistake. I look at the clock. Then the harder I try to convince myself to drift off again, the more sleep eludes me. Although I fight the urge, I keep peeking at the clock in much the same way I watch a scary movie—through partially open fingers. The desperation becomes more intense as the minutes and hours quickly tick by. Instead of falling back to sleep, I become so agitated and annoyed that I'd have to be hit over the head to fall asleep. It isn't long before deal-making starts. "Okay, I don't really have to wash my hair in the morning. I can always wear the same outfit as yesterday. I'll skip breakfast and grab a coffee on the way. I might have to drive faster to get there on time." It's just no fun feeling totally exhausted in body, mind, and soul...yet being unable to fall asleep.

According to sleep experts, we need to spend at least one third of our lives sleeping. That's eight hours per night if you want to be fully alert, in a good mood, creative, and energetic all day. Over an average lifetime, that adds up to 24 years in bed. The time you spend sleeping has a profound effect on the other two-thirds of your life in terms of clear thinking, reaction time, memory, productivity, performance, weight, mood, energy, alertness, creativity, communication skills, good health, safety, and enjoyment of life. The consequences of sleeplessness include increased accident rates, health problems, and a reduction in the quality of life. You could be walking around sleep deprived and not even be aware of how ineffective you've become.

People who get the proper amount of sleep live longer, age less quickly, and have healthier immune systems.

Yet in today's frenzied culture sleeplessness has become the rage...almost fashionable. People who say they need only four or five hours of sleep are perceived as being ambitious and hardworking. It's like wearing a badge of honor. If we admit to needing lots of sleep, we run the risk of being seen as people who lack what it takes to be successful. We might even be seen as lazy.

Studies show that people who get the proper amount of sleep live longer, age less quickly, and have healthier immune systems. A good night's sleep also affects your outlook and frame of mind because it's during sleep that your brain replenishes its supply of neurotransmitters (the chemicals that regulate mood). When our sleep is reduced, our potential is diminished and our health suffers. When we are rested, our metabolism is more efficient, we burn more calories, and we have a better chance of losing or maintaining weight. Long-term memory also improves, and we can master new skills more quickly.

Are you having trouble sleeping? You're in good company. On any given night, millions have trouble getting to sleep or staying asleep. Do any of these sound familiar?

- You dread going to bed at night because you know you'll toss and turn.
- The spouse who snores loudest always falls asleep first.
- You have difficulty falling asleep and then wake up an hour later once you do.
- You wake up many times during the night.
- You wake up earlier in the morning than you planned even though you're still tired.

- You feel like you need to take naps during the day.
- You wake up in the middle of meetings.
- You fall asleep while reading or watching TV.
- You snooze while waiting for a traffic light to change.
- You're so sleep-deprived you wish you could get caffeine through an IV.

If you relate to any of these, you're not alone. Insomnia not only affects your ability to function effectively, but it can be accompanied by irritability, anxiety, tiredness, and restlessness. Insomnia has many causes, including high caffeine or sugar intake during the day, uncomfortable bedroom conditions (excessive light or noise, lack of fresh air, too much clutter, an uncomfortable temperature), excitement or dread concerning an upcoming or recent event, work shift changes, jet lag, traumatic personal experiences, and general stress.

Because sleep deprivation, fatigue, and exhaustion are so prevalent in today's hectic, stress-filled society, many physicians consider such commonplace complaints as low energy level, moodiness, irritability, and lack of alertness to be within the "normal" range of functioning. They sometimes dismiss these conditions as not being symptomatic of any valid medical concern. But let me tell you, it is *not* normal, and you *do not* have to go through life feeling this way.

Nearly half of all people who suffer from insomnia choose to self-medicate, according to some estimates. There are better ways to get a good night's rest. Rather than using prescribed or over-the-counter drugs, try these:

- Relax periodically during the day. You sleep better when you go to bed rested.
- Set aside a period of relaxation before bedtime to purposely quiet your mind.
- Dim the lights early, turn off the TV, and stay away from the computer.
- Avoid reading anything that stimulates your brain.

- Steer clear of ambitious planning or problem-solving right before bedtime.
- Take a warm, candle-lit bath and sip some warm milk or a steamy cup of herbal tea with chamomile.
- Apply some lavender-scented body lotion on your hands and feet.
- Wrap up in a cozy robe and fill your evening with soft music and candlelight.
- Snuggle up in front of the fireplace with a comfy blanket and pillow.
- Read from a good novel, a humor book, a magazine, or something inspirational.
- Make your bedroom a restful, clutter-free sanctuary with calming colors, textures, and scents.
- Use a lavender linen spray on your bedding to promote calm, peaceful sleep.

Establish your own routines and patterns that will trigger your mind to go to sleep. Do you remember changing into flannel pajamas, having a snack, brushing your teeth, turning down the covers, having a bedtime story, and saying prayers before bed during your growing up years? You can benefit by having bedtime rituals now too.

Improving your sleep patterns and habits could vastly improve your quality of life or even save your life. Wouldn't it be wonderful to know you can lay your head on your pillow tonight and drift off at once into a deeply refreshing sleep? And awaken revitalized tomorrow morning? Implementing the suggestions in this book, and especially in this chapter, may help you get the shut-eye you've been trying to dream about.

Sleeping Secrets

One suggestion many "how to get to sleep" books offer is to read something boring until you get sleepy. The most boring book I could find was the manual for my new vacuum cleaner. I didn't fall asleep, but I did learn where to find the button that recoils the electrical cord. Eventually, when the bags under my eyes looked like they hadn't been unpacked for weeks,

I came up with some survival tips to relieve the problem and break the stress–sleeplessness cycle.

- Develop a daily sleep routine or ritual that signals your mind it's time to sleep.
- Avoid drinking caffeine.
- Do something calming before bed. This means not watching a violence-filled movie or reading a murder mystery with an intricate plot.
- Reserve your bedroom for sleeping and lovemaking only.
- Periodically during the day, and particularly before bedtime, do something for relaxation. You'll sleep better when you go to bed relaxed.
- Read from the book of Psalms: "I will lie down in peace and sleep" (Psalm 4:8 TLB).
- Read from the book of Proverbs: "You'll take afternoon naps without a worry, you'll enjoy a good night's sleep" (Proverbs 3:24).
- Talk to God. It's easy to rest in peace when you know your heavenly Father is awake!

30

Sanity Secret #25

Laugh and Rest

In my *Stress Survival* workshops, I often hand out red clown noses to the audience. At one session I encouraged a group of senior executives to wear them during a portion of the program. The moans and groans coming from them would have made outsiders think the group was being led into a torture chamber. Most looked around the room to see if anyone was going to consent to this irrational and ridiculous request. Finally they loosened up. With noses in place, some even jumped up on their chairs, made monkey noises and gestures, and displayed their new look to the rest of the group. Laughter soon filled the room until most of them clutched their stomachs and doubled over. It was contagious. The more they laughed, the louder they laughed! Soon everybody broke into applause.

Humor and fun are natural to us, but sometimes we get so adult we forget how to play. Lack of humor in life can lead to despair and hopelessness. Eventually someone in a white coat will take you away, put you in rehab where you get to draw and color and string beads, and when you begin to laugh again, you get released.

My belief in the power of laughter and humor is based on personal experience as well as ancient wisdom found in the Bible, which tells us, "A cheerful heart is good medicine" (Proverbs 17:22 NLT). It is also supported by cutting-edge scientific research, which shows that laughter positively influences the body:

- energy levels are heightened
- tension is reduced
- body temperature rises giving us a "warm all over" feeling
- breathing becomes deeper and diaphragmatic
- endorphins are released
- immune system is strengthened
- muscles contract and relax, giving us an inner workout

Laughing may be one of the healthiest antidotes to stress! Our bodies are so miraculously made that when we laugh or even simply smile, blood flow to the brain is increased. As a result, endorphins are released, along with a lot of other biochemicals and powerful antidepressant elements that contribute to an overall sense of well-being and comfort. Before long the level of stress hormones drop. Apparently this decrease in stress hormones allows an increase in white blood cell production, which increases our immunity to illness. Isn't our Creator incredibly awesome!

One author, the late Norman Cousins, did extensive breakthrough research when he chose to fight a crippling form of arthritis by having friends and family bring him a supply of funny movies and books. During the day he watched comedies, read humorous literature, listened to jokes, and laughed as much as possible. He found that for every hour of laughter he got two hours of pain-free sleep. Eventually his disease went into remission, and he lived longer than expected by his doctors.

Laughing is like jogging on the inside. Along with deep breathing and healthy air exchange, a good laugh creates the same "high" or good feeling as exercise. In fact, just a few seconds of hearty laughing is equivalent to several minutes of aerobic exercise. It's a lot like giving your cardiovascular and respiratory systems a good workout. And the best part? It doesn't require any spiffy outfits, special shoes, elaborate equipment, or specific scheduling. Laughing is affordable and accessible!

* * *

She who laughs—lasts!

For those times when you're alone, assemble your own "humor first-aid survival kit"—a special tote bag filled with funny literature, comics, cartoons, joke books, comedy movies, and anything else that will jump-start your funny bone. Go to the gift shop and start a collection of comical greeting cards. Create a scrapbook of cartoons clipped from newspapers and magazines. Keep it handy for days when fun is missing from your life or you're having a hard time unwinding or getting to sleep.

Make a conscious effort to bring laughter into your life. This will also help you develop your own unique sense of humor. And your awareness of the funny side of everyday situations will be heightened. At times nothing brings more relief than laughing at ourselves. Even when things go wrong, we'll probably be able to tell friends and have a good laugh about it someday...so you might as well start right now. Consciously decide to narrow the gap between an incident and when you begin to see the funny side of it.

I have more laughs at myself than at anything or anyone else. One reason is because I suffer from "I can't believe I said that" syndrome. Since I seem to like putting my foot in my mouth, I'm seriously considering getting some chocolate shoes.

One time I was giving a keynote presentation at a conference and decided to say something I'd been considering for a long time. I referred to a coffee advertising slogan as a way of making my point about having a purpose in life. As I quoted from the advertisement, I also added my own comment: "If Folgers in your cup is the best thing about getting up, then you've got problems." My point was that we needed a better reason than a cup of coffee to get motivated, so discover your purpose in life. The dilemma was that I was speaking to Proctor & Gamble executives. Proctor & Gamble manufactures Folgers!

Another time I was a guest at an annual networking banquet where I'd been the main speaker a few times over the years. Because the attendees had been in my audience several times, most of them remembered me and called me by name. Since I couldn't possibly know all of them as well, as they knew me, I was relieved to see they were wearing name badges. Whenever someone called me by my first name, I was pleased that I could do the same by discreetly glancing at their name tags. After boldly saying hello to Lucy, Ethel, Ricky, Fred, Wilma, Betty, and Liz, I slowly clued in. It was Cher's badge that was the final give-away. What I didn't realize until too late was that the group's theme for the evening was "famous people" and each attendee was wearing a well-known person's name.

I've learned that I can be my own sitcom and have a good laugh at myself!

When we think of some of our past experiences and the things we may have heard as children, it's not surprising we often hold back from having a good laugh. Do any of these comments sound familiar?

- "Wipe that smile off your face." (Hidden message: I'm not laughing, so you don't have the right to laugh either.)
- "Get serious." (Hidden message: If you're smiling, you're not paying attention.)
- "When are you going to grow up?" (Hidden message: When you get to be an adult, you won't have anything to laugh about.)
- "Settle down." (Hidden message: You're acting like a child.)

Maybe acting childlike once in a while isn't a bad idea. The next time you're feeling overstressed, relive your childhood and act like a kid again. There's a difference between being *childish* and being *childlike.* To fight stress and tension, relearn playfulness. Do something goofy. Grab an umbrella, walk in the rain, and splash in the puddles. Invite friends over and have a water fight in the backyard with squirt toys. Make animal shadows on the wall. Find some crayons and draw a picture or just doodle. Rent a favorite childhood movie, read from *Winnie the Pooh* and other children's books, buy a bubble-blowing kit, build a paper airplane, fly a kite. In summertime ride a merry-go-round, eat Popsicles, have an ice cream cone, or build a sand castle. In winter make snow angels, go sledding, and drink hot cocoa with marshmallows. Now that Cliff and I have grandkids, we're even more likely to do these things again.

One thing I've noticed that little ones often do is throw their hands up in the air while shouting "Ta da!" I read recently there is a scientific study that has concluded that lifting your arms up into the air can also lift your spirits. In my church we often raise our arms as a gesture of praise and worship to our heavenly Father. Apparently throwing wide your arms and embracing God and life not only makes life worth living, but may, from a physical standpoint, make it last longer. Euphoria is good for the body, and joyfulness expressed physically may act as a protective influence against the caustic effects of stress.

Let's recapture our childlike sense of playfulness. A day of revisiting times when life was simpler is a good, inexpensive stress buster. Play and laughter are great ways to change your perspective and bring balance into life. Remember, "You gotta laugh a little!"

Humor Hints

- Angels fly because they take themselves lightly.
- Life isn't about how to survive the storm, but how to dance in the rain.
- Start a file of comic strips, funny greeting cards, jokes, and humorous stories to kick-start your funny bone.
- Assemble a comedy survival kit, and create some humor triggers to get you laughing.
- Learn to poke fun and laugh at yourself without personal put-downs.
- Plan to regularly integrate laughter into your life rather than waiting for it to happen.
- Sing in the shower. Use the soap for a microphone.
- Try your hand at telling a joke a day or a hilarious story of an embarrassing moment.
- Learn to reframe reality and see the funny side of life.
- Choose to laugh each day—even if you're by yourself.
- Take humor breaks. I love to read the funnies, Calvin and Hobbs, the Far Side collections, Erma Bombeck, Dave Barry, and Barbara Johnson.

- Get out the board games and arrange to play with family and friends.
- Have a basket of silly hats, glasses, noses, masks, wands, and feather boas handy. Put them on when you're mowing the lawn, driving in heavy traffic, or feeling frustrated.
- Don't just watch sitcoms; try your hand at writing or telling stories of your own hilarious adventures.
- During a committee or work meeting, give everyone a stuffed animal that makes a whining, bleating, or growling sound they can use as a way of making a point or objection.
- "Laughter is a corrective force which prevents us from becoming cranks" (Henri Bergson).

Rest Your Stress Away

Are you sick and tired of feeling sick and tired? Would you like to be renewed, restored, relaxed, replenished, revitalized, and rejuvenated? Stressed-out women need words that begin with "re"! The first sanity secret God gave us for getting refreshed, reenergized, and recharged is the ancient principle of the Sabbath. Keeping the Sabbath, the seventh day of the week, as a day of rest, allows us to experience all these things and more.

> For in six days God made Heaven, Earth, and sea, and everything in them; he rested on the seventh day. Therefore God blessed the Sabbath day; he set it apart as a holy day (Exodus 20:11).

After creating the world in six days, God rested on the seventh. He didn't do it because he was worn out. He did it to set an example for us. God gave us the Sabbath to protect us from getting into a condition of overstress and to protect our sanity. He created a day for us to be restored mentally, physically, emotionally, and spiritually. Even Adam needed a day without checking email or answering a cell phone. People and nations around the world have observed the Sabbath for centuries. Only recently in our Western culture of 24/7 have we forsaken it. Among some churchgoers the idea of Sabbath has become foreign. Many people are so involved in the process of Sunday service—teaching Sunday school, overseeing the nursery, singing in the choir, ushering, driving a bus, preaching the message—that it's simply become another workday, even though they are glad to contribute to God's work. Later, along with non-churchgoers, they often use Sunday to catch-up on household chores, yard work, and shopping that didn't get done during the week. Or some take part in sports activities and entertainment events. Many of us have no real concept of the Sabbath as a day of pure rest. Our lack of knowledge is killing us.

Imagine a time when people didn't say TGIF (Thank God It's Friday) but TGIS (Thank God It's Sabbath!). That was the best day of the week. Do you remember when businesses didn't operate on Sunday? (If so, you must be over 50.) There was an unwritten law that businesses shouldn't expect their employees to work on the *day of rest.* While I grew up with every store in town closed on Sunday, kids today are growing up with many stores open around the clock. Our overwhelming focus on progress and profits has essentially eliminated the God-given pause that refreshes.

One Sunday morning after our church service, people lingered to chat as I hurried for the door. I had too many things clouding my mind to join in: fine-tune my notes for a talk I was to give on a cruise ship in Hawaii about living stress free (could I relax enough to actually *be* stress free?), finish packing for the trip, arrange for someone to feed the cat and bring in the mail, get to the gym for an hour—okay, maybe half an hour. As I walked out the door, a deacon shook my hand and said enthusiastically, "Be sure to enjoy the rest of the Sabbath!"

❋ ❋ ❋

Seven days without a Sabbath makes one weak.

With much guilt I thought of the commandment I'd learned as a child: "Remember the Sabbath day, to keep it holy" (Exodus 20:8 NKJV). Growing up, Sunday was a day set apart from the rest of the week. We attended church in the morning, where we got to hear the choir and my mom sing a solo before listening to Reverend Morrison preach his message. Then came a home-cooked dinner of roast beef, mashed potatoes, gravy, corn, baked squash, and warm-from-the-oven rolls with butter, all served at the dining room table. Afterward we'd help Grandma into the car, pile in behind her, and take a quiet drive in the country, stopping at the dairy for ice cream cones. All stores were closed so there was no shopping, and we didn't do any work. Everything had been taken care of the day before, and the entire house was tidy and sparkling clean. Mom told us it was because this was the Sabbath, a day set apart for God. On Saturday she would head for the store to get whatever we would need until Monday. If we ran out of milk, eggs, or anything else on Sunday, we had to borrow from a neighbor or do without.

These days the Sabbath has changed so much that it no longer feels different from any other day of the week. We've bought into the lie that there is no time for rest, and affirm that notion with our overloaded schedules, never-ending to-do lists, incessant emails, and relentless cell phone rings.

The word *Sabbath* comes from the Hebrew word *Shabbat,* meaning to rest or cease from work or exertion. It's a day when we're to stop thinking about what we want to do and spend time considering the things of God. From the beginning of creation, Adam worked six days and rested on the seventh. The ancient Israelites honored the seventh day since it was the day on which God rested after creating the earth. This was the day they worshiped God with their families and refrained from their labors.

In the book of Exodus, the children of Israel escaped the bondage of Egypt and began their journey to the Promised Land. When they were starving in the wilderness, God miraculously provided manna for them to eat six days of each week (Exodus 16). God clearly instructed them to gather enough to eat for one day and no more. If they took more, it would spoil by the next day. On the sixth day, though, God told them to collect enough for two days. This extra manna lasted through the Sabbath without spoiling. This allowed them to rest on the seventh day. In fact, when they awoke on the Sabbath, there was no manna—the ground was bare. I'm sure they got the idea!

> We long to find rest and renewal in our busy lives. Make a decision to take one day a week off and use it for rest and relaxation.

The early Christians kept the Saturday Sabbath and considered Sunday a feast day—the Lord's Day—to celebrate Jesus' death and resurrection.

Laws restricting work on Sunday were instituted later, though more for political than religious reasons. The Puritans in America established an even more disciplined Sunday code of conduct that included no public dancing, singing, or merriment of any kind.

Ways of observing the Sabbath have changed with the times, yet the necessity for one day of rest each week remains. Built within us is a vital human yearning for a refreshing time away from the daily routine. All we have to do is look at the flood of books, magazine articles, radio programs, and TV shows designed to give us tips on how to find peace and restore spiritual balance to our lives to know people hunger for rest. The more hectic our schedules, the more our empty spirits yearn for the peace and serenity of honoring the Sabbath.

We long to find rest and renewal in our busy lives. Make a decision to take one day a week off and use it for rest and relaxation and time with God. Our bodies and minds and spirits need this break desperately. We simply can't keep racing 24 hours a day, 7 days a week, and expect to stay sane and healthy. There will always be more to be done at home and at work. We need to be diligent about setting limits as we create our own sanctuaries amid the demands of modern life.

Even so, the Sabbath is more than just time off. It's a time for stronger connection with God. It's a day when we put aside all other things to honor our relationship with him. The Sabbath doesn't mean we do nothing. People are always doing something. But the Sabbath provides an opportunity to step back from our regular schedules—for a moment, an hour, a day—and consider and give thanks for the wonders of our lives and the One who gives us life.

Resting

- Try it! Rest for one day this week.
- Let yourself off the hook when resting. Don't beat yourself up with feelings of guilt. Recognize that when you come back to your tasks, you'll be more creative, effective, and productive.
- Take time to enjoy *being* rather than *doing*. You are a human being...not a human doing.

- Develop the habit of calming your mind and stilling your soul.
- Make your Sabbath a day when you can get immersed in silence, stillness, and simplicity.
- Oddly, it takes a lot of energy in the beginning to slow down and be apart from the world, so be prepared.
- Meditate on God and his Word. Regular meditation isn't always easy and takes practice.
- Remind yourself that God also rested on the seventh day.
- "Observe the Sabbath day, to keep it holy. Work six days and do everything you need to do. But the seventh day is a Sabbath to God, your God" (Exodus 20:8-10).

The First Resort

Oh, the utter extravagance of his work
in us who trust him—
endless energy, boundless strength!
Ephesians 1:19

Would you like to have endless energy and boundless strength? It almost sounds too good to be true, doesn't it? Yet in Ephesians 1:19 God promises to work in us who trust him, and he says he'll do it with utter extravagance. According to my thesaurus, that means with sheer, sumptuous splendor and lavish opulence. *Wow!* I love the way The Message Bible paraphrases this verse. It tells me that God doesn't hold back anything once we place our complete faith in him.

When I'm struggling to overcome stress, I lean on God and trust in his Word that says, "The law of the Lord is perfect, reviving the soul" (Psalm 19:7 NIV). Getting God's Word into my heart changes my thinking and stores up inner reserves of strength for handling future stresses. When you and I bend our knees as well as our hearts and offer a simple prayer, whether at home, at work, or at church, God comes to us with the answers we need and shows us a way out of the stress. Make the act of turning to God your first resort rather than the last.

❋ ❋ ❋

The Spirit of GOD will come on you...
And you'll be transformed.
You'll be a new person!
1 SAMUEL 10:6

Peace and Joy to You!

❊ ❊ ❊

The world is round and the place which may seem
like the end may
also be only the beginning.
IVY BAKER PRIEST

Before reading this book, you may have felt overwhelmed, overloaded and overextended. Maybe you were frustrated, frayed, frazzled, and fatigued. Taking the time, money, and energy required to nurture yourself may have seemed like a self-centered extravagance and a narcissistic indulgence. Now you know that isn't true. You've discovered by caring for yourself you can also better care for the people you love and cherish most. As the flight attendants remind us when we're traveling with someone who is dependant on us, we must put on our own oxygen masks first so we are capable of helping another. Our natural tendency is to look after the needs of others even if we're not fully equipped. The truth is that we can't give away what we don't own. And so many of us are attempting to do just that!—give to others even though we're empty.

Discovering ways to nurture yourself back into balance and pamper your life into wellness is just the beginning. Practicing the sanity secrets to create a sanctuary from the demands of modern life involves making a lifelong commitment. It doesn't stop once your energy levels are soaring, your health is good, you've lost those ten pounds, work–life balance has been restored, your finances are in order, you meet the partner of your dreams, or you get that fantasy job. Make sanity secrets part of your daily life even when everything is going your way.

There are situations and events happening all around us that drain us of our fuel. Some circumstances won't go away, and they have the potential to wreak havoc by keeping us in a constant state of tension. If we weave into our lives the sanity savers and survival hints, we fortify ourselves against raging storms.

My precious friend, to stay stress free and find rest in the midst of your chaotic world, I encourage you to pray. Make prayer your first resort. Don't wait until you've exhausted all your own resources. I learned a long time ago that I'm really not capable of running my own life—but I know the One who is, and I can go to him first! As you follow God's leading and implement daily nurturing self-care, you'll find that you more fully experience the beauty, simplicity, and power of living life according to his principles and purposes. Leave the stressed-out life behind and follow the abundant life.

❊ ❊ ❊

Knowing that I am not the one in control gives great encouragement.
Knowing the One who is in control is everything.
ALEXANDER MICHAEL

About the Author

Invigorating, captivating, stimulating describe Sue Augustine when she offers audiences the principles, skills, and inspiration they need to experience extraordinary results. Sue has a unique talent for inspiring and challenging men and women to make the powerful, positive choices that will transform their lives and careers. Through her keynote addresses, seminars, workshops, and books, she speaks internationally on personal effectiveness and excellence.

Due to her exceptional ability to influence men and women and compel them to take action, Sue's services are sought after by numerous distinguished corporations, businesses, professional associations, school boards, shopping centers, hospitals, and nonprofit groups. She has been featured in several business publications and regularly appears on international television and radio shows.

What is truly remarkable is knowing where Sue came from. After surviving a severe illness and a devastating personal situation, she became a successful entrepreneur and corporate trainer in sales before attaining her goal of speaking professionally. Sue knows firsthand what it takes to turn tragedy into triumph and dreams into realities.

Sue is the author of *Turn Your Dreams into Realities; When Your Past Is Hurting Your Present; With Wings, There Are No Barriers; Simple Retreats for a Woman's Soul.* She is also a contributing author to the bestselling Chicken Soup for the Soul series.

Aside from her speaking career, Sue is married, mother of two daughters, grandmother of four, and actively involved in her community in Ontario, Canada. She serves on the Board of Directors for her home church and Niagara Life Centre, a nonprofit family counseling center.

To contact Sue Augustine or book her for an event, check out

www.sueaugustine.com

or e-mail her at

info@sueaugustine.com

Other Great Harvest House Books by Sue Augustine

Turn Your Dreams into Realities

Do you want to travel? Build a house? Volunteer? Spend more time with your kids or grandkids? And what about smaller goals—coordinating a family reunion, working on a deck, or planning a vacation? Whatever your dreams, acclaimed motivational speaker Sue Augustine offers 101 powerful strategies that will take you where you want to go. Discover how to...

- identify your God-given passions and dreams
- use your unique abilities and talents to achieve your goals
- overcome doubts, fears, and insecurities
- break big dreams into doable action steps

Packed with enthusiasm, creative ideas, and hands-on suggestions, *Turn Your Dreams into Realities* will transform your life as you put these principles into practice and reach for the stars. Achieve more than you ever thought possible!

When Your Past Is Hurting Your Present

Is your past dictating your present? And your future? Do you want to break this destructive pattern and move on to a happier life, but find it impossible to do so? Sue understands. She too was once held captive by a painful past. With compassion, empathy, and a touch of humor, Sue shows you how to...

- identify, release, and change how you respond to the past
- trade bitterness and resentment for peace and joy
- set goals for the future with passion and purpose
- understand God's incredible timing and direction

If you're struggling with a difficult past that's harming your present and crippling your future, begin today to cut loose the baggage of the long-ago...and start to see your fears conquered, your dreams renewed, and your future become bright with new possibilities.

Simple Retreats for a Woman's Soul

Do you long for the pure and simple things in life? Have endless responsibilities taken the fun out of your days? Are you experiencing more stress and anxiety, and less peace and joy? Drawing from her professional expertise and sharing from her own experiences, Sue helps you find new meaning in the ordinary experiences of everyday life.

Each of these short chapters will help you recapture the joy of such simple pleasures as welcoming the wind in your hair, going barefoot, and escaping in a good book.

Take a break and enjoy the kind of life God has designed for you.